# THE ARTIFICIAL BODY IN FASHION AND ART

*The mixture and range of cultural forces at play in this scintillating manuscript takes us on a cultural magical mystery tour that is as exciting as it is surprising, as provocative as it is erudite, as original as it is imaginative, and as thrilling as it is perverse.*
Joy Sperling, Denison University, USA

*A profoundly innovative study that presents surprising and far-reaching insights into the complex intersections between the phenomenology of dolls, masquerade and marionettes and post-modern subjectivities.*
Mary Gluck, Brown University, USA

*Using several social science disciplines, Geczy undertakes a valuable overview of the changing significance of the doll in previous centuries and today. His analysis reveals important changes that are taking place in women's conceptions of the female body.*
Diana Crane-Herve, University of Pennsylvania, USA

*This book is a completely fascinating read that takes you far beneath the surface of appearances by stripping bare a myriad of meanings of dolls in our lives, from baby to adult. It makes you think, and re-think, by drawing on diverse histories of theatre, art, fashion, aesthetics, technology, religion, philosophy and psychoanalysis, literature, film, gender and cultural theory. Geczy brilliantly guides the reader in this rich account that cannot be pigeon-holed by discipline—it is a must read for all interested in the relationship between our minds, bodies and soul.*
Alexandra Palmer, Royal Ontario Museum, Canada

*Painting a broad canvas Geczy provides a rich and detailed landscape that links ideas stretching from Jane Munro's* Silent Partners: Artist and Mannequin from Function to Fetish*—a cultural history that traces centuries of evolution of the artist's mannequin within the context of an expanding universe of effigies, avatars, dolls, and shop window dummies—to Yuval Harari's* Sapiens: A Brief History of Humankind*, which provides an evolutionary history of our species towards an unfolding future that witnesses the fusion between natural bodies and cyber limbs in a scientific odyssey involving non-organic-life engineering. Geczy adds an important piece in the jigsaw of the scholarship on dolls and masks, that examined the boundaries of the animate and inanimate in dolls and representations.*
Efrat Tseelon, author of *Masquerade & Identities* (2001), University of Leeds, UK

# THE ARTIFICIAL BODY IN FASHION AND ART

## MARIONETTES, MODELS, AND MANNEQUINS

ADAM GECZY

Bloomsbury Academic
An imprint of Bloomsbury Publishing Plc
BLOOMSBURY
LONDON • OXFORD • NEW YORK • NEW DELHI • SYDNEY

**Bloomsbury Academic**
An imprint of Bloomsbury Publishing Plc

50 Bedford Square
London
WC1B 3DP
UK

1385 Broadway
New York
NY 10018
USA

**www.bloomsbury.com**

**BLOOMSBURY and the Diana logo are trademarks of Bloomsbury Publishing Plc**

First published 2017

**British Library Cataloguing-in-Publication Data**
A catalogue record for this book is available from the British Library.

ISBN: HB: 978-1-4725-9596-6
PB: 978-1-4725-9595-9
ePDF: 978-1-4725-9597-3
ePub: 978-1-4725-9598-0

**Library of Congress Cataloging-in-Publication Data**
A catalog record for this book is available from the Library of Congress.

Cover image © Antonius Antonius Getty Images

Typeset by RefineCatch Limited, Bungay, Suffolk
Printed and bound in India

To my sons Julian (Scaramouche) and Marcel (Harlequin)

# TABLE OF CONTENTS

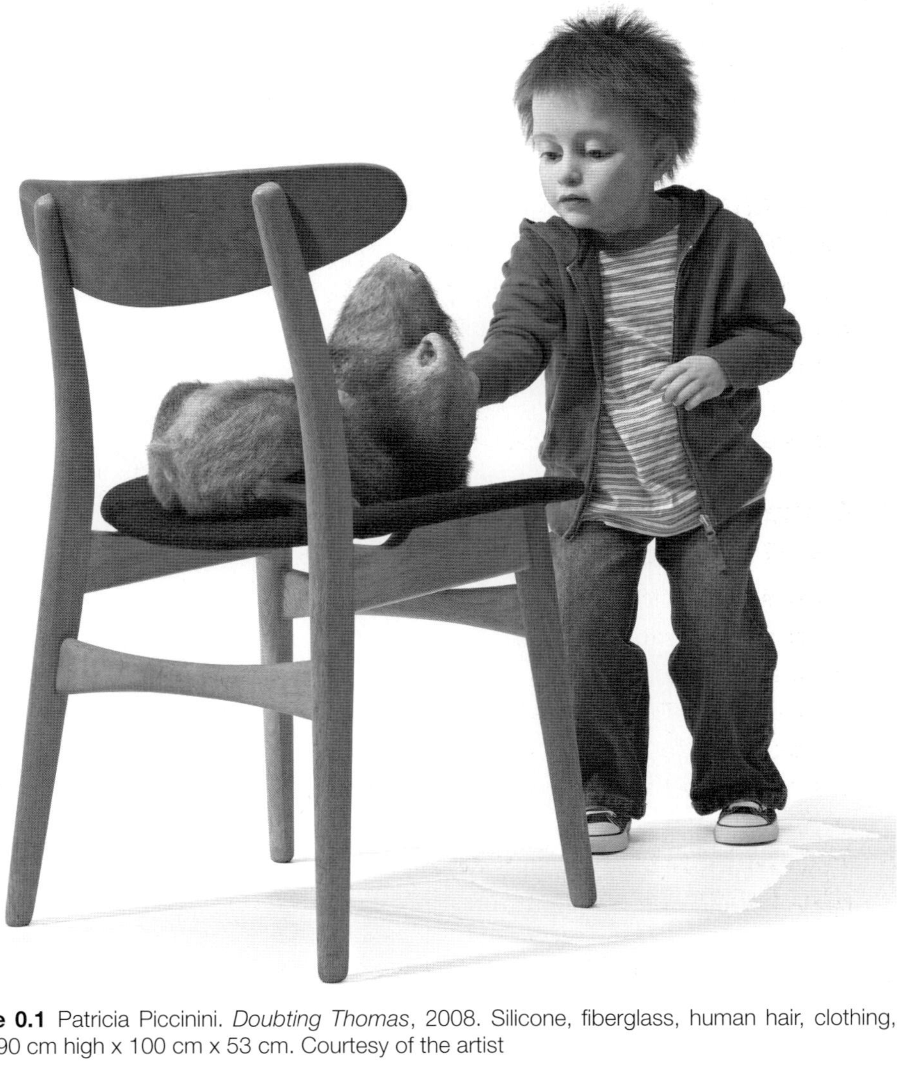

**Figure 0.1** Patricia Piccinini. *Doubting Thomas*, 2008. Silicone, fiberglass, human hair, clothing, chair. 90 cm high x 100 cm x 53 cm. Courtesy of the artist

# LIST OF ILLUSTRATIONS

## Figures

# Plates

# ACKNOWLEDGEMENTS

This book owes itself to many people who have given advice, have introduced me to examples of which I was ignorant or provided conditions for research. Thanks to Jennifer Hayes and Domenica Lowe from the library at Sydney College of the Arts, the University of Sydney, who have helped in providing obscure sources from distant lands.

The Institut Internationale des Marionnettes in Charleville-Mézières gave me two weeks of hospitality that were invaluable for research and writing. Ulrika Celik for her beguiling grace and continued, loving fascination in the project and reading my drafts. Also Marquard Smith and Kenneth Gross for their generous time and expert counsel. Jonathan McBurnie, my mentor in all things Batmanian and mutant. Victoria Hodgkinson, my informal librarian, and to Katherine and Daryl Hogkinson, who have always loomed large in the world of cosmetic plasticity. And as always, my trusted friend and colleague, Vicki Karaminas.

# INTRODUCTION

*It is not difficult to credit that statues may have appeared to ooze with sweat, shed tears, or exude something which resembles drops of blood, since wood and stone often gather a mould which produces moisture, and not only display various colours themselves, but take on other tints from the atmosphere, and there is nothing to prevent us from believing that heaven sometimes employs such portents to foreshadow the future. It is also possible that statues may give out a sound which resembles a groan or a sigh, which is caused by a fracture or splitting of the particles of which they may be composed, and produces a louder noise if it takes place inside. But the notion that articulate speech, so clear and abundant and precise, could proceed from a lifeless object goes beyond the bounds of possibility, since neither the human soul, nor even a god, has ever spoken or conversed without possessing a body which is organically constructed and fitted with the various vocal members.*

—PLUTARCH[1]

*Let us recall Hegel's famous reply when one of his students criticized him because an empirical detail did not fit with his theory: "too bad for nature."*

—SLAVOJ ZIZEK[2]

There has arguably been no time in history when words such as *natural* and *pure* are used in such profusion: on products and advertisements from food to clothing to lifestyle. Psychoanalysis has taught us that an effusive expression of something usually emanates from an anxious need to compensate for what is actually lacking. The paradox of our contemporary moment is that, in the age of the rife rhetoric of naturalness, we as human beings have never been so unnatural. Clearly, this requires more definition, but for now it is worth pausing to reflect on the extent to which our bodies are artificially modulated by our environments, and the extent and availability of the possibilities to do so. This may be from the fluoride in our water, which unbeknown to most, has exponentially reduced the incidence of tooth decay, to the likelihood that someone we know born in the last twenty years has been the product of intravenous fertilization, thus in a different category of ontic possibility from someone who came into the world under "natural" circumstances. Add to this the amount of people who now find it acceptable to improve their bodies cosmetically, whether that be through dental whitening or breast implants. But the truth of these is that neither blindingly white teeth nor melon-like breasts are natural, yet their desirability and their increasing normativity has rendered them so, much as a bodybuilder—whose Hellenic build is made possible by chemical supplements—with so little body fat can barely walk before a tournament, is called "fit." The age of the technologized body that grew out of the 1980s has rendered the distinction between prophylactic or restorative bodily mediation, on one hand, and voluntary and arbitrary bodily mediation, on the other, harder than ever to define. The contention of this book is that we are in a radically new period in our consciousness of body, other and self. Put simply, in the humanist age, Pinocchio wanted to become human; in the so-called post-humanist age, humans aspire to become Pinocchio. In so doing, we attempt to internalize an imaginary other. There was once just the doll, now we wish to become that doll. In charting this qualitative transition of self, this book begins with the doll and the puppet's role within the social imagination, and the way in which the doll, the projected, artificial self, has become incorporated, folded back onto the natural body that defined it, so as to consign the difference between natural and artificial to an historical narrative, to the past.

Puppets, dolls and marionettes are as old as the very earliest civilizations, with evidence of dolls in the ancient Egyptians, Minoans, Etruscans as well as the Chinese. There is plenty of reason to argue that they are caught up with the formation of civilization itself. For although a puppet, for example, is a constructed, stylized and artificial being, it has, since early antiquity, functioned as a powerful vehicle for conveying messages that would be too difficult, risky or explicit if handled by real bodies, much as a fairytale holds perennial truths beneath the fantastic and rationally implausible. This means that dolls and puppets—fake, substitute bodies—played a role in helping to reflect on the fluid ordering principles of social relations from politics to gender.[3] Evidence of dolls since antiquity reveals that they were prevailingly present in the formation of the individual, as an imaginary other that then assisted in the formation of one's own psychic imaginary leading to the safe phantasy of the unified self. The often ritualistic contrivances of the doll has therefore been important to personal adjustment, and as a modulator to individuals as social groups. Put simply, dolls, puppets and marionettes are the visible presence of fantasy to ensure that we are protected from the horror of the fantasies of self and social identity. In the sympathetic phrase of a German anthropologist, the doll is the *treueste Spiegelgefärtin*, the "faithful mirroring companion."[4]

Because of this, dolls and body-aliases are also widely used as tools for early stages of learning, and for adult counseling.[5] Moreover, masks are an accepted tool for therapy, given that it acts a shield and is a spur to acting out fantasies, fears, traumas.[6] Punch and Judy shows and their ilk are not only tools for children's amusement, but also effective for communicating with children, their mischievous nature providing vivid warnings about possible dangers like crossing the road or bumping into undesirable strangers.[7] The ersatz body—either external the body or assumed—allows the spectator to cathect, or graft, her (as it was predominately in antiquity) anxieties and premonitions with far less fear of recrimination, diminishing the sense of inhibition. As Kenneth Gross, in his study of our relation to statues, explains, "statues, public and external as they are, have the character of those highly cathected psychic images or 'internal objects' that people the space of mind. We are not just buried in our statues, our statues are buried in us."[8] Such an observation has forceful ramifications for the way we relate to inanimate anthropomorphs such that the lines between art, psychology and life are all but annulled since the puppet and doll are essential to the phantasy of self. In practical psychology, for instance, there is a sizeable amount written about the usefulness of "anatomically correct" dolls, that is, dolls with genitalia, in assessing cases of child abuse.[9] On the other hand, the contemporary RealDoll, expensive and lifelike dolls used as sex toys, allow for a level of violent engagement, deplorable in itself, but criminal on a real body. There are also numerous cases of men who claim to have relationships with their dolls. Pathos or perversion, the healthiness of this is up for speculation.[10]

But it would be a mistake to leave the analysis there as the doll may not only be considered as external to the body. Well before the new contemporary conceptions of body and self, the puppet is not only a prevalent metaphor for a certain type of person who is easily manipulated, but also for both theater and religion. In religion, there is the universal notion of God, or a god, being the sublime puppet master—satirized in the figure of the Wizard of Oz—who pulls the strings of fate. Zeus, the Greek king of the gods, is also supposed to have played with clay figurines. The game of chess is also a similar activity in which two opposing forces manipulate the ciphers pertaining to statecraft. Beyond these schematic applications, the notion of the puppet helped to establish humans within an environment of law and method that was outside of their control, and within which humans were only agents acting according to a preordained order, and in accordance with the limited resources of movement assigned them. On the other pole of power, Thomas Hobbes also described his Leviathan as a massive automaton.

After Descartes, the role of the self and the other becomes an issue in earnest. With Descartes, the subject shifts from thinking to a being that thinks, from *cogitans* to *res cogitans*, thereby creating a breach in being and thinking while sealing it in the same gesture. Or as Slavoj Zizek puts it, Descartes "patches up the wound he cut into the texture of reality." He continues:

> Only Kant fully articulates the inherent paradoxes of self-consciousness. What Kant's "transcendental turn" renders manifest is the impossibility of locating the subject in the "great chain of being", into the Whole of the universe—all those notions of the universe as a harmonious Whole in which every element has its own place (today, they abound in the ecological ideology). In contrast to it, subject is in the most radical sense "out of joint"; it constitutively lacks its own place, which is why Lacan designates it by the matheme S̶, the "barred" *S*.[11]

It is first worth taking note of Zizek's aside with regard to ecology here, which has to be seen as part of the same campaign for technological humankind's highly encoded return to nature. For the rest, Zizek elaborates on the Lacanian thesis that the constitution of the self as bounded subject only occurs by dint of a fundamental unboundedness, or incompleteness. Hence "The Paradox of self-consciousness is that it is possible *only against the background of its own impossibility*: I am conscious of myself only insofar as

I am out of reach to myself qua the real kernel of my being."[12] Our relationship with artificial selves is therefore fundamental to the very make-up of our being, since it is not only persistence and presence of the other, but the artificial other, which allows us not to confront that we, human subjects, are intricate fabrications. To put this into more technical psychoanalytic parlance, the doll, the body-other, plays the role of *Vorstellungs-Repräsentanz*, which is what stands in for what is missing (in ourselves). To use Zizek's words again, it is "the signifying representative of the missing representation."[13]

What is more than curious, however—and the ironies of such historical symmetries are writ large in this book—is that the theatrical phenomenon of the commedia dell'arte enters just before the inception of the Cartesian subject. That is, the beginnings of what Kierkegaard would later characterize as the ironic conception of self, the self that constitutes itself through occupying multiple positions, and who is skeptical of notions of unilateral, inviolable personal witness. This relationship is already pregnant in the formal nature of theater itself. Since ancient times, theater has involved the conflict between individual will and destiny, the effects of which may be expressed as comedy or as tragedy. This fundamental friction asks the indelible question whether the subject is a complex and cruel illusion who is really a cipher, shell, or puppet leveraged by something or someone else. To what extent an actor is a puppet of the script, the plot and the direction, may depend on the kind of theater, according to history or genre. While theater was always open to improvisation, the improvisatory performance was dominated by puppet theater, inevitably, since puppets were fabricated from the beginning to represent a role, type or condition.

While it is established that dolls have had an enduring role in the child's psychic evolution, well before the invention of psychoanalysis, its relation, both material and metaphoric, to the modern subject is quite particular. It is a relation that this book traces in two phases, from humanism to posthumanism. Plato made occasional mention to puppets in his *Laws*, such as descrying the unquestioningly obedient as "for the most part puppets,"[14] or indulging in the commonplace speculation that we are puppets of a higher power.[15] When Kant turns to subjective moral agency, he retains some of the regular meaning in principle, but otherwise radically reorients it to deal with the nature of imperfect knowledge, which nonetheless is bound to a higher moral order. If we somehow grasped the immensity of things, if God and the eternal might in their awful majesty would stand unceasingly before our eyes, we would be gripped with such fear that our actions would exist not as moral decisions but as pure obeisance:

> The moral worth of actions, on which alone the worth of the person and even the world depends in the eyes of supreme wisdom, would not exist at all. The conduct of man, so long as his nature remained as it is now, would be changed into mere mechanism, where, as in a puppet show, everything would gesticulate well but no life would be found in the figures.[16]

As Zizek argues in his reading of this passage, Kant identifies a radical predicament. Namely, that in terms of "things-in-themselves" we are just a mechanism, while in the world of occurrences and appearances (phenomena), we are part of a flow of larger causes and our immanence as developed mammals. Our freedom, which is our capacity to judge, is caught somewhere between the realms, creating a kind of deadlock from which we cannot escape.[17]

It is as if with the free modern subject the doll is not expelled—I am no longer a puppet but a free modern agent—but rather enters through another door. It represents the very limits of freedom once and as a result of that freedom being granted. This is yet another way of considering the existential disturbance of modern alienation—but it is also very useful to help in reflecting on the new phase of the cyborg and the artificial body in the posthuman age and the now age of the anthropocene. Here, the identification with doll is no longer external, it is either imbricated or wholly embraced, where the horror of the indeterminacy of agency is in transforming into the determinate object of the doll. This can be rendered as self-transformation, or through serious congress—affective, intellectual, sexual—with a nonbiological "being." To admit of such a possibility can be read as the technological end result of Romanticism's valorization of suicide as the ultimate statement of personal will (I had no choice in my birth, but I have in my death), except that we live on—through transformation, modification or identification— as something else, as various members of the technological undead. Why the extraordinary spate of vampire books, movies and televisions series in the last decade or so? The zombie genre has flourished also. In line with such speculative symmetries, it is worth noticing that Kant's time witnessed a profusion of automata of a sophistication hitherto unseen. The passion for automata, which in many circles bordered on mania, was caught up with "philosophical toys" and the rationalist view put in train by Descartes that humans were machines with a soul.[18]

It is thus in the formation of the self-positing and free subject that the doll assumes a level of importance, manifesting in droves in all artistic genres. In modern drama, for instance, the idea of the "living doll" was a popular one, especially in cabaret. But in conventional theater, the so-called formalist model, in which the living actor subordinates him- or herself to the words of the absent poet is a contested one, since it reduces diction to oratory and leaves gesture to a minimum. True enough, in Shakespeare's time, for example, the manner of acting was less spontaneous and "humanist" than what we find in great modernists from Chekhov to Ibsen, but when it came to the main actors in the drama, a certain human pathos was inevitable. Shakespearean drama demands for wide emotional range that wooden acting formalism cannot sustain.[19]

For this reason, modernist drama struck up a relationship with puppets and dolls that explores the limits of human will and consciousness, and to dwell on human agency, social stratification and what it began to see as the fictions of human irreducibility. This growing skepticism comes to an important head with the work of the Belgian Maurice Maeterlinck. Best remembered for his play *Pelléas et Mélisande* (1893), which inspired Debussy's famous opera, Maeterlinck also wrote some highly influential marionette plays, which as the name dictates, were disposed toward artificial bodies, it is critically agreed that they were more intended for living actors.[20] This was because Maeterlinck needed to find an alternative form of dramatic expression that delivered something more than the temporal and immediate activities of humanity, dispensed with naturalism and in its place was able to disclose the more profound spiritual core. Instead of lucid, speech took on an incantatory quality, and bodily movements could appear uncomfortable and contrived. As Harold Segel explains, "the plays embody a metaphysical viewpoint for which Maeterlinck devised what he regarded as an appropriate dramatic style."[21] To him, the fragile body was only to be a vehicle for something more essential. Well before the Brecht and Beckett, Maeterlinck disturbed the imaginary screen between actor and spectator with mechanical and highly contrived form of theatrical mise en scène that was steeped in a deathly atmosphere.

Much of this willful reduction of humans into mechanical objects can be traced back to the still remarkable and much commented on philosophical narrative by Heinrich von Kleist, "Über das Marionettentheater" ("On Marionette Theater").[22] Not that this is the first text that seeks to confront human nature with his uncanny counterfeit counterpart, but it is certainly one of the most intriguing texts of the time. Influenced by Schiller, who distinguished between the naïve and the sentimental, and by Goethe, whose Wilhelm Meister had a special fondness for puppet theater, Kleist weaves together a series of observations that are as baffling as they are original. Kleist's narrator runs across a mysterious "Herr C.," who proceeds to expound a theory that the movements of marionettes have a superior grace to that of humans because they lack self-consciousness and are indisposed to hesitation. Kleist thereby evinces a distrust of human consciousness, and the essay is widely interpreted as a romantic defense of unconscious processes. While marionettes, required a puppet master, they were nevertheless regulated by the basic laws of gravity which the human body perforce defies. Yet, this is precisely what we look for in most of our dancers.[23] The deeper allegorical thrust of Kleist's narrative is directed to humanity's wrong turn, the Fall. For it is the Fall that has cleaved humanity from being in harmony with the world. Kleist's Herr C. relates a story of a handsome young friend of his who lapsed from spontaneous grace to vanity after he saw his reflection and became self-conscious of his beauty. It is this change that is emblematic of the Fall, and which characterizes the difference between humans and their mechanical counterparts. What Kleist's heavily cited texts helps to expose is the very fragility in humanity's conception of its worth and its capacities, and that the artificial alibi may be more than an alibi but a rival.

With artificial bodies, connection between innocence and terror is central. The animated doll brings with it the ancient desire of animism, whose most enduring myth is told in the story of Pygmalion, who brings life to his own statue.[24] But the doll is also the harbinger of death, the lifeless double that is the uncanny reminder that we will all end up dead. More specifically when it comes to the modern evolution, or passage, in humanity's relationship to artificial bodies, the eighteenth century gives us everything from which to draw. There are two main factors to consider. One is the automaton as a thing of technical advancement and the challenge to emulate humans on a biological and intellectual level. The automatons powered according to barrel mechanisms and clockwork are only to be seen as early forms of the contemporary robot and artificial intelligence (AI) and now the desire to research the possibility of affective intelligence. The other takes issue of affective intelligence and contends that it is an undesirable accessory, and that modern subjecthood his more of a burden than an advantage. But the renunciation of one's subjectivity is tantamount to death, and the need to renounce can be seen as tragic, as the terrible failure of the humans to come to peace with themselves. Artificial bodies are associated with joy and possibility (beauty and play) while at the same time pointing to an interminable abyss.

Despite being the era that shaped the modern code of nature and the natural, the eighteenth century was also a period that celebrated elaborate and studied forms of fêtes and masquerade that well surpassed those that originated out of the Renaissance. From Marie Antoinette's follies in Versailles, to those in Nymphenberg in Munich, the highest echelons of society would dress up as shepherds and shepherdesses, or as figures from classical antiquity. These serve as examples of the developments from the commedia and of the courtly masque in so far as it finds people self-consciously acting out pre-established stereotypical parts in a manner of being that, while less stylized than masquerade, is all the more perverse in the sense of playing out a world that is as yet impossible. In anticipation of the conclusion of this book, this impossibility is made possible with the inception of the technologized body from the 1980s onward.

In the swelling world of diversions and entertainment, in addition to puppets and automata, another significant invention was the waxwork. Rationalism and humanism created acute scrutiny as to what it meant to be human, which created a healthy audience for the first waxworks exhibitions staged in Paris by Philippe Curtius, who became the teacher and mentor of Anne Maria Gosholtz, later Tussaud. As her biographer, Kate Berridge notes, "Just as Curtius modeled the celebrities of the day in wax, for a time a couple of enterprising impresarios enjoyed the success on the back of their famous look-alike marionettes."[25] Tussaud marginally escaped the Revolution and was subsequently employed to make death masks, which included the king and queen, as well as Robespierre and Marat. In literature, the waxwork sideshow attraction finds its vivid testament in Mr Jarley in Dickens's *Old Curiosity Shop*. To the delight and astonishment of his audience, he alters the likenesses of famous personages into writers or other people familiar to them. But it is still the eerie oddity of the waxworks that haunts the main character, Nell, as they draw to mind the "perpetual nightmare" of Quilp,[26] the grotesque and avaricious dwarf. They were never truly benign. She slept among them, with their "great glassy eyes"

> and, as they stood one behind another all about her bed, they looked like living creatures, and yet so unlike in their grim stillness and silence, that she had a kind of terror of them for their own sakes, and would often lie watching their dusky figures until she was obliged to rise and light a candle, or go and sit at the open window and feel companionship in the bright stars.[27]

The ghoulishness of the approximation of life is the waxwork's most lasting accomplishment. But it is also its thick reek of death that also makes the waxwork so sympathetic to celebrity. As if embalming one's popularity, arresting what is uncontrollably transient, it is a mark of fame to have one's double made and displayed, especially in the flagship Tussaud's in London. In any such museum, fans can be photographed standing next to the latest newly fashioned celebrity doppelganger.

The greatest lure of the waxwork museum has always been in the darker potential of the uncanny double, not just in the death mask, but in the replicated figures of criminals in history. How many of us who have visited a wax museum and have stared into the wax faces modeled on convicted killers, or of those who met a horrific end, with protracted fascination, despite knowing that it is all inert matter? Harnessing the figure of the doll to explore the sinister and the macabre was part of the Romantic era's preoccupations with what overreached human limits. The results penetrated into the uncanny and the horrible. The consequences of Dr. Frankenstein's Promethean dream are well inscribed in the popular consciousness, but perhaps less well remembered with the exception of German speakers is E.T.A. Hoffmann's novella *The Sandman*, where the fascination with robotics is brought together with the darkest of children's tales in which the protagonist, Nathaniel, falls in love with Olimpia, who turns out to be an automaton, which drives him insane. This story, to which we will return later, can be read in a number of ways, including the way the loved one is a projection of the lover's desires, and more recently, the way in which people follow models of physical perfection that are simply not "naturally" human.

Hoffman's tale is one dark and memorable example of a large amount of literature that emerged out of the nineteenth century where dolls came to life and vice versa. Carlo Collodi's *The Adventures of Pinocchio* appeared in 1883, while Lewis Carroll's *Alice's Adventures in Wonderland* appeared in 1865. Both of these enduring tales are enticing because of the way they explore very basic human desires through the lens of a child, using motifs deriving from dolls and other forms of child's play. Carroll's tale is an intricate surface of all forms of mimetic play, where animals speak and where playing cards become soldiers. Not only is it a graphic testimony to the way in which children breathe life into inanimate objects, it also searchingly tells us that all is not as it seems, and reminds us of the potential for the human mind to embroider and fabricate. The strange becomes familiar so that Alice, the only "normal" being in the motley gatherings, is made to feel out of place.

Appearing just before the birth of psychoanalysis with Jean-Martin Charcot, and subsequently Freud (whose *Studies in Hysteria* was published in 1895), the latter half of the nineteenth century brings conflicting states of mind to the fore, in which human mental experience begins to be categorized and socially situated. It is instructive to note that the word *homosexual* first appeared in 1886, coined by the German psychiatrist Richard Freiherr von Krafft-Ebing. For some time previous to this, homosexuality had been referred to as "inversion," but it was only in the late nineteenth century, culminating poignantly in the Wilde trial in 1895, that homosexuality is essentially created as social phenomenon. The birth of homosexuality's relevance to the subject of dolls lies in the way in which they are both associated with the strange, and thus, the queer. This is in no way to make the absurd argument that anyone who plays with dolls, marionettes or puppets is gay or queer, rather more to insist that they are both examples of what stands outside the general, imaginary and ideological framework of what counts as normal, and what exists outside a chain of accountable causality. Whereas a normal, "straight" person assists in the propagation of the species, the doll and the queer is unproductive, and therefore, a threat to a rational social ecosystem.

This analogy will have growing importance at the end of this book with the conception of the technologized body whose mediations are often outside the measures of utility and which no longer comply with older conventions of suitability and normativity. In fact, the relationship between the artificiality and queerness is a compelling and highly subversive one. Judith Halberstam and Ira Livingston draw attention to the way in which the gendered body exists among a maelstrom of shifting co-ordinates in which the ideological, technological and biological meet. Writing at the end of the millennium (1995), they rightly describe the ways in which the body exists constantly as mediated both from inside and from without, as representation. Sexuality becomes an increasingly mobile and fabricated element with changing forces in which the borderline between passive and active is progressively challenged.[28]

Dolls as they were used and appear since modern art have been fairly generously examined, including the Surrealists' obsession with them, for obvious reasons. Salient among them, although central to the still rather loose Surrealist clique, Hans Bellmer gives us some of the most lasting images of dolls, which he dismantled then reassembled to become contorted shapes reflective suffering and ennui. Bellmer was himself influenced by the other adaptation of Hoffmann's *Sandman* in Offenbach's *Tales of Hoffmann* as well as dolls from the sixteenth century, which had rounded joints. Bellmer's dolls are rearticulated into disturbing yet visually eloquent morphological jumbles in which childhood innocence is harrowingly violated. His first book of these figures had these dolls in *tableau vivant* settings, grotesquely recasting a convention that grew out of the eighteenth century. Bellmer was vocally opposed to the Nazi regime, and his dolls are read symptomatically in terms of the atrocities after they came to power, and the cataclysms of the Holocaust and World War II. But other pointers can be added to the list. For what is just as true, and which has not yet been considered in the healthy amount of literature on Bellmer that has grown out of recent years, is how through science and technology the body has been exaggerated into untold proportions from overpumped bodybuilders to what trash lifestyle magazines, blogs and websites refer to as "plastic surgery disasters." In light of these, Bellmer's work can be read afresh as the way as the self made other, sometimes laughably, other times unspeakably.

If we are to accept that Bellmer's the strongest exponent of Bellmer's legacy is Cindy Sherman, then we fall back into the hands of the predicament—predicament because it defies unity and facile explanation—of queer. For while Bellmer's work might easily be read as a misogynist, deeper exploration runs into more ambiguous, and sinister, conclusions. Equally, Sherman's feminism is far from reducible, nor is it coherent. With a career that began in the late 1970s, Sherman's work is witness, and in retrospect, testimony to the watershed described in this book, from the body that observes the doll to the body becoming the doll. And in a more subtle sense, her work addresses the more vague division between the psychological roles that we all play and physical acts of subjective reattribution and transformation. Leigh Bowery springs to mind, but there are far more brutal and unnerving from the man who had surgery and facial implants to look like a cat, to the Japanese man who spent a small fortune making himself look like Michelangelo's *David*.[29] From the very beginning of her career, Sherman has always dressed up. The female complement to Bellmer, Sherman treats herself as a doll-like cipher, but in the grotesque doll-like configurations themselves. These figures can be viewed as the Dorian Gray inner core of the contemporary age of forced and bodily perfection that is less perfection and more caricature. In a more sinister way, they play out what is commonly burlesqued in popular media in features about "plastic surgery disasters," the trashy exposés on celebrities' cosmetic excess gone awry.

Any investigation into the forays of stylized otherness will ultimately devolve to the fashion model. Before the individual identity of the supermodel in the 1980s, models were initially intended as living versions of mannequins—the French for model is *mannequin*. It is precisely at the time of the supermodel, when the model is given a subjective face, that the lines between artificial bodies, natural bodies and desirable bodies become more uneven and obscure. By the 1980s, cosmetic surgery surged in popularity, while anabolic steroids generated the new superbody immortalized by Schwarzenegger and Stallone in action film.[30] But it is in the present, new millennial era that the notion of aspiring and fashioning one's body to a media (as opposed to classical) ideal takes a new step in the way in which people wish to turn themselves in Manga dolls or Barbie, or more bizarrely, into animals. It is as if the dynamic has come full circle: from dolls imitating humans to humans wanting to be dolls. The latter is the most perverse and curious aesthetic celebration of the technologized body.

As suggested several times now, this bodily revolution is a manifestation of a much deeper change in psychology and technology. The most ambitious claim of this book is that we have reached a *qualitative* alteration in the way in which we think and treat our bodies. This change is in isomorphic, or symmetrical with similar shifts that have occurred in society and politics over the last twenty to thirty years, which include postmodernism and the age of a crisis in revolution and of democracy—the new globalized word order of the new millennium.[31] In theorizing epistemic historical breaks, Paul Hazard is one good example, demarcating the relatively short period of 1680–1715 as when the classical period was brought to the end in what became a seismic wave of scientific and philosophical questioning.[32] At these watersheds, whose onto-genesis can only be delineated retrospectively, there is almost always a paradoxical relation. In regard to the body and self, the looming question is that at the very time, with technology and globalization, when we have the opportunity to achieve the humanist project that, in the words of Stefan Herbrechter, "this very humanity disappears into the posthuman, the inhuman and the transhuman. And does this announce a disappearance, a return or re-invention of the human?"[33]

In answer to this question, this book proposes that we can no longer see the doll as external to ourselves, *but as different in degree but not in kind*. Most noticeably since the 1980s, developments in fields such as the biomedical sciences, including genetic engineering, prosthetics, nutritional supplements, and cosmetic surgery, have caused us to question what constitutes optimal bodily health and beauty. They also raise the bugbear of what constitutes a natural body over one that is artificially mediated. Although there is no precise answer for this, what is for certain is that the modern, and now postmodern body, is the locus of competing agencies, from chemical to perceptual. What is certain is that we live in a world that is presided over by archetypes of beauty and happiness that reflect a certain form of physiological excellence. Both the star athlete and the fashion model are highly mediated identities, their bodies, faces and all else besides created from the rigors of training, dieting, and perhaps, cosmetic surgery. Whereas in antiquity, the ideal body was maintained as a suggestive if mythic tie to the Greco-Roman concept of what nature stood for, in the modern and now postindustrial age, such equivalence is unthinkable. Nature, as Adorno states, is an ideal that allows humans to think that there is something outside of them that does not rely on them, is invariable and transparent—it is therefore a myth and ideology of transcendence to which humans impossibly aspire, but which to humans, as it were, impossibly belong.[34]

Prophetic of this shift is the 1984 film *Blade Runner*. Ridley Scott's film is the subject of a welter of critical reflections, and is an important marker in the ways in which humans have confronted their humanity in relation to technology. The film also revives the venerable question about whether humans are playthings, puppets, of an anonymous Maker. It is useful to turn again to Zizek who has deliberated on this aspect of the *Blade Runner* in detail:

> The last impersonation of this figure [the "Thing which thinks"] occurs in the *noir*-renewal of the eighties, in the guise of the new kind of father which characterizes "postindustrial" corporate late capitalism, a father epitomized by Tyrell in *Blade Runner*, a lone figure of the uncanny, ethereal, frail materiality, devoid of a sexual partner. This father clearly materializes the Cartesian Evil Genius: a father who exerts domination over me not at the level of my symbolic identity; but at the level of what I am qua "Thing which thinks."[35]

In reflecting on the void of origin, the replicant must contemplate his or her monstrosity. Rachel starts to cry when Deckard reveals to her that her memories are all just constructs inserted in her head to give her the illusion of humanity. Yet, as the patient viewer of this film, it is more in the crying that allows her to "become" human, well beyond the problem of accurate memory, since after all there is no such thing.

At about the same time as Scott's film, Donna Haraway penned her polemic, the "Cyborg Manifesto"[36] in which she called for a new way of thinking the female in the context of a re-ordered, technologized universe. Underpinning her thesis is the need to find a structural alternative to the humanism represented with Descartes, and later, Kant. Haraway is an important early marker in what is now an established field of inquiry. Against human individualism and the preciousness of the irreducible human soul, in the words of Elaine Graham, the cyborg chooses "to fashion an ironic, subversive exemplar to a non-dualistic, post-gender, post-colonial, post-industrial world."[37] Further, "Haraway argues that the cyborg's hybrid status as both organism and cybernetic device, calls into question the ontological purity according to which western society has defined what is normatively human."[38] But the question that hangs over this alternative, or "third way," is whether it is a third way at all, or something that either "improves" on the human or acts as a primitive form of repression.

From the humanist viewpoint, however, it is not hard to see that one of the tensions of *Blade Runner* is that it has a foot in both the cyborg and humanist camp, since Rachel clearly places value in what she perceives she is not. Yet at the most extreme, now some thirty years after this film, the need to reflect, attain or maintain humanity—understood here in its most commonsense post-Enlightenment sense—appears less and less exigent. One only need take the unprecedented, and truly "posthuman" phenomenon of someone like Blondie Bennett, who not only has submitted to countless surgeries and other cosmetic interventions, but also undergoes weekly hypnotherapy to make herself more vague and stupid.[39] This is one instance of the Nietzschian *Übermensch* returned to us as a bad joke, not a bang but a whimper.

It is a case that certainly gives Freud's gnomic statement that "Man has, as it were, become a kind of prosthetic God," a rather bathetic ring. But let us look at the rest of the passage:

> When he puts on all his auxiliary organs he is truly magnificent; but those organs have not grown on to him and they still give him much trouble at times. . . . Future age will bring with them new and possibly unimaginably great advances in this field of civilization and will increase man's likeness to God still more. But in the interests of our present investigation, we will not forget that present-day man does not feel happy in his God-like character.[40]

This has now changed. Not only is humanity comfortable, or "happy" with the new improvements, but it is also no longer feasible to separate those "organs" that have "grown on," and those that have not.

Films and televisions series after *Blade Runner* bear witness to this. These seem to have jettisoned the residue of romantic pathos and engage directly with the replicant, who either takes precedence, or vies creditably with his or human counterpart. For example, in *The Machine* (2013), the protagonist, a computer scientist played by Toby Stephens, ends his days with the female artificial life form he had a hand in creating. No longer does Frankenstein turn on his maker; technology triumphs with a new equanimity. In *Ex Machina* (2015), AI is pronounced "only a matter of time": the creation "Ava" (after "Eve" no doubt) overcomes both her maker-captor and her-would be savior. But unlike Frankenstein, she, in the end, melds seamlessly with the world. The BBC series *Orphan Black* (2013–2015) is about a number of women who have been cloned, who refer to one another as "sisters." Released almost contemporaneously is another television series, *Almost Human* (2013–2014) in which police officers are accompanied by a combat-equipped android to face a dystopian future where crime rates are exploded. The end of this book examines two celebrated manga movies, *The Ghost in the Shell* (1995) and its sequel (2004), both about cyborgs in a futuristic age. Ventriloquizing Kleist, the second film contains the line: "Humans are no match for a doll, in form or in elegance."

This book is structured as a series of discrete studies in a roughly chronological order. In addition to the central argument of this book that today's technologized body requires a dramatic rethinking of the natural self, the chapters demonstrate the extent of the manifestations of the ersatz body, the body double, the doll and the mannequin since modernism. Beginning conveniently with a corollary between Descartes and the mechanical body, the first chapter on the commedia dell'arte draws the relation between the mind–body split and the way in which bodies are typologized and stylized. Chapter 2 deals with the automata of the eighteenth century, while the following chapter examines the doll as it surfaces more prominently in early modern literature, from the lesser known texts of Jean Paul to the more celebrated of Kleist, Hoffmann and Rilke. It also looks at the drama of Maeterlinck and Craig's theories of acting. Chapter 4 examines the work of Bellmer and Sherman, and ends with examples of hyperrealist sculpture in contemporary art, which are used by some artists to advance modernist concerns, but also the way they reveal thresholds of such concerns, and our ability to relate to the nonhuman. The next two chapters trace the living doll from the fashion model (which actually began as a doll), to Barbie to bodybuilders, and then the contemporary inclination to have oneself transformed into a living doll through repeated cosmetic procedures. The final chapter is a meditation soul and body with reference to the two *Ghost in the Shell* manga films.

What are the moral conclusions of this book? This is hard to say as posthumanity presents an engaging and still-unresolved moral conundrum. For it does not deplore moral codes or commonsense, but rather acknowledges a new order in which both the sources and the aims of humanism have been reconfigured. One is the natural body. If ever there was one—since humans have always mediated their bodies—then the possibility of one in the present era is more remote, and exposes itself to be of a mythic benchmark. And when we pause to consider how much our communications are with machines or through them, we might begin to rethink communication itself, and the lines that join the world we live in, and the kind of bodies we inhabit.[41] A central aim of this book is to suggest that these changes—despite the neologisms such as "posthuman" and "anthopocene"—are perhaps not as abrupt as they seem, but were imminent within modernism, and perhaps, the shadow cast by the modern body itself.[42]

# 1
# CLOTHES OF CARNIVAL: PERSONAL PUPPETEERING AND ROLE PLAY

*Ah! ah! ah! ah! How I have made them scared! Here we have some fools who fear me, me who fears others. I'faith! It is only about playing face in this world. Had I not played the lord, and had not played the hero, they wouldn't have bothered nabbing me. Ah! ah! ah! ah!*

—POLICHINELLE, IN MOLIÈRE, *THE IMAGINARY INVALID*[1]

In accounting for major changes in human awareness and activity, the logical place to turn is historical circumstance: the climate of knowledge and need. Social changes that transpire from a particular leader, or upheavals such as war or natural disaster are easy to accept as part of the vicissitudes of change. However, the causes of changes in consciousness and knowledge are harder to position. The alterations of worldview instigated by Kepler and Galileo are to a great extent precipitated by growing sophistication in lenses and the burgeoning of world travel. And the major landmark that followed from their example was the introduction of the Cartesian cogito, in which the mind is deemed independent from the body, and in which the only worldly certainty is that we think and know we are alive. Descartes spent his entire professional life careful to duck accusations of apostasy, but his system, widely agreed to be the beginning of modern philosophy, is central to the schism between rationality and religion that would only continue to widen. In this light, we can begin to speculate more deeply on the phenomenon of the commedia dell'arte and its historical complement of the masque as it grew out of the sixteenth century. People had always dressed up, even to the point of knowing that their own enactment in social and personal settings are equivalent, yet never before had there been such a stylization by which theater was organized.

The commedia began with a relatively prescriptive framework of costumes and character types that were the armature for improvisation. The term commedia dell'arte was coined toward the end of the seventeenth century,[2] and was preceded by "commedia a braccio," "commedia all'improviso" (or improvisa), "commedia di gratiani," "commedia a soetto," "commedia d'ostrioni," "commedia italiana" and "commedia di zanni."[3] By this time, it was embraced throughout Europe and persists to some degree to this day (if only as an historical echo) as a theatrical institution. Many commentaries about the commedia and improvisation tend to emphasize the role of language,[4] while underplaying the extent to which improvisation steers the actor toward the body, toward the physical and embodied aspect, inherent but subordinate to spoken language. In his analysis of the influence of the commedia on Molière's *Don Juan*, Franco Tonelli remarks that

> The specificity of the Commedia dell'Arte resided in the shifting of the theatre's center of gravity from words to mimic and action. The spoken word became but one element among all others, often improvised, created, readapted, at any rate conditioned by a theatrical mode more akin to the "happenings." Thus, the specificity of the Commedia signals that the matrix of their entertainment was a blatant transgression of the dominant theatre's norms; for here it is not the text that becomes action, rather it is action that becomes text. As forms of entertainment, their performance privileged movement over linear narrative, space over temporal development.[5]

Or to use the words of Gustave Attinger, the commedia dell'arte is "a plastic conception of cinema," plastic here understood in the sculptural sense of clear tangibility.[6] As traveling actors, placing action before language also made them more universally accessible.[7] This would later prove congenial to presound cinema. After all, the most famous modern inheritor of the commedia's stylized movements, and in masking and dressing up to support improvisation, was Charlie Chaplin. But either way, improvisation opens up a zone of uncertainty for the actor. Well before film, the fragility of the theatrical machinery was part of the thrill.[8] Occurring at the same time as the entry of women into live public theater,[9] improvisation also sounded a thoroughly modern tune since it reflected the equivocal nature of existence itself—think of Hamlet vacillating between his perception of himself as isolated individual or as a plaything of forces beyond his ken.[10]

With this form of theater, instead of the hand occupying the puppet, or controlling the strings of the marionette,or tweaking the arms of the doll, it was the body that entered the sheaf of costume, and the container of a character type. Commenting on a later exponent of the commedia, the Catalan dramatist Joan Brossa, David George notes that "Commedia characters are non-human, and as such play an important role in Brossa's idea of theatre, which is unsentimental and denies psychological realism. They are easily identifiable types, able to be quickly portrayed."[11] The respective actors don clothing encoded, or associated, with particular actors who are expected to respond in particular ways according to prescribed character traits. In this way, the body enters into prefabricated mechanism in order to animate it, as a hand enters into a puppet. The commedia is conceived as a decisive turning point in notions of dramatic character and a challenge to theatrical convention.[12] But this was evidently also a symptom of new material and psychological conditions. Just as, traditionally, dolls were both the material and the symbolic other for self-reflection and self-growth, they were also the reminder that the world had an order independent but inclusive of the individual. With the commedia, the actor effectively renounces his or her particularity, to participate in a generic order, functioning as a doll for the audience. But there was more to this, since the inherently improvisatory nature of the commedia also meant that the "doll" also had its own inner power. This was pure theatrical artifice laid bare because one knew from the very beginning that the character was not real, but a stereotype. For all accounts the notion of clear order of humans within a definable universe was scuttled. The commedia dell'arte, it would seem, was the cultural manifestations of Cartesian doubt, and the comedic embodiment of uncertainty in the modern world.

Originating in mid-sixteenth century Italy, the commedia dell'arte evolved out of Mannerist drama. Here, Mannerism has more than one definition, but it is broadly understood in art the jettisoning of stylistic harmonies associated with Renaissance humanism in favor of a more jarring aesthetic that was reflected the uncertainty of the individual in the face of church and state. One of the most cited watersheds in the way art reflected the change of values was in the Sack of Rome in 1527 due to troops out of control following the sudden death of the Holy Roman Emperor, Charles V. Pope Clement VII was driven from the Vatican and thousands of priests murdered, churches and monasteries sacked and pillaged. This was taken as a sign of the permeability of the Church and that of faith itself. With Luther already in 1521 having incited Charles and the former Pope, Leo X, by refusing to retract his *Ninety-Five Theses*, the sack was widely seen as inaugurating a new direction. The loss of an absolute figurehead also left a spiritual

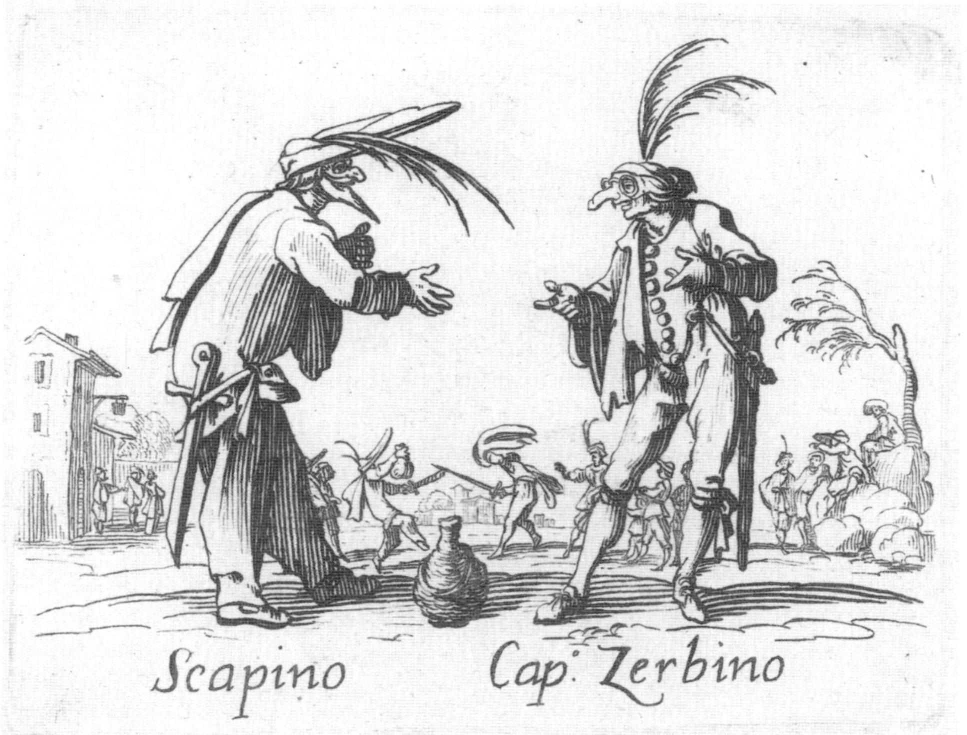


**Figure 1.1** Jacques Callot, Scapino and Zerbino, masks from the commedia dell'arte (early 1600s) engraving. Image: National Gallery of Art.

vacuum. Yet, the treaty of Cateau-Cambrésis between Henri II of France and Philip II of Spain in 1559 marked a period of relative peace, which it has been argued, also opened a way for forms of enjoyment exemplified by new and revived comedic forms that would coalesce into the commedia dell'arte.[13]

The art of this period, understood as the cusp of the modern world, varied from the Renaissance in numerous and quite marked ways, mainly through recourse to discordant relationships, and a growing emphasis on conceits and fancies. This could be seen not only in the birth of the commedia,[14] but also in the painting and music of the period. While composers like Carlo Gesualdo relied on musical dissonances that would anticipate the music of the twentieth century and its distrust of melody, painters such as Pontormo would place their figures in unfathomable settings worthy of the Surrealists, while Parimigianino rejoiced in jettisoning natural bodily proportion, stretching figures to give them an alluringly serpentine but out-of-this world elegance. The statuesque portraits of artists such as Bronzino and Allori were characterized by a striking inscrutability, and their faces have an opaque, sculpted quality as if the sitter were wearing mask. A common property to painting as well as sculpture (Giambologna) was a tenseness and torsion to poses and gestures. While Renaissance artists such as Piero della Francesca placed his figures with a strong, harmonious architectonic order, or imbued them with a lyrical naturalism (Leonardo), the figure of Mannerist art was undeniably one that was out of sorts with its surroundings, uncomfortable in the world, hence improvising a role rather than participating in a harmonic, closed circle of divine immanence.

The masks used in the commedia helped in the stylization of character by obscuring facial attitudinizing, hence minimizing psychological import. Other signs of Mannerism, as Paul Castagno observes, included "typification of form (lack of individuality, conventionality), focus on surface treatment (costume, excessive ornamentation), lack of dimensionality or depth, exaggeration and distortion, and emphasis on parts versus the unity of the entire design."[15] He correctly states that the commedia lays the ground for modernist art, especially in the slackening of links between form and representation.[16] While modernist visual art is a (heroic) struggle with different forms of abstraction, drama experimented with various abstractions of affect. As Arnold Hauser remarks in his huge study of Mannerism: "To mannerism . . . all things presented themselves in distorted forms, under a cloak of concealment that made their true nature impossible to ascertain. The mask was never laid aside, the cloak never thrown off."[17] On the other hand, the active assumption of otherness and the renunciation of self, was a ploy that sought to go beyond appearances through the visible display of deception. Hence, the paradox of masquerade is that it presents something more authentic through the skin of the inauthentic. It is a reversal no different from the classic psychoanalytic insight about disavowal: "I don't care what he thinks" means the very opposite.[18] Thus, modernist subjective particularism and individuality is haunted by, or only enabled by its opposite; the stereotype. And it is precisely through the stereotype that categories of identity are cast into radical doubt.

The emphasis on type is also something germane to comedy. As Constant Mic observes, if there is some engagement with character in comedy it is not in the same regard as with tragedy because the comedic character embraces a particular condition, a certain stereotype:

> The vice or the character trait that he presents has to be intimately integrated into the person, confounding completely with his personality. In the contrary case, if the comic trait has not entirely absorbed into the personality of the one who acts on stage, if it remains isolated and lives on in him like a kind of parasite, it can provoke laughs. Each comic character is a type, and every human being that is like a certain type, and is possibly reducible to several banal traits already has a certain comic element. Comedy is dominated by types; in tragedy, on the contrary, the living personality of the hero contains and absorbs the complex unity of vices, faults, the various traits that the type schematizes. Bergson makes a striking example for this point: comedies often take a vice or human weakness as their title (*The Miser*, *The Gambler*, *The Distracted One*), whereas the title of dramas is generally the name of the person.[19]

With the commedia, this was stretched to the point of challenging the nature of personality and individuality. For the circumscription of characters into types meant a double-movement of conformity and then a set of exceptions for the sake of dramatic surprise. But it was also such simplification that made their popularity extend beyond the upper classes, of whom only a fraction were stimulated by the more "commedia erudita," whose conventionality and abstruse references had a tendency to ponderousness. The French Parlement of the sixteenth century sought regularly to ban the commedia dell'arte, while courtly and public approbation, charmed by its satire and ribaldry, ensured it remained.[20]

## Precursors: Atellan farce

Drama begins with language itself, with spontaneous storytelling that evolved into more and more improvisation through gesticulation and demonstration in support of a narrative. When it entered into a more or less formal framework is unclear, however one of the earliest examples can be found in the *ludi Osci*, Oscan plays, but better known as Atellan farce. Atella was the Oscan town in Campania, and the first versions of the associated style were written in native Oscan. This form became popular in Rome after about 400 BCE and persisted well into the first century CE. These were bawdy satirical plays that centered around a handful of characters, Bucco, Manducus, Pappus, Samnio and Dossenus (or Dorsinus), all with distinctive traits tailored for explosive, exaggerated encounters. Bucco was stout glutton; Manducus, the avaricious, big-jawed ogre with an insatiable appetite. Predating Pantalon, Pappus was the jealous old coot who got in everyone's way, while Samnio was a bit like Harlequin, the nimble trickster and foiler of plans. As the name would imply (*dorsalis* means "back"), Dossensus was the hunchback; an abrasive, devious, often intoxicated troublemaker whose later equivalent was to be Pulcinella. Others entered occasionally such as Sordus ("deaf man"), Cocommonon, the lunatic and Maiales, the campy castrato.[21]

Moving between set scripts and improvisation, Atellan farce evolved to become a popular and effective instrument of social satire. In 23 CE, Tiberius found the spate of comedies, both scripted and otherwise, scurrilous enough to banish all the *histriones* from the region. One group that was singled out for special scrutiny was the practitioners of Atellan farce. One of the reasons for considering them a threat was their appeal to the general public as they were one of the earliest forms of what we would today categorize as B-grade popular entertainment. Often performed in public places and more ad hoc than other dramatic forms, they inevitably drew from events of their time and fed on public sentiment. Their power of penetration into the public mind was great enough to incite persecution, as when Caligula had an author of an Atellan farce burned in the arena, and Nero had an actor called Datus exiled for mentioning Claudius and Agrippa, both of whom died under suspicious circumstances,[22] a mention that was meant to bode the same for him. Suetonius tells of an occasion of popular ferment against the unpopular Emperor Galba, who reigned for a mere seven months (68–69 CE). As R. Reynolds explains in his essay on the criticism of people in Roman theater:

> When the Atellan actors struck up a *notissum canticum* which began "Venit Onesimus a villa," all the spectators took it up with one voice and sang it through several times, beginning at this line. The exact nature of the allusion is unknown. Onesimus may well have been an avaricious master; the song was in that case sung by his town slaves regretting his return from his country estate. For Galba's return from Spain had been proceeded by a number of legends about his avarice and meanness. Some think the name should be Dorsennus, the name of the well-known stock character in the Atellan burlesque. Others prefer to read "Io Simus," though Galba is known to have been hook-nosed. But the point of importance is that again the Atellan actor was the mouthpiece of the crowd and the representative of public opinion.[23]

These are isolated examples and other commentators suggest that the farce largely stopped as such, as farce.[24] In any event, the forays into theatrical activism would not last however, for by the second century, the Atellan genre was almost wholly superseded by mime. Its influence on Roman drama should however not be underestimated as the dramatist Plautus gained his earlier experience as an actor of Atellan farce and then of mime, and his proficiency in Atellan theater played a cardinal role in his proficiency as a comedian in his own plays, in which he was also an actor.[25]

Insofar as the actors inhabited these types as ciphers or constants, Atellan farce is the closest early approximation to the commedia, however with distinct points of difference. Little is known as to the nature of the clothing, although masks were widely used in all forms of drama since ancient Greece. Atellan actors relied on their own actions and their costumes would have varied, or were sometimes nonexistent, with the emphasis on word and gesture. The main point of character reference for the Oscan period appears to have been dominated by masks, the bodies were clothed in traditional togas and tunics.[26] The off-hand, brazen nature of this form of theater also owed itself to the simple fact that it was a simplification and a vulgarization of the more literary form of dramaturgy.[27] If a particular play had a script, it was relatively loose, and any hole could be filled with spontaneous ribaldry and ham-handed comedy. There is also plenty of evidence of paraded priapism with hilarious prostheses, overt homosexuality (albeit not a discrete concept then), and transvestism, the latter particularly conducive for farces of mistaken identity.[28] In the words of Pierre-Louis Duchartre, "if the farces were often lacking in propriety they possessed, on

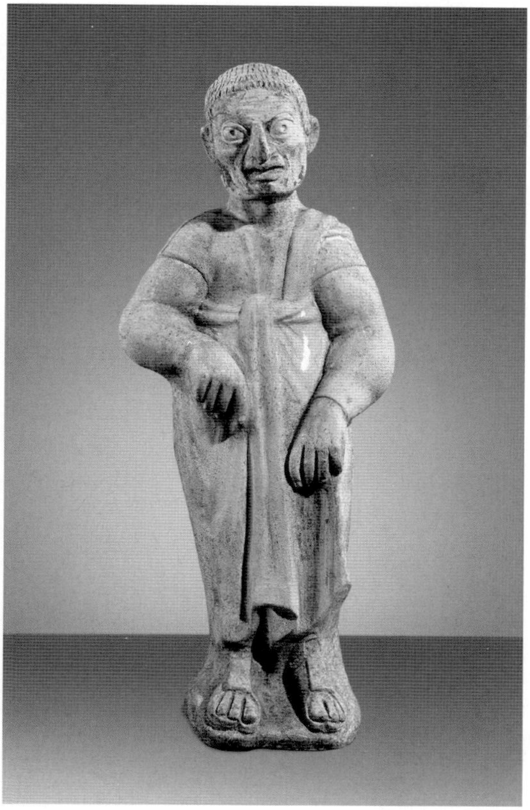

**Figure 1.2** Actor from the Atellan farce, sculpture, Italy, tenth century. London, British Museum. Photo by DeAgostini/Getty Images.

the other hand, the more essential quality of life, as is witnessed by the ancient bas-reliefs and frescoes."[29] Thus, the Atellan mode consisted in the pagan rituals of Pan and Dionysus simplified down into the contemporary, popular vulgate, shorn of their sacred import and reveling in their physicality. When we turn to Plautine drama's debt to Atellan farce, some scholars persist with the view that one of the ways that Plautus removed himself from Atellan farce was to do away with the mask. This has been increasingly discredited while converging on the notion that Plautine masks were less unnaturalistic than symbolic, with outlandish and often animalistic traits.[30] Yet, Plautine drama, while involving caricature and exaggeration, noticeably did away with the use of stocks types, with one detail of evidence being that Plautus was disposed to individualizing his masks by retouching them.[31]

These comic routines, using stock characters designed to make the audience erupt with laughter, would later come to be known more broadly as *lazzi*.[32] But it was the commedia dell'arte that was conducted along these lines using generic characterizations and closely linked costumes. There is evidence of consistency with set costumes from the Atellan period, especially with regard to Pulchinella, who will be discussed shortly, but the comparisons are still very slight. To be frank, the costuming of the commedia dell'arte is in direct lineage to the superheroes of the late modern era, or more precisely and more contemporaneously, cosplayers, albeit that cosplay enjoys a different kind of sociocultural organization. And in film, irrespective of which actor played a hero, his functions and powers were nonetheless the same. The stock dress and mask, "while impersonalizing the actor" notes John McDowell,

> heightened the type so that characteristic pieces of business may be associated with the part until they became traditional. With the emphasis on type, the interest was centred on what the type-actor did and on how he did it. The traditional costume was always recognized, and that, coupled with the bare outline in the scenario, made it necessary for the performer to be a man of action, and to appeal to the eye. This, then, led the actor to assume poses and make gestures, usually exaggerated or grotesque, which left little to the imagination of the spectators. The most striking observance, in this connection, is the vividness with which the movements and positions definitely picturize the situation.[33]

Physicality and visuality through impersonalization is key here. For while social commentary was well and truly deployed, in the commedia there is also a pervading sense of alienation of the individual, which is articulated through constant conflict and irresolution of the plot, the closure of the end being but a punctuation mark in what would eventuate in yet more disruptions and mayhem. Understanding this alienation is crucial, for while Atellan actors inhabited their characters to simplify known events through allegorizing them, for the benefit of a crowd hungry for expressive acknowledgment of their frustrations and suspicions, the commedia is a far more reflexive and solipsistic. The masks, for instance, not only transform the actors into genera, but are a barrier that can be interpreted in a number of ways, beginning with the insufficiency and incompleteness of communication and the difference between audience and actor, person and puppet, despite their codependence. There is no doubt that the commedia was a readaptation of Greco-Roman farce, but with great modifications and operating under a different concept of society and self, an issue to which we will return.

The distinction between Atellan farce and the commedia was therefore not only that the latter deployed motley costumes but in the masks themselves. As Efrat Tseëlon observes, "In the ancient world or in tribal societies, the mask had a fixed role—transformative, protective, empowering; its modern and postmodern usages are multiple and shifting, metaphorical and real, expressing danger and relief."[34] What is noteworthy is that this a transition that is not attributable to the shift from paganism to Christianity, but more to the evolution of the free modern subject who, in being granted freedom is suddenly faced with an intolerable alienation. It is alienation from God and society as well as, conceivably, from the body itself.

The other major forerunner in the chronology leading to the commedia dell'arte was the carnivals of the Middle Ages. These took several forms, namely, as public fêtes involving performing troupes of jongleurs, dancers and tricksters, to the dressing up by the upper classes during group festivities. Dressing up would continue as a popular constant to climax in the courtly masque of the seventeenth century. With its origins in pageants of the Dukes of Burgundy in the time before the Renaissance, the masque was

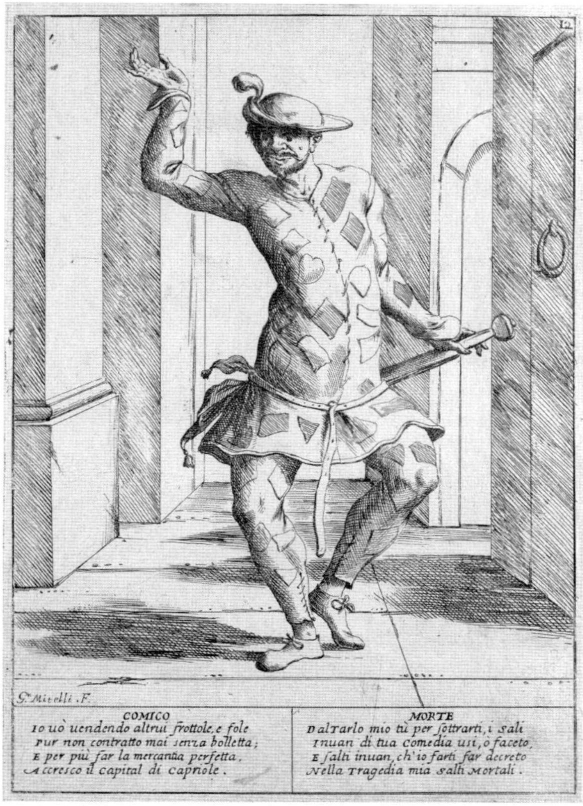


**Figure 1.3** Giuseppe Maria Mitelli, Harlequin, 1678, engraving. Photo by DeAgostini/Getty Images.

something between pagan ritual and theatrical play. Its continuing popularity lay not only in its motley display, but also that it allowed for those behind the mask to become someone or something else, temporarily unencumbered by their everyday identity. Another precursor was the dumbshow. Also developing from the Middle Ages, the dumbshow was a pantomime at the beginning or middle of a spoken play used to complement the main action with what was more metaphoric or allegorical. A famous instance of this is the pantomime within *Hamlet* (III, ii). By this time (c. 1600), the commedia dell'arte was on its way to becoming a cultural institution. In many ways, it conjoins the Atellan genre with the dumbshow. It is worth remembering that while antiquity had dolls, there was no known institution of puppet theater as such. Moreover the dumbshow did not use a conventional set of defined character types.

# Pulchinello and Punch

Shortly after its popularization by the early seventeenth century, the commedia also branched into *grand guignol*, and the Punch and Judy show. Punch—the Anglicized version of Pulcinella, Policinelle, Punch, Jan Klassen and Petroucka, among other variants that also extend to Hanswurst in Germanu—arrived in England in 1662, and was acted before he evolved into a puppet at the end of the century.[35] Pullus Gallinaceus, thence Puccio d'Aniello, condensed to become Polecenella with the Neopolitan dialect, bears a strong resemblance to Maccus of the Oscan mimes, the generations that took over from farce. Maccus was a bastardization of Bacchus, but really referred back to the companion of Dionysus (the Greek progenitor of Bacchus), Silenus, the fat old man who was permanently drunk, bawdy and free of inhibitions. Like the Punch we know, he too was masked, hunch-backed, pot-bellied and hook-nosed. A similar figure was excavated in Herculaneum, and also drawn on the walls of a Pompeiian guard room before it was effaced by nineteenth-century tourists.[36] (He also seems to have precedents in the flabby cheeks and oversized mouth in Bucco.)[37] But the parallels go far deeper as Michael Byrom explains:

> Pulcinella in the Italian Comedy carried an assortment of comical weapons—sometimes used as a scepter, including a *conchiglia* (horn), a *scopa* (broom), a *sciuscella* (wooden sword), a *squarcina* (splap-stick), and occasionally an inflated bladder. In the marionette shows the horn and sword were certainly seen, while the slap-stick seems to have been reserved for the glove-shows. Now, all these implements were common stage properties in the Atellan farces. The slap-sticks used in both ages were pieces of split wood or cane or bundles of sticks held in the hand which served the *zanni* [a commedia character type] to gesticulate and to beat with and play the fool. In addition to this, the speaking instrument or *privetta*, called in England the "swazzle," was known to have been used by the Oscans in Rome; and although it does not seems to have been part of Pulcinella's equipment on the live stage, it was a common feature of the puppet shows. Another indication, perhaps, that Pulcinella was originally a puppet?[38]

This is a striking and strong claim, albeit couched as a question. The comprehensive evidence of continuity between the early Oscan traditions and the commedia dell'arte of the Mannerist period onward, should not deter from the main thesis here, which is to argue of a much widespread and more complexified deployment of this system of theater.

For by the end of the seventeenth century, the commedia had become relatively ubiquitous across Europe, and had developed fairly specific forms of dress and gestural patterns that took it away from the more "literary" or scripted theatrical forms. As Catherine Velay-Vallantin observes, at this time at end of the seventeenth century, the commedia began to have a very particularized set of movements amounting to the respective characters, with mechanized movements, with an acrobatic element that had a strong visual effect.[39] It is also no coincidence that marionette theater, specifically dolls controlled with strings, appeared in central Europe in the sixteenth century.[40] Polichinelle appeared in France for the first time in 1649, and a little later thanks to the Brioché father and son troupe (from the Italian, Briocci), he was turned into a marionette. This coincided with the time when the living members of the commedia began to mimic the movements of marionettes.[41] The mechanical body was also the beginning of the modern body, and of course, the thinker of the seventeenth century to have entrenched the notion of the body as machine was René Descartes.

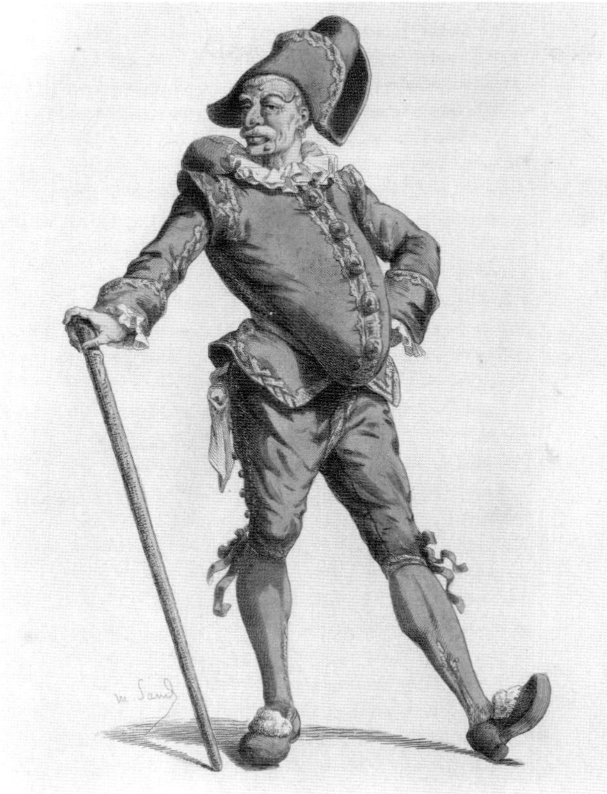

**Figure 1.4** Maurice Sand, Polichinelle in 1820. Engraving from the ommedia dell'arte study entitled *Masques et buffons, comédie italienne*, Paris 1860. Venice, Casa di Carlo Goldini. Photo by DeAgostini/Getty Images.

## Commedia clowns and the mind-body problem

By the sixteenth century, which also marks the beginning of modern science, it became increasingly customary for thinkers to conceive of bodies as machines. This conception was key in making the transition from a world ruled by abstract design to one governed by systems and laws that could be understood and replicated. As Paul Valéry observes, it was thanks in large part to Descartes that we were able to do away with occult methods and beliefs on which so much of medicine was based. By using the metaphors of pumps and bellows within the body, he was able to show physiological principles that related to the way life functions and operates.[42] While salutary, such explanations had several ramifications, for the certainties of reason came at the price of renouncing the abstract forces of a Godhead. To conceive bodies as machines was also to step into a deeper psychic turmoil as to the source and direction of things.

The notion of the body ruled by mechanical principles was taken up by some of the earlier writings by Descartes well before the *Discourse on Method*, but published posthumously. Titled *The World and Man*, this was Descartes's first attempt at a systematic natural philosophy. His treatise on *Man* asks for us to consider that bodily functions.

> All follow naturally, in this machine, from the single provision of its organs, neither more nor less than do the movements of a clock or some other automaton, from its counterweights and its cogs; so that we must conceive on their account in it no other vegetative soul, not sensible, nor any other principle of movement and life. . . .[43]

The body is described in terms of pneumatic and other mechanical technologies:

> The nerves of the machine that I am describing can be compared to the pipes in the mechanical parts of these fountains, its muscles and tendons to various other engines and springs which serve to operate these mechanical parts, its animal spirits to the water that drives them, the heart to the source of the water, and the brain's cavities to apertures. Moreover, respiration and similar actions which are normal and natural to this machine, and which depend on the flow of spirits, are like the movements of a clock or mill, which the normal flow of water can make continuous. External objects, which by their mere presence act on the organs of sense and thereby cause them to move in many different ways . . . are like strangers who on entering the grottoes of these fountains unwittingly cause the movements that take place before their eyes. For they cannot enter without stepping on certain tiles which are arranged in such a way that, for example, if they approach a Diana bathing they will cause her to hide in the reeds, and if they move forward to pursue her they will cause a Neptune to advance and threaten them with a trident.[44]

This is a remarkable, and exhaustive portrait that sets out to consider the human body in an objective and materialist fashion. Descartes's biographer Desmond Clarke considers that while not mentioned in his correspondence, it is nonetheless highly likely that the inspiration for these metaphors derived from the engineer and architect Salomon de Caus, who in 1615 published his *Explanation of Moving Forces, with various machines both useful and decorative: to which are added various designs for Grottoes and Fountains*.[45] According to de Caus, a machine is "a combination and firm connection of timber or other material, which has the power and movement either from itself or from any other source."[46] Among other things, his book had designs for hydraulic machines that could make similar sounds and movements to those of humans and animals.[47] Influenced by his brother, in 1644, Isaac de Caus produced a design for a group of automated birds powered by a water wheel and pegged cylinder that, as will become evident in the next chapter, was the basis of the most famous automata of the following century.

Despite such specialized antecedents, it would be Descartes who was perhaps the most influential in entrenching the analogy of the body as machine. Another famous, corresponding, parallel arises in the *Leviathan* (1651), where Thomas Hobbes compares society to a huge automaton. Shortly after Descartes death, the machine-body analogy had penetrated into several orders of life, as evidenced by the entry on the marionette in Antoine Furetière's dictionary of 1690:

> MARIONETTE. Subst. woman. Small puppet moved by levers and which appears animated, like a Saltimbanque, which is behind a small theatre and is made to speak, play and dance to give pleasure to children and people. Ironically one also calls a young woman a marionette. Descartes says that beasts act only as marionettes, and that the agitation of their blood acts in lieu of the levers; that one can but admire their small manners (*petites addresses*), as the levers of a clock which, without a soul, marks the hours better than any human could.[48]

In his commentary on this passage, Michel Manson observes that it returns to a theme already present in antiquity, that of animism which is applied to religion and magic as well as toys.[49] The object, the machine is in effect given life as a result of brute perception, but also belief and imagination.

Descartes's adoption of the mechanical principles of the body set him on the decisive direction to positing the mind-body division. As he states in what is now his most famous document, the *Discourse on Method*, "the soul by which I am what I am, is entirely distinct from the body; and even if it is easier to know than the body, it would still be what it is even if the body were not to exist."[50] It was also by setting the mind up as something discretely different from the workings of the body that opened up the question as to its foundation and orientation. Hence, Descartes ushered in methodic doubt, which was essentially to change the question as to what is true to the how something can be known. In doing so, Descartes made humans responsible for knowledge where before it had been God who was the chief guarantor of truth; certainty became a matter of individual judgment. Descartes fundamentally unmoored human principles from the binding principles of deity, and placed the burden of knowledge on the shoulders of humans. While scholars of Mannerism such as Hauser place Descartes in opposition to earlier thinkers such as Michel de Montaigne, whom he sees as thoroughly embodying Mannerism from a literary and theoretical perspective, it is the Cartesian split that is important here; and it is the contention here that the commedia dell-arte is modernized incarnation of comedy in the classical comedy-tragedy division. Unlike its antecedents in Oscan theater, the commedia dell'arte quickly evolved to have an intimate and manifold relationship to dolls and puppetry. The modern subject may be independent; the modern subject literally pulled its own strings, but this was also a condition for the plague of uncertainties.

Despite its forerunners, the claim that the commedia dell'arte is a cultural phenomenon unique to the modern era must align to the notions that Descartes helped to shake up and shape. But it is also this alignment that brings to the fore something that the commedia dell-arte achieved through comedy, which was a strong emphasis on otherness, and the estrangement of the other, analogous to the estrangement of the body from the mind. As Domenico Scafoglio presciently observes, comedy had always been conceived according to the actions and lives of others: "the comic figure is always the same albeit in different ways, being foreign to the culture he lives in: in Rome one said the Atellan dramatists came from Atella; the comedians of Roman theater were slaves, and so again foreigners; the buffons from urban European societies came from the country or were thought to be; the masques of the Commedia dell'Arte of the sixteenth to the eighteenth century were generally ethnic masques that represented under typologized forms, neighbouring cultures."[51] In their anthology of documents on the commedia, Ferdinando Taviani and Mirella Schino divide the various professionals of the commedia spectacle into not only actors, but also "charlatans, buffoons and beggars."[52] In further support of this, the *zanni* is known to be the "dispossessed immigrant worker."[53] They were all from the lower orders of society, and were they not in entertainment, mostly undesirable.

It does not take much to extrapolate that the commedia were also a dramatic solution to the otherness of the body to the mind. As living dolls, they were, as it were, all body, all machine, each one reflecting a particular appetitive state. Moreover, by actors inhabiting preexistent types with their attendant rules of voice and action they insert themselves into the body of the other that gives them a certainty that they do not have as individual human beings. The entire body becomes a mask, and the costume allows for theatrical stylization analogous to the controlled bodies of puppets themselves. It was a highly positive avowal of the body as machine. The best example of this is preserved in the etchings of Jacques Callot from 1621 (see Figure 1.1), and later in the works of Claude Gillot (Plates 1 and 2). Apart from their technical mastery, the most recognizable aspect of these small works is the very lack of naturalism to the poses: They are arachnid, simian, serpentine and amphibious; contorted, bent and tensile; the forms are not humanoid but not human, pulled by invisible strings or as if inhabited by an inner mechanism, or armature. But their expressive, animal aptitudes are noticed immediately.

After all, as Descartes argued, the body was much easier to know than the mind. With the bodies as machine-like, and the characters as preordained, audiences were given an anchorage of certainty within the comedic chaos. In this regard, there is also a connection to be drawn between the commedia and madness in the age of reason, as described by Michel Foucault in his seminal history *Madness and Civilization* (1960): Reason, as epitomized by the Cartesian *cogito*, necessitated a less well defined other for its subsistence; with the birth of reason also comes the birth of its shadow, madness.[54]

In contemplating dualities between body and mind, madness and reason, it is worth returning to the physicality of the commedia, which it inherited from the Oscan theater. In the early days of the commedia, upon its entry into France, remarks Duchartre, "The jovial and crude naturalism of the art of the Italians, in contrast to the French theatre, which inclined rather more to reason or logic, oftentimes seemed intolerably vulgar to many contemporaries."[55] But the physicality was not limited to slapstick and melodrama, it was also a way of making the body act out the expressions of the face, while the face was static because it was covered by a mask. In this regard, the strategy of the pantomime artist is no different from the marionettist: "The art of playing with the mask, then, is not conceivable without a perfect knowledge of pantomime. When once this is mastered all the muscles of the actor's body co-operate in his interpretation and perform the expressive function of the muscles of the face."[56] This can be expressed more obliquely but more beautifully by Paul Verlaine's poem "Pantomime" whose third stanza runs: "That scoundrel

Harlequin has been/Kidnapping Columbine/And pirouettes four times."[57] This transferal from face to body also suggests that emphasis is less on facial pathos, but a more corporeal, sculptural form of expression. At best, the audience loses consciousness that the actor is wearing a mask as the body enters into its own affective processes.[58] Curiously enough, the masks raised occasional antagonism by contemporaries of the seventeenth and eighteenth centuries, associating them with demonic behavior.[59] Such superstitions have their literary roots since Alchino is one of the devils mentioned by Dante in his *Divine Comedy* (XXI and XXII). Equally "Erlequin" can be found in old French legends to be a mischievous imp.[60]

While the commedia would continue to have a life in modern times, this life was episodic and sporadic. It returned as an historic form, or in specific festivals as in the masques of Venice, where it is not so much as played but referenced for the sake of tourism. It did, however live on in the puppet theater whose appeal was primarily to children. One literary anecdote serves to round this section. Bearing in mind the forays into the sexually and politically subversive in the commedia dell'arte and in Atellan farce before it, the tendency to rebelliousness within this tradition ends, notably enough, with a puppet: Pinocchio. In Collodi's well-known classic, chapter ten has the puppet child view a *Punch and Judy* performance. But on seeing Pinocchio, the performance is momentarily disrupted, suddenly contravening the directions of the puppeteer. This is revolt against authority is a motif in the book, where Pinocchio regularly disobeys his elders, finally to triumph by being endowed with his own free will.[61]

## Representations of the commedia dell'arte in art

The earliest painting to have represented the commedia dell'arte is supposed to be from 1571 to 1572, a group scene of a players before a noble audience by an unattributed Flemish artist (formerly thought to be Jacques Pourbus).[62] Given their motley visuality, the commedia would continue to enjoy a strong presence in the genre painting well into the nineteenth century. It appears that artists were not only drawn to the striking, and to the contemporary eye, recognizable nature of the costumes, but also used commedia themes as a vehicle for lascivious or elicit themes.[63] This was also true of arguably the greatest artist of the commedia, Antoine Watteau, whose scenes are not as formal and proscenially staged as the painting of his predecessors, but lost in a dream, the costumes congenial to the musical stillness and ethereal pantomime in which intimacy and deceit are harmoniously married. But one painting, unusually large of the artist (1.85 m x 1.5 m), stands out: *Gilles* depicts a Pierrot character in the foreground flanked by the rest of his costumed troupe, which appear on the lower right of the canvas, as Gilles is standing on the rise, in a nimbus of his own isolation (Plate 3).

The stark but still elegantly emblematic nature of the image may be due to its first intended use as a sign for a café whose owner, Belloni, had once been an actor. But this does not detract from the compelling oscillation between frankness and enigma. Ostensibly, the painting is a paragon of humanism: His face appears honest and passive, at once imploring yet withheld. But to any viewer who spends any time with this work, it becomes noticeable that the core of the tension is precisely that he is being so human, yet in costume. He has assumed a role which he is not actively playing, unlike the figures we see below who have a more active and mischievous air. It is also unclear whether, according to a humanist reading at least, he wishes momentarily to escape his guise and communicate to us as a person as such, or whether he comes to us as having permanently, pathologically, assumed his character and appears to us as this proxy. What then he presents to us is made interminably ambiguous apart from the tautological fact stated in the title. In his examination of Watteau and the art drawn from the commedia, Günther Hansen describes the art as depicting a world in which "authenticity can no longer be found," where the figures lie suspended between "appearance and being, between stage and world."[64]

In many respects, Watteau's painting is a coda for the decentered modernist subject. Pierrot and Harlequins would continue to be a staple of both academic and modern art—from Gérôme to Cézanne (Plate 4) to Picasso—and their meaning would expand to suggest the artist himself, not only to propagate the myth of the mute who must express himself in words, but also as the outsider and the madman. Such iconography was also the expression of the venerable Platonic skepticism about the artist as the purveyor of seductive but false truths. Ultimately, to play the doll was to renounce the transparency of self, to displace the notion of nuclear self, the Cartesian *cogito*, to become a perverse or even degraded being. The modernist artist as outsider would have growing affinity with the outsider to biological body: the automaton, the doll and the marionette. If the artist trafficked in representations, in a world different from the real one, then the artist might have the right to occupy this world as well. From the eighteenth century, there was a growing interest in the possibility of machines that could form complex human functions, but also the obverse, of the human falling in love with, or wanting to become, a machine. This is to be seen plentifully in not only literature and later art, but also in the craze for making robots and automata, the subject of the chapter to follow.

# 2

# A SOUL IN CONTROL: THE ART OF THE AUTOMATON

*My friend, there are three models, the man of nature, the man of poetry and the man of acting. The one of nature is not as great as the poet who is in turn not as great as the great actor, the most exaggerated of all. The latter climbs onto the shoulders of the poet, a large wicker mannequin that houses its soul, shaking this figure fearfully, even to the extent that the poet no longer recognizes himself.*

*The sensitive man obeys the impulses of his nature and precisely only expresses the cry of his heart; the moment he tempers or forces the cry, he ceases to play himself and an actor takes over.*

—DIDEROT, *THE PARADOX OF THE ACTOR*[1]

One of the curious ironies of the Enlightenment period is that the same period when the subject began to defend his (usually his) unique status, independent thought and so on, was also when the first successful robots and automatons were being built. These figures and contraptions were based largely on mechanics devised from clockwork. In the eighteenth century, Descartes's metaphor of the body and the machine was now a reality, or at least a concrete alias. There had been examples of automata well before, but in the eighteenth century, they became more than eccentricities by becoming powerful mechanisms by which to understand and contemplate the nature of life, physiology and creativity. Since the mechanical body was no longer a metaphor, but a perceived reality, it brought questions of free will and consciousness into sharper relief, and also enlivened speculation, that would later be articulated by Kleist, as to whether free will and consciousness were indeed desirable. Diderot also articulates this in his paradox of the actor: A good actor must dim his expression, in essence mute his humanity, in order to divulge a more compelling humanity on stage. While this case is told to be untenable by most actors, that need not matter, for the point in question is that Diderot found it necessary to make such a point.

Interest in mechanical bodies reached a peculiarly new pitch in the eighteenth century. This is not entirely attributable to technological advancements. In his detailed study of simulated bodies, Marquard Smith observes:

> The human's functioning, previously God-given, later comprehended in terms of thermal and fluid dynamics, and operating through the matter by which it is constituted,

> becomes a motion machine where the physiology of humours is replaced by the physiology of nerves, where the brain is a motor that drives a complex organism with a circulatory system a nervous system circulating energy. (The entry for *nerve* in Diderot's *Encyclopédie*, published between 1751 and 1772, claims that the "essence" conveyed around the body is referred to by some as "animal spirit.")[2]

The ingenuity of the machines of this time is to be seen as motivated, accelerated, by Enlightenment humanism, which questioned the very nature of human expression and feeling, and as famously formulated in the philosophy of Immanuel Kant, the limits of human perception and agency. Hence, the self-contradictory question, subtending Diderot's hypothesis, was whether automatons are better at being human than humans.

This historic question is certainly worth turning to when reflecting on the disconcerting film *Her* (2013) by Spike Jonze, in which the hapless protagonist (Joaquin Phoenix) falls desperately in love with the voice of a highly sophisticated computer operating system, "Samantha." A (weaker) film, *Automata*, from the following year, directed by Gabe Ibáñez, has robots accomplish the impossible and assume consciousness and disobey their human makers, contravening a supposedly unbreakable protocol. This is made possible by someone appropriately named "the clocksmith." When Wallace, an executive from the company that manufactures the robots, accuses one of the new breed to be "just a machine," it retorts that such a comment is the same as calling a human "just an ape." Replete with historical subtexts (that in the overall film devolve to so many clichés), "clockmaker" refers to the mechanisms of the eighteenth century that derived from clockwork, while the distinction between humans and animals has Cartesian overtones, but ones overturned recently by animal ethicists. But it is also present with the Zooma range of domestic robot pets, which the child is meant to nurture as much as enjoy. To what extent is looking after an animate toy the same as looking after a real dog?

While concepts of a subjective inner nature had been alive since at least Augustine, those of naturalness, social duty and personal rights were relatively new. Was the automaton that evolved at the same time a foil, facilitator or corrective? The answer is that it was all of these, but it was also a means of humans understanding themselves as the automaton was literally the embodiment of technological wish for precision and freedom from nature. Paradoxically, the body-machine was a perverted realization of the Cartesian model, symbolically transcending the workings of nature in the aspiration of reason in and for itself. This dream predates the dystopianism of extreme rationalization; however, a corrective was offered by F. W. Schelling, who equated perversions of nature with monstrosities. Another corrective is that the two most famous of automata, a duck and a chess player, were both fraudulent. But what is even more provocative is that their fame has lived on as has the desire to believe in them.

## Early automata

One of the earliest citable examples of automata comes from the hands of Ktesibios, also the first head of the Alexandrine Library, who is reputed to have invented the first cuckoo clock. Subsequently, in Alexandria, the mathematician Heron wrote about hydraulics and pneumatics, and is reputed to have invented the aeolipile, or Heron's engine, the first steam engine, or turbine. There are also some recorded instances of automata in ancient China, as reported by the Lie Zi text of the third century BCE. Yet, the description is more than mildly implausible, describing a lifelike figure that sang in tune, danced and winked its eye.[3] Automata would continue to be reported and described, as when Liutprand, an ambassador from Cremona, visited Theophilius's palace in Constantinople in 949, and declared to see all manner of lifelike, mobile lions and singing birds.[4] Little is preserved, however, as to how these were set in operation, and the accounts are hard to verify.

In the middle of the fifteenth century, Johannes Müller, otherwise called Regiomontanus, fabricated a fly out of iron propelled by cogs that walked about on a table, and an eagle out of iron or wood that is said to have flown toward the King of Nürnberg. According to other sources, it stood at the country gate, nodding and flapping its wings on the king's approach. In the sixteenth century, also in Nürnberg, Albrecht Dürer's stepfather Hans Frey built hollow statues that consumed water, much in the manner of earlier Arabic automatons that drank and expelled wine. Hanns Bullman, also active in the early sixteenth century, fabricated a variety of figures based on clockwork that also registered themselves rhythmically. Some could also launch bullets. A short time later, Caspar Werner made a ship that navigated itself on a tabletop inhabited by a woman beating a cymbal, and at the helm was a boy who moved his head while guiding the rudder with both hands, while at the rear lay a Cupid with

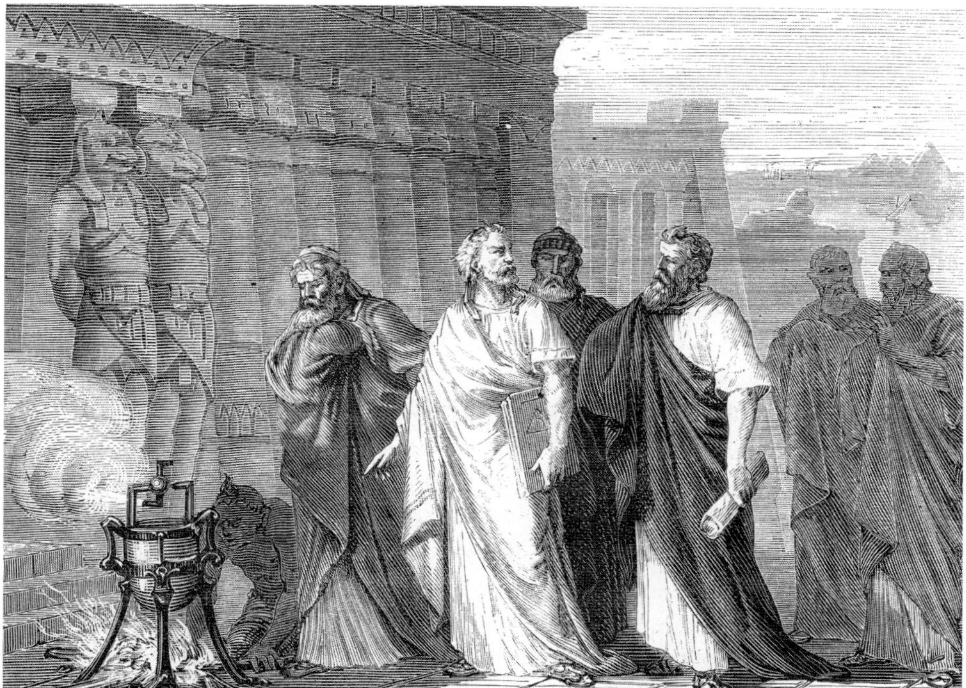

**Figure 2.1** Heron performs an experiment with an aeolipile before the students of the School of Alexandria. Anonymous engraving, nineteenth century. Photo by Universal History Archive/UIG via Getty Images.

his bow ready to shoot one of the audience with a small arrow.[5] In 1540, Gianello Torriano, an engineer from Cremona, made Charles V a figure of a girl that could play the strings of a lute. More apocryphal is the tale that Descartes himself brought with him a mechanical replica of his late daughter, Francine, on his journey to meet Queen Christina of Sweden in 1649. If this is shrouded in doubt, we do know that Descartes did have several automata constructed for him, which included a small machine simulating a rope dancer most likely before he formulated the hypothesis that animals are without souls.[6]

With the exception of the last example, the appeal of automata was largely one of spectacle. As Anthony Grafton explains, in fifteenth-century Italy, automata were mostly a feature of theater, pageants and public events, where it was common for artists and engineers to work together on contraptions whose primary purpose was to inspire wonder and delight.[7] Arguably the most celebrated maker of automata of this period was Giovanni Fontana, whose creations included a devil, a rabbit that emitted fire from its rear and a bird that could fly. His collusion with the supernatural was confined to his fake figures, yet Fontana was openly contemptuous of the superstitions of his time. He toyed with such figures, "as a deflation of stories told by magi and theologians alike. Magicians invoked devils. Fontana showed how to create a mechanical male devil, with movable eyes, tongue, horns, arms, and wings, as well as his fire-breathing she-devil."[8] Fontana also ridiculed the belief that statues could have souls. Indeed, it was despite, and because of, such widespread belief in the paranormal that fed the enthusiasm of Fontana and his contemporaries to supply highly evocative mechanical alternatives. Fontana, as Grafton observes, "could already build a partial replica of a human being, and by doing so, he showed not only, as Archimedes had said in another context, that he could move the world, but also that he could disenchant it."[9] The ingenuity that Fontana lavished on his apparatuses and in debunking his contemporaries would not prove to have a lastingly rationalizing effect for the simple fact that the impulse to foist belief onto the artificial being was too strong. The presence of automata, while reinforcing the humanness of humans, also reinforced the opposite: not only by offering practical understanding on biological mechanism, but at the same time emphasizing humans' compunction to assume life in the lifeless, and moreover, to forego the natural for the artificial.[10]

## Pygmalion and Pygmalionism

Greek mythology has its share of animated figures, from the automata in the forge of Hephaestus (the equivalent of Vulcan) to Talos the bronze giant that circles Crete thrice daily on lookout for invaders. Hephaestus was not only the god of fire and metalwork, but also sculpture, and the most famous mythological sculptor was Pygmalion, a Cypriot artist who fell in love with a woman statue wrought from his own hand. Made familiar and famous by Ovid's *Metamorphoses*, Pygmalion is introduced as a man who disliked women ("Abhorr'd all womankind, but most a wife"[11]), but sculpted a figure of incomparable perfection and fell in love with it. After making a sacrifice to Venus, the goddess of love grants life to the inanimate statue who lives on to have Pygmalion's child, Paphos, who goes on to found the city bearing his name.

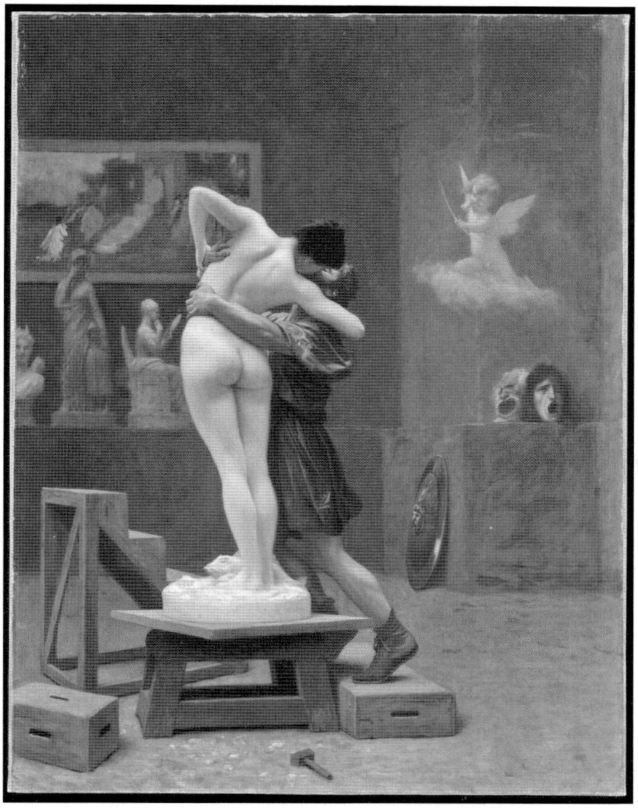

**Figure 2.2** Jean-Léon Gérôme, *Pygmalion and Galatea*, 1890, oil on canvas, 88.9 cm × 68.6 cm. The Metropolitan Museum of Art, New York.

It is a myth that has itself given life to countless retellings in drama, narrative and image. But what is of special interest is that Pygmalion is enamored of a lifeless object to the exclusion of all women alive. Marquard Smith places the Pygmalion story centrally within what would become, from the eighteenth century onward, its own pathology, hence, Pygmalionism—the tendency to fall in love with inanimate objects and wish to bring them to life. As he points out, from the Enlightenment onward, spurred no doubt by Descartes, the passion for Pygmalion is quite striking, citing a variety of texts such as André François Boureau-Deslandes's *Pygmalion: ou, la statue animée* (1741) and Rousseau's most influential dramatic piece "Pygmalion scène lyrique" (1762).[12] Schiller also devoted a poem to Pygmalion, "Die Ideale" (1795–1796) as did Dryden about a century before (1697–1700). Interest in the story would continue to this day where Pygmalionist creationism has been given a futuristic touch, a revival nourished by growing probability of artificial life. Pygmalionism, the psychological diagnosis, relates to a particular form of autoerotism since Pygmalion fell in love with the statue he himself made. It grew together with the many sexual diagnoses that emerged from the middle of the nineteenth century. Smith also notes that terms such as *normal*, *normalcy* and *abnormal* appeared at about the same time.[13] This occurred a century after the conceptualization of nature and the natural.

These ambiguities also appear in Rousseau's *Pygmalion*, for when Galatea comes alive she exclaims "C'est moi" then reverts in bafflement, "Ce ne'est plus moi"—it's no longer me, but arrives at assurance when she turns to Pymalion himself: "Ah, encore moi" (ah, still me). It is a web of multiple narcissisms, starting with Pygmalion's own magic and devolving to his own created other. It is not a perfect reciprocality, but rather a relationship in which each one partakes of his or her own narcissistic mirroring, something with which a Lacanian psychologist would quite agree. In his analysis of Rousseau's play, Paul de Man also observes that in the stages before its animism, Pygmalion is not all assured, finding the statue "aptly monstrous," and when it is "brought to life" it "feeds upon colder fires than those burning on sacrificial altars." Since she is an exception to the rule, she effectively casts everything into doubt; we can no longer be sure of the status of objects, or language itself.[14]

## Vaucanson

In expanding his notion of the body as a machine, Descartes remarked that the human body was simply a better one than the kind produced by human hands. Yet, he concedes that "bodies constructed by human artifice" have helped him understand biological functions, "For I do not recognize any difference between the machines made by craftsmen and the various bodies that nature alone composes," only that the human mechanism was far subtler and diverse in its intricacies. Descartes asserted that "It is certain that all of the rules of mechanics apply to physics, and that everything artificial is also natural; it is no less natural, for example, that a clock keep time by means of its inner works than a tree bear fruit."[15] As Geneviève Rodis-Lewis remarks, Descartes effectively reverses the distinction between the artisan and nature advanced by Aristotle in his *Physics*, where nature is spontaneity in motion whose finality is immanent, while the artisan's finality is driven by intent.[16] Thus, Descartes announces that "As art imitates nature and men are capable of making various automata which move but have not thought, it seems consistent with reason that nature produce its own automata, though far superior to our artefacts."[17] But most conceivably, Descartes's conviction that the human machine was just an optimal version of what can be made outside of the hands of God effectively threw down the gauntlet to the possibility of challenging this view.

The *home machine*, as it was called in the eighteenth century, could also be assigned human characteristics not only in movement, but in what could be achieved. The simplicities of animation and discharging a particular anecdotal function, prevalent in the previous centuries, transitioned to automata that sought to vie with their human counterparts. For unlike the earlier automata, those of the eighteenth century were not just for show, and more germane to Descartes's use of them, they were a means by which to gain a better understanding of the human organism and how it functions.

Operating on a very different register from Descartes was Spinoza, who also urged a different thinking about the body. Well before what would become called the philosophy of embodiment—regularly invoked to distinguish humans from automata, explaining that our systems of knowledge are intertwined with the aesthetic, perceptual, bodily systems[18]—Spinoza proposed a "bodily thinking," as it were. As Gilles Deleuze states,

Spinoza "proposes to establish the body as a model: 'One does not know what a body wants. . . .' This declaration of ignorance is a provocation: we speak of conscience and its decrees, of the will and its effects, to dominate the body and its passions—but *we do not even know what the body wants*."[19] In passing this question to the eighteenth century, it is curious to add that the means of answering it was not only in dissecting and observing the body, but by attempting to build artificial bodies.

While previous automata had been to some extent reliant on finesse and illusion, add to this a real intent on emulating the bodily mechanics. Jessica Riskin states, that a new feature of the automata of the late eighteenth century was that they were not all about external appearance but also emulated process and function:

> Cartesian dualism, which had exempted consciousness from mechanist reduction, and "hypotheticalism," which had allowed for an infinity of possible mechanisms underlying nature's visible behaviours, gave way to an emergent materialism and to a growing confidence, derived from ever-improving instruments, that experimentation could reveal nature's actual design. These developments brought a new literalism to automata and a deepening of the project. The designers strove, not only to mimic the outward manifestations of life, but also to follow as closely as possible the mechanisms that produced these manifestations.[20]

Hence, Jacques de Vaucanson (1709–1782), by far the most celebrated inventor of the period, stipulated that his mechanisms were instruments of instruction. In a letter to the Abbé Desfontaines, he defended the need to construct a mechanism over merely producing diagrams and "anatomical descriptions."[21] His mechanics were derived from exhaustive examination of the biological *écorché*, the body flailed of its skin to allow for study of the tendons and musculature (Plate 5).[22]

Vaucanson was the younger son of a line of Grenoble glove makers, who showed early proficiency in machinery by mending clocks of friends. After a brief stint with Jesuits, he quit the order to go to Paris to take up studies in music, physics, mechanics and anatomy. It was at this time that he met a well-known surgeon, Claude-Nicolas Le Cat, who was interested in developing knowledge of the human body through "moving anatomies" (*anatomies mouvantes*), that is, automatons. Another surgeon, François Quesnay, also encouraged Vaucanson to make artificial bodies that simulated certain biological functions. His first automaton was begun in 1735, completed in 1737 and exhibited in January of the following year in the Hôtel de Longueville. Called the "Transverse Flute Player," it, in many respects, mimicked the form of a flute-playing satyr by the sculptor Antoine Coysevox. Measuring about 170 centimeters, the figure sat on a rock on a pedestal. The figure boasted the ability to play eleven tunes and was a huge success, called a "masterpiece of the human spirit."[23] An example of what in Diderot's *Encyclopédie* called an "androïde"—with Vaucanson in mind this was defined as "an automaton with a human form (*figure*) and which, by means of some well-placed springs etc., acts and performs other functions exteriorly similar to that of man"[24]—it was made largely of wood; the main feat of the android were to simulate the passage of human breath. A chief reason for simulating the statue was not solely for aesthetic reasons, but also to accommodate the complex medley of cogs and levers, which were too plentiful for a single body shape to house. The source of the breath was in nine bellows that corresponded to three pipes leading to three reservoirs located in the chest of the figure. These conjoined to one single pipe leading to the mouth whose "tongue" levered up and down in accordance with the opening and closing of the mouth and jaw.

Foreseeing that the novelty of his invention would inevitably fade, Vaucanson, who had already profited considerably from the invention, embarked on a new project, this time a figure of a provincial shepherd that not only played a flute, but also a tambourine. As Jean-Claude Heudin, in his book on artificial bodies comments, "Vaucanson was able to make discoveries that an autopsy could not, such as the amount of stress required to exhale at such a rate, which the inventor judged to be around 56 pounds."[25] Significantly, Vaucanson was not simply motivated by the interest in fabricating a curiosity, but by exploring the possibility of mastery of an artistic endeavor, therefore something quite particular and expressive. Like an artist, the automaton could perform a function not common to everyone.

The third contraption was by far the most sophisticated. "Vaucanson's duck" of 1741 was made with more than one function: It drank, ate, paddled in the water and even ejected its waste. Onlookers could see it ingest and later expel the waste as a small green pellet. To do all this necessitated a fairly large and complex machine, whose working

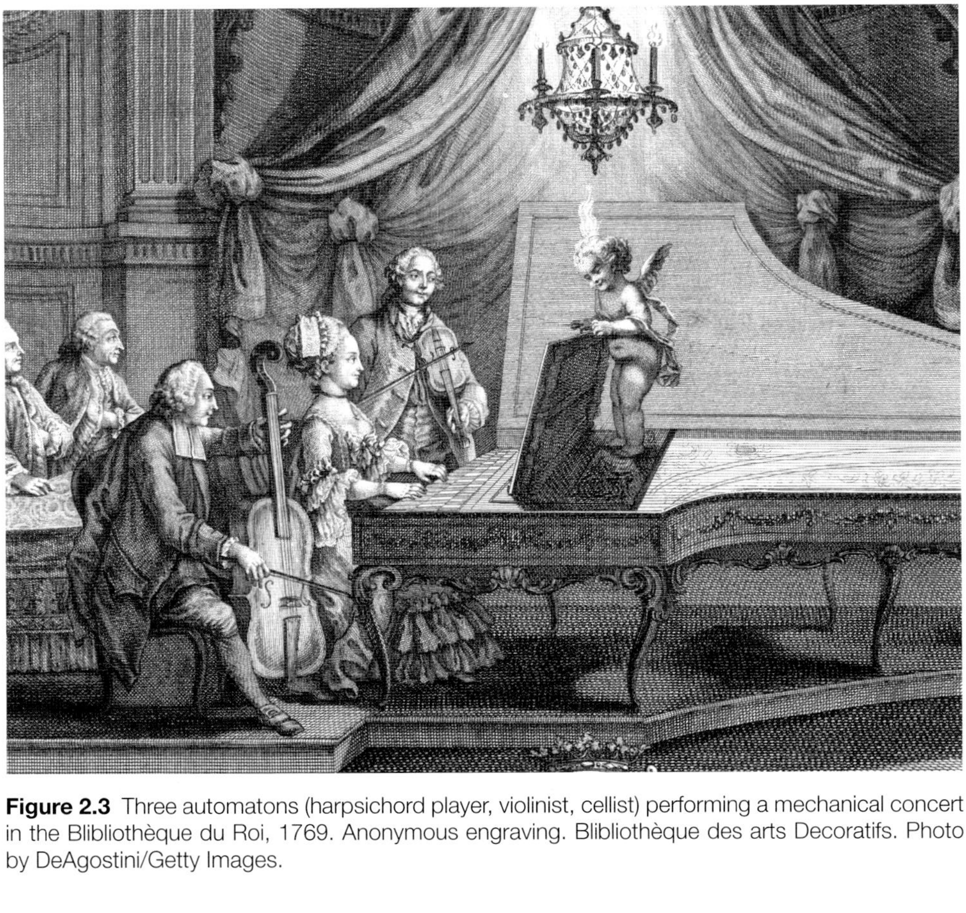

**Figure 2.3** Three automatons (harpsichord player, violinist, cellist) performing a mechanical concert in the Blibliothèque du Roi, 1769. Anonymous engraving. Blibliothèque des arts Decoratifs. Photo by DeAgostini/Getty Images.

viewers could observe, which served as its pedestal. To achieve this, Vaucanson had studied the animal's morphology in exhaustive detail, inside and out. For as well as its biological "functions," it moved very much like a duck. In a letter to the Abbé Defontaines in 1738, Vaucanson testified: "My second Machine, or Automaton, is a Duck. . . . The Duck stretches out its Neck to take Corn out of your Hand; it swallows it, digests it, and discharges it digested by the usual Passage."[26] Its inspiration is most likely an artificial swan that a mechanician called Maillard showed to the Paris Academy of Sciences in 1733. Powered by a paddle wheel, it moved through the water while its head swayed from side to side. Unlike Vaucanson's duck, it was only intended to simulate the animal's movement, not its physiology.[27]

As intended, contemporary witnesses were astounded. The astonishment continued on the machine's resuscitation for the 1844 International Exhibition in Paris. But it was also found that the feat of simulated digestion was more a "mystification" than something properly achieved.[28] In effect, even biomechanics, when rigorously applied, required a level of illusionism. But Vaucanson was always motivated by philosophical and quasi-scientific concerns, to reveal biological mechanisms through artificial equivalents and to test the horizon of what at that time can be produced artificially.[29] Not only wealthy, he quickly became a celebrity across Europe, with Voltaire calling him the "rival to Prometheus."[30] Spurred by such fervent interest, Vaucanson went to work on an android that imitated the circulation of blood, which he sought to achieve with a complex network of rubber tubing. This venture was cut short by his appointment in 1741 to inspector-general of silk manufacture. Little is left of this, and the famous duck was taken by the fire that consumed the Nijninovgorod in Russia in 1879. The other two earlier automatons disappeared in around the same period. But what did remain was the demystification of certain biological processes: They obeyed physical laws and were not at the behest of some mystical or divine process.

Choosing to focus on the duck's digestive tract, while simpler than simulating the circulation of blood, was also a revisioning of Aristotle. For although he twice referred to animals as "automatic puppets," he was careful also to draw some rather significant distinctions, one of which was the nutritive faculty that is essential to maintenance and growth and must be held in balance according to the nature and activity of the body.[31] Subsequently, physiologists had debated over whether digestion was chemical or mechanical. In many ways, medicine up until the mid-nineteenth century was in the shadow of Aristotelianism, conceiving the body as a whole that flowed and secreted. Well into the early 1800s, physicians did not see themselves as treating specific diseases, but rather stemming and regulating flows, digestion and circulation chief among them.[32] To conceive of a machine that consumed, processed and excreted was, in effect, for the eighteenth-century mind, to simulate physiology. But in truth, Vaucaunson's duck performed its famed function imperfectly. Explaining his claim that the duck digested through dissolution he deferred to another occasion. The food stayed at the base of the tube from the mouth, while the "faeces" were of a wholly different substance that had to be loaded up before the digestive performance.[33] The massive machine was more or less a highly labored form of showman's misdirection, which is perhaps what prompted one disaffected viewer to write off the machine as "nothing more than a coffee grinder."[34] (A few decades later, with the declining fortunes of France after its serial humiliations of the Seven Years' War, machines like these were associated with the unproductive fripperies of a dissolute court: once the "dearly beloved," after 1763, Louis XV was dealt a welter of pejoratives, among them the "vile, imbecilic automaton."[35]) But what Vaucanson's ventures demonstrate is the need to make possible through artificial means artistic creativity, on one hand, and digestion, on the other, thus to defy the limits of what machines were thought to achieve.

Shortly after assuming his new position, in 1744 Vaucanson created an entirely automatic weaving machine. Similar to the former automatons, it used a metallic cylinder that was powered by a hydraulic system. The cylinders could be changed according to the kinds of weaves wanted. But it was only until the next century that a more comprehensive and commercial machine was achieved. Joseph-Marie Jacquard (whence the Jacquard loom) melded an earlier mechanical type invented by Jean-Baptiste Falcon that used perforated cards with the cylindrical drum of Vaucanson, which powered the needles. Jacquard's invention constituted the first machine that responded to modifiable programs, hence the first sequential, industrial automaton. It was, in effect, the first computer. Computers, then, arose out of the combination of technology derived from the first androids and clothes production—something worth considering with the birth of the fashion model, the mannequin that wears clothes.

Although outstanding, Vaucanson was by no means an isolated case. A notable contemporary was a mechanic from Stuttgart, Friederich von Knauss (1724–1789). After becoming curator of the collection of clocks and clockwork of Charles de Lorraine in Brussels, in 1753, Knauss set about creating machines that wrote automatically, although they cannot specifically be called androids.[36] He moved to the court of Francis II of Austria, where in 1760, he presented the amazed emperor another automatic writing machine. As decorative as it was curious, its center comprised a sphere that could open into six parts, like a flower. On the flat base above this mechanism were two small figures: a goddess and a genie divided by a vertical tablet supporting a piece of paper. The goddess's traced letters on the paper. At particular intervals the goddess figure would place the pen in a pot of ink, while the paper was replaced. As with Vaucunson, this was powered by a cylinder, but also controlled by a keyboard whose keys corresponded to a letter. While this still exists in the Gewerbe Museum in Vienna, Knauss is reported to have made others, such as a flute player and four talking machines, but they have not survived.

In the footsteps of Vaucanson and Knauss, the father and son partnership of Pierre and Henri-Louis Jacquet-Droz were also clockmakers who made several androids that became celebrated toward the end of the century. Realized from 1770 onward, three examples—the writer, the draftsman and the musician—remain well preserved in the Art and History Museum in Neuchâtel, Switzerland. It is also largely thanks to this family that Switzerland gained the reputation of a land of master clockmakers.

The most complex of the three, the drawing figure, was some seventy centimeters high and seated at an ebony table. Having both a movable head and eyes, it places the feather pen in the ink, shakes its head and places its hand at the top of the paper. It starts writing at the pull of a lever. The entire core apparatus is located in the figure's back, and the central piece is a cam cylinder. It can write up to forty letters or motifs in an angular, but still recognizably acceptable, style. It was made principally by the father with the help of Jean-Frédéric Leschot, as the son was still quite young. Similar in conception to the writer, the draftsman could draw four things: a butterfly, a dog, and the profiles of Louis XVI and Marie Antoinette. Differing from the first two, the third is the body of a girl sitting at an organ. With both movable head, eyes and hands, after each piece of which she could play five, with a movement of her body and incline of her head, she defers to the audience. Even her neck moves to give the illusion of breathing.

One direct predecessor of Jacquet-Droz was Friedrich von Knauss from Darmstadt who traveled to France and Flanders, where he made several writing automatons, the first of which he showed to Louis XV in Versailles in 1753, which he subsequently sold to the governor-general of the Spanish Netherlands, Prince Karl Alexander von Lothringen. Knauss also entered the prince's service as part of the "Physical Cabinet" (*Physikalischen Kabinett*). Under these auspices, he fabricated two superior writing apparatuses, culminating in 1760 with the two-meter high "All-writing Wondermachine" (now in the Technischen Museum, Vienna).[37]

## The art of automata

While figures and animals with more prosaic movements were beginning to be produced as expensive curios,[38] the choice of action of the most accomplished automata by Jacquet-Droz (as with Vaucanson) was not by chance, for each automaton symbolized the three arts of literature, visual art and music. Instead of choosing an action such as sewing or wielding an axe, both of which we refer to as indeed mechanical actions, the automatons performed actions that are believed to transcend the mechanical with the creative. Notably, their respective mecano-artistic contributions also evolved from an era that had heavily imbibed the classical style. Their genesis therefore predates the Romantic era with its ethos of the irreducible passions of the human soul, and its rebellion against the overly constrictive artistic forms and armatures. In German Idealism of the eighteenth century, spontaneity was a concept different from the one we have inherited from the Romantic era. As Zizek observes:

> What eludes utilitarianism is precisely the element of "spontaneity" in the sense of German Idealism, the very opposite of the everyday meaning of spontaneity (surrendering oneself to the immediacy of emotional impulses, etc.). According to German Idealism, when we act "spontaneously" in the everyday meaning of the word, we are not free from but prisoners of our immediate nature, determined by the causal link which chains us to the external world.[39]

The regulated moves of the automaton were therefore highly congenial to this notion. In her essay on musical automata and German *Einfühlung* (feeling) and *Empfindsamkeit* (sensibility) of the eighteenth century, Adelheid Voskuhl examines two significant treatises of the period, one by C. P. E. Bach and another by the flautist Johann Joachim Quantz. She concludes that "When elaborating the criteria for good musical performance, however, both authors are comfortable in describing the arousal of affects as calculated, controlled, and pointed effort and with describing the human body in this process as machinelike."[40] Moreover, the early Romantic writer Jean Paul Richter, better known as just Jean Paul (the writer remembered for his coinage of the word *doppelgänger* and who will be discussed further in the following chapter), responding both to the automata of the era and such contemporary writings on how music ought to be played, challenges the limits of automata and the machine-like model, but also the limits of what audiences deduce from means of expression deduced from a machine-like model. Voskuhl is also one of several commentators who notice the predominance of women in such roles, drawing a parallel between rules of female deportment—from table manners to musicianship—and quasi-mechanized discipline.[41] Women also noticeably dominate the polychrome medical models of this era with their opened stomachs revealing the distribution of bodily organs.[42]

Indeed, we see one key example of the blurred line between real automata and people behaving as such in Mozart's *Cosi fan tutte*. (Mozart also participated in the interest of marionette-operas that blossomed in his time.) Here, two women make a wager that they will change their minds about their love for their fiancés if they swap roles, but unbeknown to them, their lovers swap roles as well. As Mladen Dolar notes of this duplication,

> Love doesn't finally triumphantly defeat all, but love is easily defeated. . . . There is something in love that is like a machine; it is not a set of predictable emotions: there is a mechanical predictability in its emergence that can be mechanically induced. Women, proverbially unstable and capricious, now appear to be the best embodiment of this of this mechanical character, exemplary machines, *les femmes machines*, puppets.[43]

Dolar goes on to observe that "the mechanical doll is a metaphor of, and a counterpoint to, autonomous subjectivity; autonomous self-determination and the automaton seem to go hand in hand."[44] This condition is confronted on a very particular level with music, particularly that of Mozart's era, which seeks to strike a balance between rhythmic discipline and episodic emotion. To investigate forms that are meant to be quintessentially human through inhumanity provides the ultimate challenge to our humanity and the authenticity of our affective response, or indeed in what that authenticity consists.

Thus, with the confusion created between whether mechanically generated images and music can be either natural or expressive, we have shifted dramatically from the reflections of the previous chapter in which the machine was limited to the body, and where bodies played out as machines. While debate was well alive in both music and theater, a converse case evolved in parallel: that of the automaton simulating a disciplined mind. Something in line with this vein of thinking can be found in one of Denis Diderot's most enigmatic texts, *Neveu de Rameau* (*Rameau's Nephew*), in which the eponymous Nephew muses on his inability to achieve excellence, and is unable to resolve whether he is person of genius or an imbecile. What we learn, though, is that the genius is centered and controlled. They are capable of self-definition and are not molded by arbitrary social wiles. While this stance may point to Nietzschean strength, it also relates to the machine. And we know that Kleist, whose essay places the machine's movements above those of men, had read Diderot's essay.[45]

While the limitations of these early androids are self-evident—the bodies are constrained to what was chosen for them to do and their respective "programs"—the choice and the aim still remain nevertheless instructive. Moreover, the contraptions by the Jacquet-Droz duo had evolved from the Vaucanson model through a substitutable cylinder with encoded spikes. In substituting the one for another encoded cylinder, the range of what these figures could write, draw or play was effectively infinite. Another incipient form of computer, the popular versions of these exist today in curiosity and gifts shops in the form of the musical phonograph cylinder and the music box. Following the line of the Jacquet-Droz family came a number of other makers who had been apprenticed to them and who in the first half of the nineteenth century left a series automaton magicians, draftsmen and writers in their wake. Of the more creditable contemporaries included Jean-David Maillardet, a French clockmaker in Berlin who created an automated soothsayer that he called "The Great Magician." His brother Henri created an automaton in the form a child that both drew and wrote.[46]

While having the disembodied heads of the French royal family among the draftsman's repertoire may have been darkly prophetic, Marie Antoinette herself indulged in the fad for mechanized dolls. Never one to worry about spending exorbitant sums of money, at a high price she bought an automaton made together by the courtly cabinetmakers Abraham and David Roentgen and a German clockmaker Peter Kintzing (Plate 6). It was female and clothed in a replica of a dress belonging to the queen. The queen's doctor described it as follows.

> With a short time the queen acquired a small, automated female figure of eighteen to twenty inches tall that proficiently plays different musical airs on a small dulcimer in the form of a small piano. This figure, with its elegant features, proportions and bodily adjustments, measuredly hits various chords on the instrument with a little metal hammer that it holds in its hands, which move with great accuracy and precision. As well, while playing the airs, she moves her head with various expressions in her eyes and her look that are very pleasing, making for a surprising illusion. She sits on a seat placed at a table of superb wood that also supports the dulcimer; and the mechanism is enclosed and hidden within the table's thickness.[47]

Unlike the figures by Jacquet-Droz, this one distinguished itself through its miniaturization. What is also worth observing is that the forced semblance to Marie Antoinette through similar clothing was not deemed uncanny or disconcerting, but rather curious and charming. The sinister aspect would come later in the period after Marie Antoinette lost her head. But unbeknown to the queen, she was the sponsor of the first famous *mannequin*, whose etymology comes from the Dutch *manneken*, a diminutive form of "man," and thus, "little man," except, of course, the figure was female. Like all of its predecessors, the apparatus was based around a core cylinder that gyrated by a mainspring. The mechanisms were hidden in the dress and in the table itself. On show at the museum of the Conservatoire des Arts et Métiers in Paris, it can still play the musical airs, which are extracts from Gluck's opera *Armide*.

# The chess-playing Turk

In keeping with the tradition for the ongoing attempt to show how automata could rival humans in disciplines that involved will, sentiment and subjectivity, namely, the arts, one of the most famous automatons of the period was Wolfgang von Kempelin's masterpiece of mystification, a life-size figure dressed as a Turk complete with fur-trimmed cloak and turban, with a long pipe in his left hand, who sat behind a large mahogany chest of about a meter wide. While arguably not an art, no other game involves as much choice, consideration and invention than chess. It has long been at the forefront of endeavors with artificial intelligence that reaches something of a climax with IBM's "Deep Blue" computer, which, after first losing, beat Gary Kasparov in a rematch in 1997, making it the first computer to defeat a world champion under tournament conditions, and rousing again the hoary debate about when artificial intelligence will supersede that of humans. One highly striking aspect of this encounter was that the victorious second game was played with what the expert audience clearly discerned as a style, not a formula, but with intuition.[48] Another important difference from previous automata is that the movements of

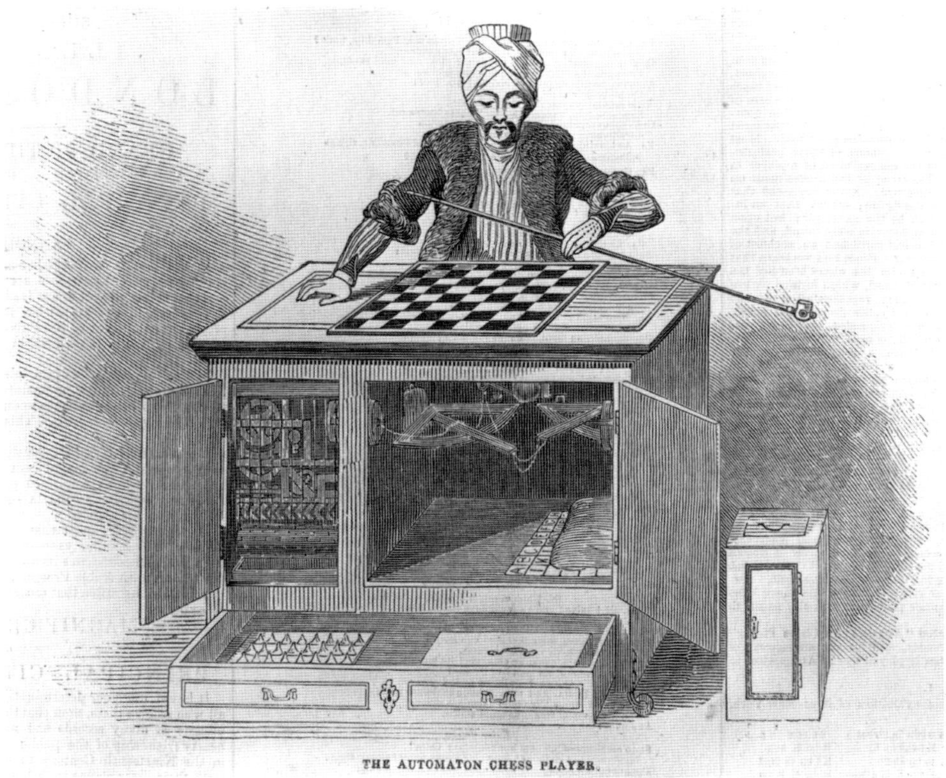


**Figure 2.4** The Automaton Chess Player as shown in New York in 1845. *Illustrated London News*. Photo by Hulton Archive/Getty Images.

Kempelin's automaton were for the sake of instrumenting decisions, and therefore, thought. The fact that Kempelin's machine was a fake does not however make it a failure. Like Vaucanson's duck, its mechanism was still a feat, and it helped to feed the fascination and rising hunger in Europe for engagement with alternative intelligence.

The leaflet used to accompany the exhibition of Kempelin's Turk at the Burlington Gardens in Saville Row, London, in 1784, is tellingly entitled: *Inanimate Reason, or A Circumstantial Account of that Astonishing Piece of Mechanism, M. de Kempelin's Chess-Player*, by the self-avowed "friend and countryman," Gottlieb de Windisch.[49]

> Among the many thousands, among the ranks, who have seen it, not one has been able to develop the mystery.
>
> Notwithstanding, say you, it can only be a *deception*, in this the inventor, and every other reasonable being will readily agree with you. But in what this deception consists, is a Gordian knot more difficult to untie, than that in days of yore, which Alexander cut asunder.
>
> 'Tis a deception! Granted; but such an one as does honor to human nature; a deception more beautiful, more surprising, more astonishing, than any to be met with, in the different accounts of mathematical recreations.
>
> The first idea that strikes you, on superficial examination of this chess-player is, a suspicion, that its movements are effected by the immediate impulse of some human being. I, myself fell into this mistake.[50]

Indeed, it was no mistake, but M. Windisch's pamphlet was typical of the sort of blandishments that lent to the very profitable "mystery." Certainly the deception could not have been achieved without a high degree of technical ingenuity. As a sly decoy no doubt, "Every move he makes, a small noise of the wheel-work is heard, somewhat resembling that of a repeater."[51] And "when he gives check to the queen, he nods his head twice; and thrice when he gives it to the king."[52] As a decoy to avert suspicion, "Even his breaches, which are in Turkish taste, have a little door which opens, to remove even the shadow of suspicion."[53]

Invoking the chess-playing Turk in a satirical-philosophical text of 1789, "Humans are Machines of the Angels," Jean Paul makes the thought-provoking hypothesis that humans are machines made by angels to discharge all their particular needs. One angel built a chess-playing machine. Jean Paul sets up an intriguing double-helix where humans are the machines of angels while humans also make machines. To ensure that this conundrum is well in place, he then comments on the similarity with the human, angel-made machines with the "well-known chess machine invented by Mr. v. Kempele" [sic].[54] But as if to console the reader, Jean Paul takes a surer step of retreat back to humanism, stating that there "a tremendous difference among the two kinds of machines" as "angels will always stand out by far against the work of a human," and, by extension, a human to the human-made machine.[55] After all, echoing Descartes, "one consists of flesh and blood—blood that no chemist can fabricate—the other out of mere wood and metal."[56] Yet, reprising ambiguity at the end in referencing the mechanical female music players, he asserts that they, their artificiality notwithstanding, "obviously seem to betray affective involvement."[57]

One of its most famous games was against Catherine II of Russia in St. Petersburg to a large and attentive audience. In the first stages of the game, the opponents appeared equal, but then to the consternation of the gathering, the empress began losing a few of her pieces. Suddenly, the automaton banged its hand on the table and corrected one of Catherine's moves. It was an authoritarian gesture that few of the human company would have dared to make. A little after the mechanical sounds that had been humming until then stopped and the android ceased moving, Catherine, seeing that she had been saved the ignominy of being defeated, gaily exclaimed, "Ah, Mr. Automaton your manners are a little coarse! Your playing is strong, I agree. But you are afraid of losing, so in your wisdom you derailed the game." Out of sorts, Kempelin asked to explain the turn of events, but Catherine assured him that she was not at all annoyed. She may have been had she seen what was in the main case that acted as the table, as it hid a Polish officer called Worouski who happened to be a very good chess player. Kempelin's Turk was not the last of its kind, but spawned a series of pranksters and confidence men who used their false contraptions to enter into courts and secure audiences with eminences. The Turk itself would continue to show life for the next eighty-five years after Kempelin's death, arriving in the United States in 1804.

It is also useful to revisit the debates about the kind of responses that automata can elicit and their validity. In his analysis of the Chess Player, Mark Sussman believes:

> The Chess Player highlights the crucial role of the observer's simultaneous belief and skepticism in evaluating the object on display, presenting a litmus-case in the development of a theatre of machines: part puppet show, part scientific demonstration, part conjuring trick. The Chess Player, which appeared driven by magnetic or possibly electrical forces, gave life for nearly a century to the ideal of an intelligent machine, an image that Walter Benjamin adapts from the "ur-history" of the 19th century.[58]

It is all but chiseled proof that one of the defining traits of humanism is to contemplate the horizon of the human, and the inhuman, but nonetheless in its image.

Despite the elaborate charade, Kempelin was a proficient builder of more autonomous contraptions and helpful inventions. Not only is his Turk said to have contributed to knowledge about building prosthetic limbs, but Kempelin also found a way of embossing books for the blind, devised a hydraulic system for Schönbrunn Palace, a canal system that could link Budapest with the Adriatic, and most astonishingly figures that could emulate speech.[59] These proved to have proficiencies that outstripped many of those by contemporaries, such as one Abbé Mical, who in the middle of the eighteenth century had made several talking machines under the wing of the great earlier scientists Lavoisier and Laplace. Kempelin's talking machines were complex apparatuses of pipes, which drew not only the movements of the human mouth but also the sounds of certain wind instruments such as the oboe, clarinet or bassoon.

Just as the dissemination, entrenchment and diversification of the commedia dell'arte reflected a changed conception of self and society, the rise of automata have to be seen as more than just an eccentric off-shoot of technological advancement. For not only were there widespread concerns that industrialization was making humans into machines, but also educated and upper-class circles across Europe and the courts they influenced witnessed an increasing emphasis on notions of "feeling," "sensibility," "taste" and "*esprit*," which could mean both spirit and wit. These are irreducible concepts, and valued as such, but also because they provided a path toward greater moral import. Hypnosis was also invented in the mid-eighteenth century, through the work of Franz Mesmer (1734–1815). Thus, "feeling" in the eighteenth century meant something different from what we have today inherited from the nineteenth century and Romanticism. For in the eighteenth century, "feeling" also meant the "the problem of feeling," which culminated in Kant's *Critique of Judgment* (1791) in which aesthetic judgment is famously construed as being without a concept.

Therefore, the automaton had a role to play in this diverse and often conflicted philosophical landscape since it was an objective "being." If its artistic tasks could arouse at least some curiosity, then it also prompted due reflection on what warranted attention. As Kempelin's hagiographer Windisch was apt to emphasize, "How high will the spirit of invention dare to soar! Is it possible to conceive any thing more rash, than to undertake to make a wooden figure play at chess; the more I think on it the greater is my astonishment; 'nor is your's,' I dare to say, less. M. de Kempelen's automaton engages the eyes and understanding, but in a very different degree, to what M. de Vaucanson's performer on the flute, does the ear."[60] This was flagrant technical one-upmanship. If nature could arouse in us "feeling," then, so too, could other products that did not arise from consciousness or subjectivity.

Clearly, such claims were not without their detractors. In his essay "Sympathy Machines: Men of Feeling and the Automaton," Alex Wetmore remarks on the enormous popularity of the machines by the likes of Vaucanson and Kempelin:

> By performing actions designed to imitate the lifelike behaviour of humans and animals, these celebrated automata could be thought of as further examples of "mechanical" copies that civic humanists associated with frivolous, corrupt private pleasures and distractions from virtue. But while civic-minded critics like Ferguson tended to describe their cultural surroundings as a morally degraded realm where the mechanical was too often overstepping its proper bounds, these exhibitions owed their success to a curious public that found spectatorial pleasure *in observing machines specifically designed to transgress their traditional limitations*.[61]

The last point is crucial. If technological advancements were possible in medicine and physics, then they might also play a part in the very qualities that were considered to make us human. And in observing such automata certainty in the nature, location, even teleological direction of such qualities, became radically destabilized.

## The end of a fantasy, the beginning of a contrivance

The examples that have already been cited are by no means exhaustive. In London in 1772, Cox's Museum opened the Spring Gardens, which, rather than containing automata designed for particular actions, had almost two dozen apparatuses whose interest lay in the

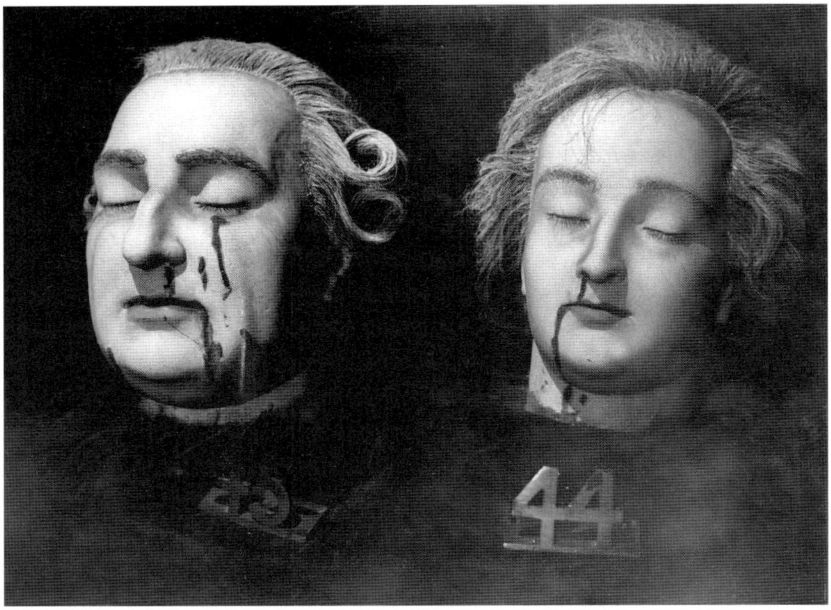

**Figure 2.5** The wax heads of Louis XVI and Marie Antoinette in Madame Tussaud's, London. Koralle 28/1937, World Wide Photos. Photo by ullstein bild/ullstein bild via Getty Images.

expensiveness of their materials and their charming mechanical conceits. Ornate in the extreme, their actions largely innocuous, such as a decorative pineapple that opened to the sound of chimes to an ornate golden chariot drawn by an equally dazzling dragon. Contemporary commentators considered these objects to be presaging an apocalypse, while others believed them to be works of art in their own right, or sumptuous oddities imparting diversionary pleasure through either their charms or simply their status as high-end commodities.[62] It was also in the late eighteenth century that the kinds of fêtes enacted since the Renaissance became increasingly more elaborate, from Marie Antoinette's follies in Versailles to those in Nymphenberg ("Nymph's Castle") in Munich, in which the highest echelons of society would dress up as shepherds and shepherdesses, or as figures from classical antiquity. It was not uncommon for people to assemble themselves as *tableaux vivants*, alluding to or recreating paintings or sculptural friezes. Marie Antoinette was even depicted by her personal court painter, Elisabeth Vigée-Lebrun, as a shepherdess, if a little frumpy and rather richly appointed for the station. The point to be drawn is that any negative element—that they were endemic of excessive leisure and expenditure incongruous with the depredations of their time—these follies were not motivated by any sinister or skeptical intent.

This would change with the French Revolution, which sought to distance itself from the courtly excesses of the *ancien régime*. The beheading of King Louis on January 21, 1793, was not only a sociopolitical watershed, but also a religious cataclysm that discredited the idea of the divine right of kings that, in turn, unmoored the modern subject from the sanctity of God. The severed heads of Louis and his Marie Antoinette are miraculously preserved in wax thanks to Mme. Tussaud, who had the stomach and the wherewithal to cast them. While wax exhibits always contained wonders and grotesqueries it was more in the tradition of the cabinet of curiosities. This was the era of the "Chamber of Horrors," the public spectacle of the most rueful recesses of the Romantic mind. As with any wax museum today, the childish follies, the historical costume cameos and the walk-ons from contemporary popular culture would not be the same without inclusion of something horrendous. Once intended as a benign fairytale fancy, Tussaud's cast of Mme. du Barry, Louis XV's last mistress, as Sleeping Beauty, can still be seen today with her automated heaving chest, but cannot be fully appreciated without also recalling her spectacular hysterics on her approach to the guillotine (so vividly recounted by Vigée-Lebrun in her memoires). Thus, while androids and automata would continue to be produced, from a symbolic point of view, the artificial body would henceforth exist symbolically on two separate poles. One is the monstrous double, the interloper, the sinister subjective perversion. The other is the example of a better, modified body that improves on human criteria, if not bypasses humanity to enter into a different class of being, thinking, and to use the sporting term also applied to automobiles, *performance*.

# 3

# DARK DOUBLES: DOLLS AS A SOLUTION TO THE FALLIBLE BODY

*Do you see, then, what has made me love and learn to value that which to-day we call the "puppet" and to detest that which we call "life" and "art."*

—EDWARD GORDON CRAIG[1]

*I do not know . . . and what does one know? She is probably one of those people who do not want to say anything, and each of us carries within us a reason not to live any more . . . one cannot see into the soul as one can into this room. They are all like that. . . . They only say banal things; and nobody doubts any of it . . . one lives for months next to someone who is no longer of this world and whose soul is now longer inclined to be; one responds without dreaming of it: and you see what happens. . . . They have the air of being immobile puppets, and so many events do not occur in their souls. . . . They themselves don't know who they are . . . .*

—MAURICE MAETERLINCK, *INTÉRIEUR*[2]

These words, uttered by the character of the Old Man, is in one of three plays that Maeterlinck wrote for marionettes, but which has also been played by people (who play marionettes playing people). Maeterlinck's work is sadly lost to most of the mainstream, although it occupies an important place in early modernist dramaturgy and can also not be omitted from any serious discussion about the relationship between human and artificial bodies. Maeterlinck's work is also historically specific and prompts the question: Granted, there are instances of automata in Geek mythology and in the annals of other cultures, just as the phantom and double make their regular appearances in stories and lore, yet what may be the reason for the rather sudden volume of literature on dolls and automata from the late eighteenth century onward? The answer lies not only in the fascination with and growing sophistication of automata at this time, but as canvassed in the previous chapter, it also had to do with humanism, and early Romantic philosophy, that sought to speculate on the scope of human capabilities. The belief that humans were essentially finite and material beings meant recourse to a Cartesianism, shorn of its theological luster. From this period onward, mannequins, dolls and automata assume a Janus face: On one hand, they are symbols of the positive onward march of science and technology; on the other, they suggest foreboding over when that science goes askew. The doll and the artificial body was also the grotesque shadow to a finite, Godless existence. The desolation voiced by Maeterlinck's Old Man is that of the recognition that character is contingent and constructed, and the soul is the pitiful illusion of vain hope, a construction of sentimentality and blind faith.

There is a remarkable—one could say uncanny—consistency in the literature of the humanist period in associating artificial life with something dismal, degraded, frightening, undesirable, even catastrophic. It symbolizes not only humanity's deepest fears, but also the dire consequences of not surmounting the hubris of trying to equal nature (or God's) grand design. As Marquard Smith puts it in relation to the *Sandman*, "In Hoffmann's tale, unlike for Pygmalion, Venus does not intervene; there is so breathing life into this doll-like automaton."[3] Thus, the stories and accounts of the life-like doll in this period are haunted by it as the symbol both of sociosexual impotence, and of religious inadequacy and doubt. It is not until the "posthuman" era that this pall would begin to rise, in fictions and in life.

By far, the most famous example of this in the popular imagination is Mary Shelly's *Frankenstein*, where the contrivances of science and modern hubris conspire to overstep human limitation only to wind up with a grisly and harrowing mistake. In his reflections on death, animism and Shelly's "new Prometheus," Marc Augé comments:

> Mary Shelly's Frankenstein is precisely one who come first to recompose a body with disparate elements taken from cadavers, then to reanimate thus recomposed body. He who assisted in the process of the cadaver's decomposition—the return to brute matter though the swarming proliferation of different forms of life ("I saw the putrefaction of death take over the colours of life, I saw the vermin inherit what had been the marvels of the eyes and brain.")—seeks to reverse the direction of this evolution. For this *miraculum cadaveris* to be possible (for Frankenstein ultimately recourse to the electrical spark), matter must have both the energy and virtuality of life—an assumption that modern science does not endorse the equation energy=life, in the sense that that would make life a matter of necessity through a pagan animist formula.[4]

The originality of Shelley's story, or allegory, is that it deftly and dramatically extends the enlightened aims of the likes of Vaucanson to find out the ways in which certain bodies function and operate into a hubristic mission of ontological self-determination. Shelly's Frankenstein ushers in the perspective of the new era that transfers emphasis from giving inanimate things life to the invigorated corpse, the shadow of ourselves, the specter of life, that presages the imminent death of the living. Freud would make considerable use of the literature of this time to elaborate his notion of the uncanny; for in projecting life onto the dead object is to only emphasize death through the lengths taken to disavow it.

## A world with no puppet master: Jean Paul

One of the neglected works in literature on automata comes from the early writings of Jean Paul, another of whose writings of a similar period was mentioned in the previous chapter. Although not his only piece on artificial bodies, "The Machine Man Along with its Properties," a satirical dialogue in his anthology *The Devil's Papers* from 1789, is perhaps his most intriguing. In its encounter between a machine man, or robot, and a human, it also presages the countless such meetings in literature to follow. The narrator states that his tale is "is only worth telling to people from the moon, or from Saturn" since they are more likely to be interested in knowing about "machine men."[5] The description does not begin auspiciously. We are taken through a series of actions that the machine botches, making a mockery of himself. He is shown wanting in aspects of writing to numeracy. "In winter he gave concerts," but since no composer was present, he made do by randomly choosing bars of music taken from a Parisian fashion magazine by of way a pair of dice. With a nod to the great automata makes of his day, the players of the music were made "partly by Vaukanson [sic] and partly by Jacquet Droz and son": a flute, a piano and an organ with pipes "made of cardboard."[6] As well as having a "Kempelin-like speaking machine," the machine himself extols the use of other apparatuses to do his bidding, such as something that wakes him up and lights the fire in the morning.[7] Drawing to its conclusion, Jean Paul states that humans excel at performing machine-like functions (*auf eine viel höhere Stufe der Machinenhaftigkeit gerückt*).[8] But it is also the case that "the more complete a being is, the more it acts together with machines," consigning them to everything that is outside of his "I" (*Ich*).[9] But with the machines doing everything, the cerebralized being, if it can be called that (*überzählende Kopf*) will tire of the Earth, rendering the next century, "unthinkable." So, asks the denizen from Saturn, is the true period of this machine man. "The eighteenth" replies the narrator. The machine man is the "genius of the eighteenth century." This is the reason why, the narrator concludes, he chose to speak to someone from Saturn, because the reader is the "machine man himself."[10]

One thinks of the poetic twist that concludes Baudelaire's preface to *Les fleurs du mal*: "Hypocrite lecteur—mon semblable—mon frère" [Hypocrite reader—my double—my brother!], which is as much a challenge as it is an accusation to spur the reader to reflect on his own complicity in the poet's dealings, in particular the willingness to follow the line of fantasmic outrageousness. The difference is that Jean Paul motions not only to our hypocrisy, but also to our hubris. A little before the end, Jean Paul mentions a world that is without *natura naturans* and is now inhabited by *nature naturata* and "just the machines without the machine master (*Maschinenmeister*)."[11] While in many respects similar to his ironic text about humans being the automata of angels, this dialogue, which also parodies the philosophical dialogues popular at the time, has the curious, and uncanny commonality with a film such as *Blade Runner*, with the awakening of the machine that realizes she is not human. The satirical tone of Jean Paul's text masks a rather harrowing, traumatic moment, which is the realization that we are far less than what we thought we were. Jean Paul's world that is bereft of a *Maschinenmeister* is a place that helps us to grasp a critical historical transition: since antiquity, the regnant metaphor had been that humans are controlled by the great puppet-master in the heavens. In modernity, the grand puppet-master had either left the building or there had never been one. The first position is one of melancholy; the second admits either of triumph due to limitless possibility,[12] or of madness.

## Kleist's *Über das Marionettentheatre* and E. T A. Hoffmann's *Sandman*

From a forgotten text to one of the most frequently cited, Jean Paul's dialogue also helps to shed light on what is perhaps one of the most quoted and analyzed texts about the agonist conundrum between humans and dolls, Heinrich von Kleist's fictional narrative, "On Puppet Theatre," which in spite of its short length, has intrigued its readers ever since it appeared in 1810. As well as its stylistic crispness and unity, Kleist succinctly draws out certain moral dilemmas within this relationship. Its opening thrust is simple to relay and well known: In the winter of 1801, the narrator meets the mysterious Herr C., who informs him that he finds the movements of puppets more elegant than those of humans because they are devoid of affectation (*Ziererei*); their limbs betray a lightness that we cannot match. Unlike puppets, whose movements are pure, humans vitiate their actions with doubt. These stirrings of consciousness, impulse and will, distract us from the task at hand. This is the inevitable, unfortunate symptom of having eaten from the Tree of Knowledge. As the dialogue concludes,

> "Nevertheless," I said, a little distracted, "must we eat again from the Tree of Knowledge to fall back into the state of grace?"
>
> "By all means" he replied, "that's the last chapter of the world's history."[13]

Expelled from paradise, we amble the earth to see "if maybe there is a back door somewhere that is open."[14] We must somehow resolve this split between our aspiration and our accomplishments, but it is uncertain whether this is ever possible. Starting with the Socratic dialogic form, the resemblances with Plato's dialogue of the cave are evident, but with Kleist the priorities have shifted, although not reversed. Both are concerned with human foibles, their actions and their perceptions, and how these are linked to the imperfect knowledge of the world. Yet, Kleist's and Plato's narratives appear to differ on one crucial point, namely, Plato leaves no doubt as to the truth of what he tells, whereas Kleist's narrative is steeped in uncertainty to the point of irony, leaving us to think that it is art, artfulness and artifice that reign, both in the content and in the telling. How we come to it and how we ascertain this is another matter.

In many respects, Kleist's *Marionettentheater* is, in coded form, a secularized version of the Fall, but with a particularly Enlightenment twist. It was Schiller who exulted in the fall in an essay in 1790 "as incontestably the most fortuitous and momentous event in human history."[15] It was a liberating moment that stirred humans to turn from innocence to reason, the instrument of freedom. It is the Fall that ultimately allows humans to be their own selves and to slough the shell of answerability to the divine. Another reading of the Fall available to Kleist denotes the opposite. Rousseau propounded that the Fall gave birth to reflection, to consciousness in which the line between being and appearance was amply drawn. In his essay "Religion within the bounds of mere reason" (1793), Kant speculated on this as well. For reason was the "mere" [*bloss*—also "naked" or "simple"] secondary surrogate for a framework of knowledge it could insufficiently grasp.[16] (Conventional translations of the text have the title as "Religion within the bounds of reason alone.")

In navigating his own path between these two poles, Kleist inserts a notion of desire that is either precipitous or premeditated. Desire is everywhere within Plato's story of the cave inasmuch as it is consequence of our inadequacy—and which eventuates in the protagonist's ruin. What is curious is that Kleist implies that our instinctual desires also cause the delay, the gap, which also drives us to create. He does not use the word as such, but the more tempered term *Ziererei*—affectation, coyness or false hesitation. Within the aesthetic circuit of the dance, desire is, on one hand, reduced to distractions of consciousness, while on the other, cast into the mold of affectation, which is artifice, false creation. Once we realize how we falsely create the world, we are lured to recreate it, falsely afresh. For Freud, this is the fetishistic spiral. For Lacan, this is desire feeding off its own ineffectual results, which leads to desiring afresh, desire desiring itself, always wanting inefficiency lest desire be fulfilled and ended. In the words of Kleist's biographer, Peter Michalzik, "Kleists's marionette is a figure without knowledge of self to which one would like to transform back into."[17] It emphasizes that humans are forever compelled to play a role that forever betrays an inner truth.[18] The play of self, the theater that is life, an endless stream of partial attainments whose only end is in the playing out itself. The marionette is liberated from the conundrum that is Being.

It is therefore with loaded irony that, at the end of the third dialogue, the protagonist K confesses to being "ein wenig zersreut"—a little distracted—from reaching a final conclusion. While his distraction may not be the result of affectation, it leaves him short of the mark of what he wants to achieve; it vitiates his grasp of the central idea. But if we reach into a deeper reading, we can surmise that Understanding is inhibited by the same agent—desire—that caused the fall in the first place, although it reaches us in a furtive, or furtively insidious form. It is relevant to Kleist's whole artistic *œuvre* that individuality is reduced to randomness. Romantic assertions of the sovereignty of subjectivity are for Kleist but pathetic consolations for a far more paramount loss. It is an abstraction that has been anthropomorphized to cover a far greater abstraction that transcends it.

Although such expressions of impasse might ostensibly resemble a Platonic bind, it is pertinent that Kleist chooses to examine this within the realm of art, which for Plato, as we know, is the invidious agent of not a double, but a triple deception. But there is another ostensible Platonism afoot here, especially when we turn to the root word of *Ziererei*, *Zier*, which means "ornament" or "embellishment." Speaking in the later language of modernists such as Adolf Loos and Le Corbusier, ornament is the unwanted, if not wicked, superfluously bourgeois paraphernalia around the essential core of form whose only purpose it is to conceal. But the difference here, and which makes Kleist's tale so baffling, is that his marionettes disclose of truth through their particular beauty. Without the inhibitions or affectations of the mind, to use the language of Kant, they reveal their purposive purposelessness (*Zweckmässigkeit ohne Zweck*, which is the very particular compulsion we have for beauty). Like shadows, they are neither living nor dead: The absence of an affective consciousness makes them more beautiful and allows them to express a more robust liveliness. We find them more affecting, yet it is *we* who are entrusted with aesthetic judgment, which conjoins the very faculty, by extension—the distraction to reason because it is without a concept—*that denies us the physical realization of this beauty for ourselves*. The marionettes are facsimiles that show us our better self. *Yet it is only in our flawed state that we are able to see this*. Our insufficiencies make us the custodians, in concept not in body, of sufficient beauty. We are condemned to watching other entities play out what we might have been. Such insights are what are vouchsafed us after the Fall.

A little later in the narrative, Kleist offers an anecdote that describes these two states, this time with young boy who his possessed of *Anmut*—grace, charm, beauty—because he carries it unselfconsciously. Kleist is most probably hinting at Schiller's treatise, *Über Anmut und Würde* (*On Grace and Dignity*) from 1793, in some respects, a reply to Kant's Third Critique since it too attempts to find an objective grasp of the beautiful. For Schiller, grace is highly subjective and internal to the singular human being. Yet, while decidedly human, grace is also not trammeled by the will. Rather it is spontaneous and "as soon as we notice that grace is contrived (*erkünstelt*), then the heart suddenly shuts down."[19] Real grace confers a certain lightness (*Leichtichkeit*) that, in turn, instills the sense of freedom, for "when something becomes strained then lightness is in no position to manifest itself."[20] Grace is the coming to appearance of higher humanity as it is the harmonized state of "reason, duty and taste (*Neigung*)."[21] But in attaining this greater humanity, we need to find a place beyond our individual intentionality and will, or in Kleist's terms, without being clouded by unnecessary decoration. With grace, we reach a state that transcends our immediate circumstances and conditions. What Schiller and Kleist share is that this state is reached through a balance between inner and outer: For Schiller, we attain our greater humanity through the suspension of desire, while for Kleist, as Maria Glotzbach points out, it is the effective unity between puppet and puppet-master. But unlike Schiller, marionettes will always supersede humans in attaining grace.[22]

The reason lies in the fact that machines don't lapse and they have no vanity. The narrator describes his own appreciating gaze of the youth whom he observed drying himself after bathing, his pose uncannily resembling the famous Greek statue of the boy removing a thorn from his foot. While he keeps silent, the boy glances in the mirror. It is a classic Lacanian moment when the subject gains a realization of self. But now that he knows of his beauty, the beauty fades. It becomes a shadow. He has fallen. His lot is to live out his tainted beauty, and when it fades, to look for the untainted beauty in others. From there on, explains the narrator, the youth spent extended periods before the mirror, which had a draining effect on his charms, "and as a year passed, there was not a trace left." The quality that left him is *Leiblichkeit*, "bodiliness," the unmediated presence of his corporeality. This transition is, as Glotzbach comments, similar to the coming-to-self-consciousness (*Bewusswerdung*) of Adam and Eve after eating from the Tree of Knowledge.[23] From thereon, grace (and hence, happiness) comes intermittently, and seldom. "The art of living" wrote Agamben apropos of Kleist, "is, . . . the capacity to keep ourselves in harmonious relationship with that which escapes us."[24]

It is worth recalling Nietzsche's statement in *Daybreak* (*Morgenröte*) that the world began with a dance. And in his essay "The Dancer" in his classic study *Romantic Image*, Frank Kermode examines the way the "language of the freely-moving dancer is more like the Image than the virtuosity of the ballerina," that is, the Image comes to us in an act that, briefly, takes us out of ourselves. Although Kleist does not feature—his central focus is Yeats—Kermode's conclusions are startlingly similar. The dance in Yeats's "Among Schoolchildren" (1926) is a temporary escape from the onus of activity and labor after the Fall. Yeats becomes preoccupied with extracting the ideal beauty from statues into a state that lives such that it is the essence of both vitality and form. Yeats's dance is not the corrupted version of Kleist's, but the import is the same because it is the aesthetic event made possible by, and which makes possible, the interval in which we forget ourselves, where we reach back into a fundamental childishness. In this, Yeats also resuscitates Mallarmé's struggle to bring chance and idea, mobility and stasis into alignment.[25] Mallarmé remarked of the dance as "a corporeal writing" that effected a "poème degagé du tout appareil du scribe" [a poem wholly divested of the writer's devices].[26]

The doll-like figure freed of subjective intent is given a more sinister face in E. T. A. Hoffman's famous tale *The Sandman* (1816), written not long after Kleist's "On Marionette Theatre." The most cited part of the story is that of the doll called Olimpia, which mysteriously comes to life and was popularized by Jacques Offenbach's *Tales of Hoffman* (1851) and Leo Delibes's ballet *Coppelia* (1870). These are various simplifications of Hoffman's tale that center on the obsession of the protagonist, Nathaniel, with the doll that eventually leads to his madness. Hoffman's tale leaves us to vacillate between our suspension of disbelief and our capacity to read its irony. For when he first meets Ophilia "in the flesh," he is struck by the perfect rhythm of her harpsichord playing and her dancing—recalling again the famed automata by Vaucanson and Jaquet Droz and son, and all their epigones. The company remark on her stiffness and taciturnity, which instead beguiles him. He is happy to take her few remarks of "ah, ah" and "Good night, love" as expressions of understanding. It is in the pared down expressions, not in any spontaneous exuberance, that Nathaniel finds love, "Oh you superior, deep soul! Only you, only you can truly understand me!"[27] In his commentary on this scene, Dolar observes,

> the problem is not simply that Olympia turns out to be an automaton and thus placed in the uncanny area between the living and the dead; it is Nathaniel who strangely acts in a mechanical way: his love for an automaton is itself automatic, his fiery feelings are mechanically produced. It takes so little to set up this blank screen from which he only receives his own message. The question arises, who is the real automaton in this situation—the appearance of the automaton calls for an automatic response, it entails an automatic subjectivation.[28]

And the question also arises: To what degree is this shift in his position willed, or a symptom of the human will itself? Clara's human love is not enough, or maybe too much—in the place of his human beloved Clara he finds his desire temporary placated in a human debasement, a doll. The doll serves the function of stripping down his desire to

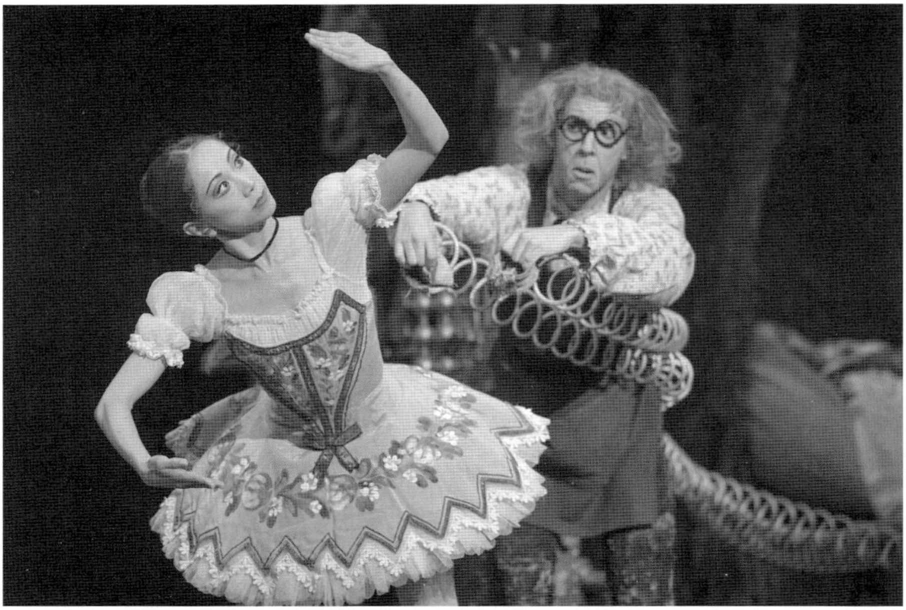

**Figure 3.1** Dancers perform on stage as the English National Ballet rehearse *Coppelia* at the Coliseum on July 22, 2014, in London. Photo by Ian Gavan/Getty Images.

its base components, which is imaginative cathexis, his need to graft meanings onto things where they do not exist. In this regard, Hoffman is playing with the reader who is in the continual process of building images from words. Ophilia is the narrative and Nathaniel is the reader. His "relationship" lays bare, in Dolar's words again, "the mechanical character of love relations. Both the subject falling love and the object can be reduced to an automaton: we have the perfect love machine."[29] But it is a perfection, which when fully revealed, is abominable. When the truth is revealed to him, Nathan explodes before Spalanzani, calling him "Satan," "puppetgrinder" (*Puppendreher*) and "devilish beast."[30] The hypocrisies of love stand bland, bald and unremitting before him. Opting not for the heroism in the face of chaos, Nathaniel, now mad, throws himself from a tower to his death.

The reflexivity and irony is of piece with Kleist's narrative. For we must recall that, throughout his discussion with the mysterious Herr C., the narrator K. interjects with numerous questions and calls for qualification, signs that maybe all is not what it seems. It starts with the possibility of unshakable belief—enshrined in the movements of the marionettes themselves—and devolves into examples that are more implausible, especially in the final episode of the fencing bear that parried every thrust of his opponent. (Because animals are untouched by the Fall, they are possessed with an ingenuousness that people lack, an ingenuousness that translates to fluidity of action.) Kleist poses a narrative in an ostensibly Platonic mode on things and appearances, but then perturbs that with expressions of uncertainty, as if to say: Here is a narrative; here are a series of ideas; believe them or not. As James Rushing persuasively argues, here Kleist expresses a loss "of faith in the possibility of regaining paradise through knowledge." Humans are simply too limited in their perspectives and capabilities. So:

> The artistic problem is how, in the limited world of human consciousness, to rise above these limits and examine the limits themselves—and how to communicate this perspective. The solution is irony. In distancing himself from the text, Kleist raises himself also above the limits of consciousness, so that he is able to "discuss" those limitations and to communicate that discussion (even though no conclusions are possible) to a reader, whose participation in the irony enables him to share the poet's perspective, to contemplate his own limitation.[31]

As with the florid and extravagant tone of Jean Paul's satirical text, irony instates the gap between belief and truth, but in so doing, drives a wedge of doubt into the possibility of something in and for itself. Can we, therefore, ever be "just" human?

For it may seem out of the ordinary to aspire to becoming the doll, and yet it is also through being unaffected and simplified that we find a region of aesthetic purity and release. In his *Aesthetic Theory*, Theodor Adorno writes of the role of silliness and clownishness that is distinct from the Culture Industry and Kitsch. The foolishness that we find in Mozart's *Magic Flute* delivers more truth than the earnestness of Wagner's *Ring Cycle*.[32] Admittedly, there are some understandable prejudices of Adorno's that we must deal with, beginning with Wagner's rampant anti-Semitism, but he nevertheless has an important point to make since it hits at the core of Kleist's cryptic narrative and what frustrated Plato about art. Adorno states:

> All works of art and art in general are mysterious. This has long frustrated the theory of art. That works of art say something while withholding it in the same breath are the terms of its mystery, which is that quality that exists beneath speech. It is apish and clownish. Once one is within the work of art in the sense of embracing it, it is not to be seen. As soon as one steps away one breaks the contract with its own immanent interrelation [*Immanenzzusammenhang*], turning back like a spirit.[33]

Adorno's "clown"—the word in German is used without an article, which gives it a metonymic resonance—is another word for the place of childishness, which the work of art yearns to inhabit. It gives us another place, another possibility, much like Kleist's marionettes or Hoffman's automaton. In all accounts, there is something absurd to aspire to a clown, a marionette or a mechanical doll. But it is only the absurdity and the paradox that safeguards the life of these objects, without which all we have is Plato's opprobrium against art or the Christian admonition of the Fall.

But the consolation that Adorno signals does not hide the darkness of Kleist or Hoffmann's texts, which for Lucia Ruprecht are "highly subversive": "Contrary to its positive connotation in Julien Offray de la Mettrie's *L'Homme machine* (Machine Man), which is representative of the materialist strand of eighteenth century philosophy, the automaton strikes a decidedly negative note in aesthetic thought."[34] It is in contravention to "the aesthetic ideology of the natural" that must eschew artificiality. To invoke Freud again, the desire for the artificial body, despite its claims to excellence, is to become beholden to damaging effects of the death drive. It is through bringing the fake and real body into close proximity, physically as well as conceptually, that also exposes human beings' vulnerability.[35] Similarly, commentators such as Annie Gilles read the literary interest in dolls from the eighteenth century onward—her reading is of works by Goethe, George Sand, as well as that of Kleist, in terms of castration anxiety. Here, the doll is both the substitute as well as the reminder of one's fallibility.[36] When we turn to art, art's representations, the reflections, may lead us to ruin like Plato's protagonist or Hoffman's Nathaniel, or it allows us to step outside of our own immanence. It confirms that in our minds and in our creative desire, we are not always "just here."

## Maeterlinck, Craig and the *Über-marionette*

Maeterlinck's radical stylizing of theater differs from the modernist drama of the twentieth century inasmuch as he was not concerned with the mechanized body as such, but rather in expressing a more accurate spiritual compass of humanity. For Maeterlinck, realist drama served a redundant purpose as it always referred back to the material and the lived, and its meaning were limited by what he saw it self-evident limitations. In intellectual and literary circles, the late nineteenth century was a time of great religious speculation that often entered the territory of mysticism. It saw the revival of the eighteenth-century Swedish theologian and mystic Emanuel Swedenbourg, whose highly novel interpretations of Christianity proved congenial to a culture attempting to find alternatives to an increasingly materialist, industrial world. Rosicrucianism also enjoyed its own special rebirth. Maeterlinck acknowledged the finitude of the flesh, but exhorted that art attend to the endurance of the spirit. This would ultimately entail the removal of human traits, which he associated only with the carapace of life, not its timeless essence. This explains what at first seems the rather baffling statement that

> One should perhaps eliminate the living being from the stage. This we might turn to an art of bygone centuries of which the masks of Greek tragedies perhaps bear the last traces. Will that one day be where the use of sculpture for a subject about which we have begun to ask quite strange questions? Will the human being be replaced by shadow, a reflection, a projection of symbolic forms or a being who would appear to be alive without being alive? I do not know. But the absence of man seems essential to me.
>
> It is difficult to predict what group of lifeless beings should replace man on the stage, but it seems that the strange impression experienced in the galleries of wax figures, for example, might long ago have led us to dead or new art. We would begin then without destinies, whose identities would no longer efface that of their hero. It seems too that all beings who have the appearance of life without having life call on extraordinary powers: and it is not said that the powers are not exactly of the same nature than those on which the poem calls. The fear that these being inspire, similar to us, but visibly endowed with a dead soul, is it not come that that they are absolutely

> bereft of mystery? Is it not that they do not have eternity around them? Is this fear, born precisely from the deprivation of fear around each living being, and so inevitable and habitual, that it is its suppression that frightens us, as we fear a man without a shadow or an army without weapons?[37]

This has been reproduced at length because it is an astonishing rendition of what at the end of the twentieth century would be reintroduced as "posthumanism": not an eradication of *homo sapiens* as such, but rather a reinscription of being, a new positioning in terms of expectations and orientation. For unlike humans, dolls are not invested with a teleology, or certainly one relieved of its transcendental imperative.[38] The speech in Maeterlinck's plays, for instance, has an incantatory quality replete with repetitions and pauses to expose the inner poetry over the content to reveal an abstract but also more than material human constant.[39] Such a re-emphasis would also shift the tragic element. And to view things from such a vantage point is perhaps to be relieved of the darkest elements of what a text such as Kleist's has to offer.

Maeterlinck's influence on the Symbolist drama of the turn of the century cannot be underestimated, and while mostly forgotten, can still help to make the programmatic clarity of still performed works such as Alban Berg's *Lulu* a little less puzzling. Of all his epigones, the dramatist most responsible for keeping his principles alive is Edward Gordon Craig. Deeply enamored of the depersonalization and stylization inherent to the commedia dell-arte,[40] Craig's staging and reflection on Maeterlinck's works caused him to overhaul dramaturgy altogether. For Craig, the director was at the epicenter of the drama and acted, less figuratively now, as puppet-master. In a philosophical sense, Craig devised a solution to the godless and decentered modern subject by inserting a new center of gravity, but at the expense of cherished humanist conditions. As Marjorie Garber eloquently puts it, "Maurice Maeterlinck in France and Gordon Craig in England were among others who saw the modernist puppet theatre as a commentary on the impossibility of verisimilitude, the destabilization of authorship and, ultimately, the vexed status of the subject."[41] Or to put this in another way, the puppet was the agonistic third term between God and man.

In keeping with Kleist's philosophical position, of which he was keenly aware, Craig regarded human self-consciousness as the actor's greatest impediment. Given that humans can never be purged of such shortcomings, Craig devised an in-depth set of theories of dramaturgy that set out to justify the elimination of human bodies from theater. As outlandish as this may first seem, Craig's polemic makes will have increasing resonance as the many examples in this book disclose themselves. His 1907 essay "The Actor and the Übermarionette" references Nietzsche's *Übermensch*, often unpleasantly translated as the "superman." Unlike Nietzche's *Übermensch*, who has found a more profound moral certainty to his will, for the "Übermarionette" the will is dispensed with altogether. According to Craig, acting must consist "in the main part of symbolic gesture. Today they *impersonate* and interpret; tomorrow they must *represent* and interpret; and the third day they must create."[42] The phase of tomorrow may be interpreted as creating a new kind of being unencumbered by mimetic values. As Craig elaborates: "The actor must go, and in his place comes the inanimate figure—the Übermarionette [supermarionette] we may call him, until he has won for himself a better name."[43] Dolls and marionettes are treated at large as quaint only because they are in the wrong hands:

> There is something more than a flash of genius in the marionette, and there is something in him more than the flashiness of displayed personality. The marionette appears to be the last echo of some noble and beautiful art of a past civilization. But as with all art that has passed into fat and vulgar hands, the puppet has become a reproach. All puppets are now but low comedians.[44]

In the effort to restore puppets to their former status, Craig invokes the words of whom he calls an "old Greek Traveller of 800 B.C. who, describing a visit to the temple-theater in Thebes" is won over by "noble artificiality."[45] And so Craig declaims

> May we look forward with hope to that day which shall bring back to us once more the figure, or symbolic creature, made also by the cunning of the artist, so that we can gain once more the "noble artificiality" which the old writer speaks of? The shall we be no longer under the cruel influence of the emotional confessions of weaknesses that are nightly witnessed by the people and which in their turn create in the beholders the very weaknesses which are exhibited. To that end we must study to remake these images—no longer content with a puppet, we must create an über-marionette. The über-marionette will not compete with life—rather it will go beyond it.[46]

Craig not only returns to Kleist, he "improves" on him, by assigning to this new form of acting an edificatory value that has philosophical and spiritual consequences. The displacement, or absorption, of the human into the object will cleanse all the noxious and unwanted emotional waste. He also prophesies the stilted types of Samuel Beckett, with their chiseled stylizations and hypnotic repetitions (as is well known the characters were). Later, Craig confirmed the consistency of his position by declaring that "There is only one actor—nay, one man—who has the soul of the dramatic poet, and who has ever served as true and loyal interpreter of the poet. This is the marionette."[47]

Craig's example, while not isolated, proved to be popular among dramatists and poets of the early twentieth century, working under the spell of the artificial richness and indirectness of Symbolist poetics. Of the dramatists, such as Adolphe Appia and Georg Fuchs, whose approaches were close to Craig's plan of action, a salient figure at this time was Vsevelod Meyerhold. Meyerhold was another who expressed distrust of Stanislavsky's quest for realism, in favor of forms that placed movement not words, at a premium.[48] Understandably, the commedia dell-arte had a lot to offer to Meyerhold's system. Meyerhold was influenced not only by the famous seventeenth-century drawings by Callot, but also by E. T. A. Hoffman. Meyerhold made use of the mask, which for him foregrounded our love of role play,[49] but which also drew attention to the way in which the barrier between what we think is our real self and the roles we play is well and truly indistinct. Where Maeterlinck's stylizations were melancholy and Craig's poetically sinister, Meyerhold's were decidedly grotesque; in all three looms heavily the omnipresent shadow of death. Meyerhold's theory of biomechanics, drawn from the work of Constructivist sculptors, led to ways of training actors so that they could perform acrobatics and engage in theatricalized combat, and which enabled them to move in a way that accented artificiality, thereby showing the body to be a mechanical system.[50] His interpretations, as in that of Gogol's *The Government Inspector*, the nature of the theatrical mise-en-scène highlighted the manner in which characters are puppets, manipulated by systems well outside of their knowledge or control.[51]

## Rilke and the puppet

Most of the critical commentary on Rilke and the puppet focuses on the *Duino Elegies*. But as a young man, he had already become impressed with Maeterlinck, after seeing several German productions. For Rilke, the best renditions of a Maeterlinck drama were to avoid recourse to *Stimmung* [mood, temper, tone, pitch] to allow for gestures that could best express feeling about which there was nothing equivocal, but extended for the sake of dramatic climax: "The marionette has only one face, and his expression is fixed for all time."[52] To this, Cristina Grazioli adds: "Its movements are reduced to the essential, visible from a distance and recognizable by a community."[53] To Rilke, exaggeration and too much effort only caused imbalance, distorting the drama out of shape. Rilke saw in Maeterlinck a definite solution to the rather aesthetically dissolute tendencies in the theater of the fin de siècle. Maeterlinck's innovations were accountable and could be applied as a technique to raise the quality of theater everywhere. In his "Letter to an Actress," Rilke advises that characterization ought to follow the example of the marionette and that to succeed at acting in a Maeterlinck play "one has to forget that one was acting." For Maeterlinck, the entire body is an expressive surface, he "did not imagine faces but bodies," which allowed him tap into what was "fundamental" to what we believe are individualized sentiments.[54] Rilke saw new opportunities for theater, as it should "have the same privilege as painting, of being able to hold the grand language of the human body and develop it."[55]

Puppets make a regular appearance in Rilke's oeuvre, with a common leitmotif of absence and surrogacy. In an early poem, "The House Where I was Born" ["*Mein Geburtshaus*"], he recalls a "salon lined with blue silk" containing "a richly silver-sequened puppet costume" [*ein Puppenkleid, mit Strähnen /dicken Silbers reich betresst*].[56] In his autobiographical novel *The Notebooks of Malte Laurids Brigge*, the main character occasionally encounters dolls, puppets and unworn clothes. In the words of Cristina Grazioli, "These figures of the poetic ritual transforming the visible into the invisible were very important for the conception of the *Duino Elegies*."[57] An overview of Rilke's work shows that puppets remain a presiding presence as not only shells of memory, but in the very Symbolist sense, as vehicles of suggestion and of the strangeness and magic from which dreams and fantastic artistic images are made.

Rilke's most sustained critical exposition on dolls is in an essay written in 1914 as a response to an exhibition of wax figures of the puppeteer Lotte Pritzel, which he had seen in Munich the year before. These particular dolls were intended as part of an artist's oeuvre, and were not expressly for children. Pritzel was well known in her time for her mannered figures with their detailed faces, elongated bodies and hands, and odd costumes that were strongly reminiscent of the languorous and menacing figures drawn by the British aestheticist Aubrey Beardsley. In 1987, twenty-five years after her death, the Munich Puppet Theatre Museum held an exhibition entitled "Dances of Vice, Horror and Ecstasy," purportedly taken from a description by a dancer belonging to a troupe impersonating her dolls on stage in the 1920s.

In keeping with the somber air of these dolls, and their reputation as sharing much with the values of the decadent movement, Rilke begins with on a shatteringly grim note: These dolls live outside of the realm of children. "The world of childhood is past." Removed from childhood, these dolls are of an adult world and even "prematurely old" and "entered into all the unrealities of its own life,"[58] suggesting an imperfect, limbotic state between childhood fantasy and the adult constructions of the world. Shortly after, Rilke falls into a reverie over the curious and ineffable aura that dwells over objects that were mediators of love or misery, but had captured a perceptible spirit because of the attention lavished on them, such as playing cards worn from countless games of Patience that become "a focal point for the sad hopes that have turned out unexpectedly."[59] But with dolls, precisely because they are focal point of so many of our emotions, the poetic, life-worn pregnancy of everyday objects is altered to reveal the falsity and failure of our efforts to ignite our own life in the lifeless. Most likely, with a similar observation made earlier by Baudelaire,[60] Rilke lamented the fact that we invest far too much in the puppets and its lack of a soul, or rather then, hollowness of the "puppet soul" accounts for one of the great childhood disappointments.[61] No amount of begging or imprecation can break the spell of the doll's inscrutability. But in this, Rilke also draws a parallel with God who became "famous mainly by not speaking to us."[62] There is a manifold alienation in our congress with the doll since we locate in it the need to overcome the basic alienation of existence, and we must face the extent to which we have duped ourselves, especially in the way we had invested so much in it. The doll is the eternal stranger. Yet, we persist in spending energy in illusion of its animism: "we are so busy keeping you in existence that we had not any time to grasp what you were."[63] Rilke suggests that despite our nervous disappointment in the doll, we maintain a disavowal of its deadness, presumably to safeguard the realization in ourselves of the immanence of death in us all, and for that, that death inhabits us all as a precondition of life.

When the puppet appears in the *Elegies*, it is a (non-)presence that is not entirely confined to melancholic loss since it is also the symbol of transformative overcoming. Puppets are a kind of pure corporeality in which the quandary of masks and appearances is resolved: "I do not want these half-filled masks,/But rather the puppet. It is whole. I want/To endure the shell and the wire and/Its face looking outward. Here. I am before it." [*Ich will nicht diese halbgefüllten Masken,/lieber die Puppe. Die is voll. Ich will/den Balg aushalten und den Draht and ihr/Gesicht aus Ausehn. Hier. Ich bin davor*.][64]

Rilke was well acquainted with Kleist's essay, having studied it in 1913, although there is no concrete evidence to assume knowledge of Jean Paul's earlier dialogue of the puppets and the angels (where humans are puppets devised by angels), however Rilke brings the two works into a compelling synthesis. Echoing Kleist, the puppet is the body divested of the complications and noise of everyday consciousness. While the puppet symbolizes pure physicality, the Angel, as configured in the *Elegies*, is the complement, pure consciousness untrammeled by physicality; one is "absolute object" and the other "absolute subject." In the Fourth Elegy, their conjunction results in a metaphysical union:

> . . . when I am in the mood,
> to wait before the puppet stage, no,
> to watch so intensely, that, so that my watching
> will finally be compensated, where an angel
> must come as player, to move the body.
> Angel and puppet: now finally a play.
> Now they come together, what we always
> divide in us being there. Now first arises
> from our seasons the cycle
> of all change. Over and above us
> plays the angel. See, the dying,
> will unlikely sense, how full of pretense
> all this is, what we endure. All
> is not itself. Oh childhood hours,
> there behind the figures more as only
> of the past and before us not the future.[65]

The space of childhood, which the puppet represents, is one of attentive presentness, without foreboding, premonition or hesitation. Although the child too will die, it has not yet internalized its mortality, and with it the terror of imminent loss and oblivion. Puppetry is, we may glean, superior to poetry, since good poetry can only come from skill that is worldly, while the puppet simulates innocence unmediated by verbiage. But in recalling the earlier essay, "Puppets" such success only works in theory, or poetically. For it is the puppet that is also the transition from childhood to maturation; the realization of its deadness leads to the confirmation that we too will meet a similar fate. As reminders of childhood, puppets are, for Rilke, figures of childhood delusion and alienation. In the words of Gross, in the oscillation of life and alienation, Rilke grants dolls "an unknowable and un*usable* subjectivity, making their burning an unusable sacrifice, an unstable loss."[66] It is tempting to add that Rilke reinvokes ancient ritual of burning dolls and effigies as a warning of death that at same time gives us temporary reprieve from our trepidation. In providing the spectacle of death, we remind ourselves that we are still alive. Alienation and comfort are bound together in their agonistic but necessary union.

But if this disappointment were to occur in childhood as tragedy, when it occurred in adulthood, it is as farce. In the same time between Rilke's crafting of the "Puppets" essay and the appearance of the *Duino Elegies* in 1919, his contemporary, the Viennese painter Oskar Kokoschka, had a replica of his former lover, Alma Mahler, made by a dressmaker, Hermione Loos. Its genesis was a matter of some obsession for Kokoschka, who lavished great attention on its descriptive and diagrammatic prototypes. He stipulated that a furry velour be used for the skin of the life-size doll of Alma for the sake of his stimulating caress. Special clothing was also made for her. When it was delivered, a witness, Edith

Hoffman, recounts that "the anti-climax was terrible" for "The doll, whom he had endowed with all the attributes of grace, attractiveness and the glamour of a love-thirsty heart, was still a doll."[67] Nonetheless, his relationship with the doll lasted for a year and a half, half the time of the real Alma, where the artist obsessively painted and drew it. But in a final fit of pique because it was only a doll, Kokoschka beheaded Alma No. 2, soaked her in red wine and removed her to the rubbish.[68]

# 4
# BETWEEN TORTURE AND TRANSCENDENCE: THE DOLL IN ART

*For with her is everything in nature is animate and inspired, and often remember fondly how she at the age of no more than one year old she saw and felt a puppet for the first time. A heavenly smile blossomed upon her face and she pressed a heart-felt kiss on its painted wooden lips.*

—F. SCHLEGEL, *LUCINDE*[1]

*How long ago and how far off it all seemed! Those ambitions were hardly more futile and childish than the earlier ones which had centred about the possession of a French jointed doll with real hair. Was it only ten years since she had wavered in imagination between the English earl and the Italian prince? Relentlessly her mind travelled over the dreary interval . . .*

—EDITH WHARTON, *THE HOUSE OF MIRTH*[2]

*And Man in Portions can foresee*
*His own funeral destiny;*
*His wretchedness, and his resistance,*
*To which his sad unallied existence:*

—BYRON, "PROMETHEUS"[3]

Let us start with a rather innocuous example. It is a smaller than life-size figure of a woman dressed in an ornate dress sixteenth-century style gown, complete with raised white lace collar, jewels and lavish details like a peacock feather fan held by a heavily bejeweled hand (Figure 4.1). She is the Countess Bathory, the "blood countess," who reputedly bled hundreds of young women for the sake of salvaging her youth. She is one of numerous historical figures (she is under the category of "Really Awful People," among whom naturally include Hitler and Nero) fashioned by the historian craftsman George Stuart whose figures, from the French Revolution to Qing China, have been shown in venues

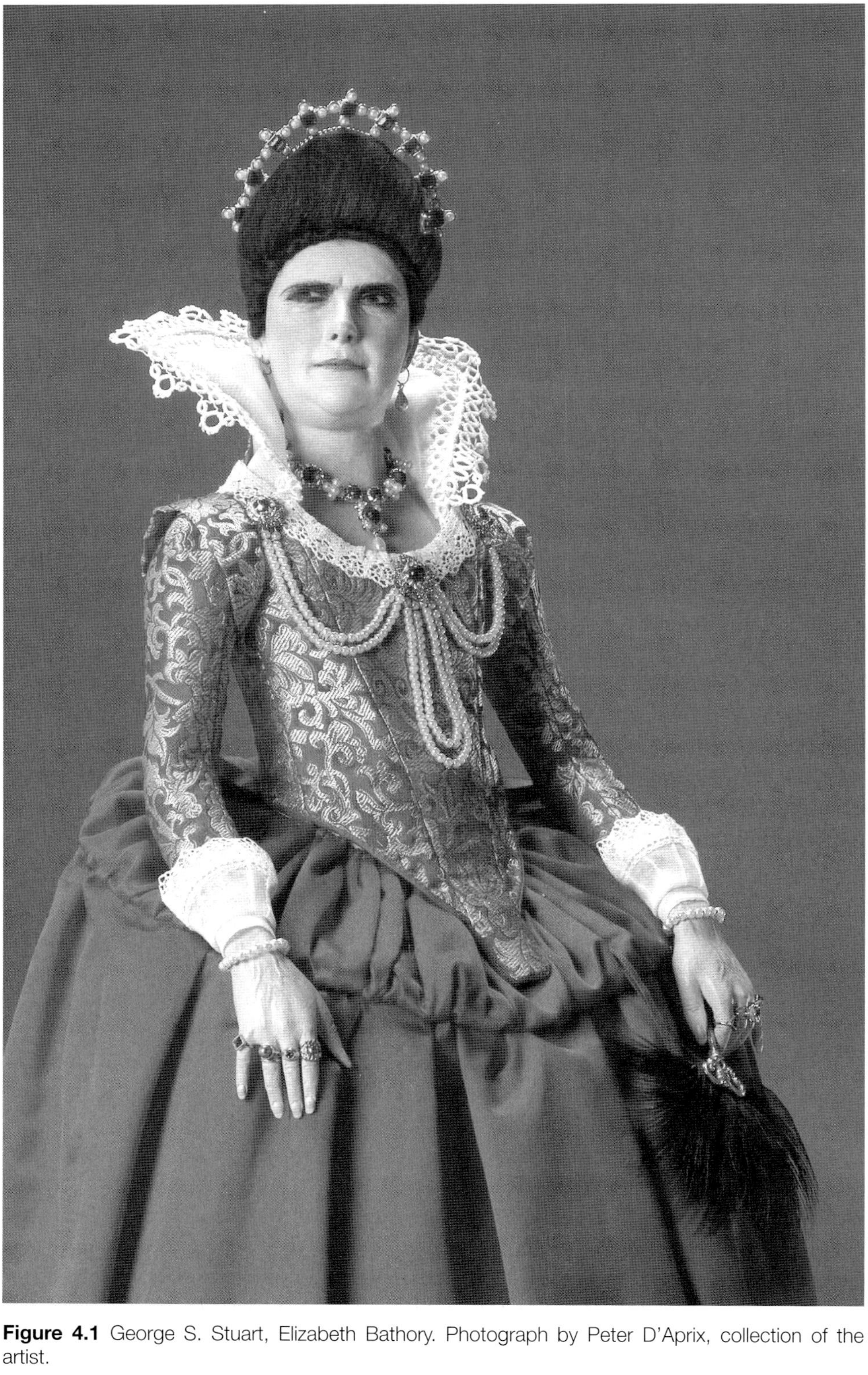

**Figure 4.1** George S. Stuart, Elizabeth Bathory. Photograph by Peter D'Aprix, collection of the artist.

such as Disneyland, but the majority of which have their home at the Museum of Ventura County in California.[4] Her figure was chosen as an example only because her deeds may be shocking but the figure is not, but rather functions as a means of sparking narrative wonder and an interest in history. Stuart's figures, based on historical accounts and imagery, are, of course, also finished with imaginative license, and are not only another instance of someone with an obsession with dolls (in the broadest sense), but also clear examples of the pleasure we take in using such figurines as catalysts for our imagination. In short, they are charming.

But charm is not the common trait of dolls and mannequins as they began to enter more commonly into art by the beginning of the twentieth century, when the visual arts caught up to literature in its preoccupation with artificial bodies. From here on, the artificial body plays a central role in resolving the relationship between humans and technology, but is also a necessary feature in the radical formalization of art. It is both a symbolic and

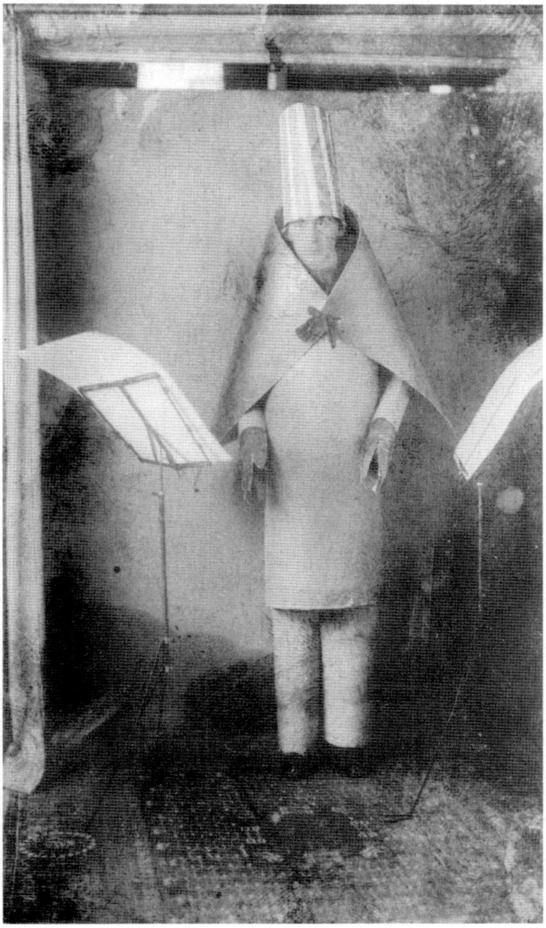

**Figure 4.2** Hugo Ball in his Cubist suit reciting poems at the Cabaret Voltaire, Zurich, June 23, 1916. Photo by Apic/Getty Images.

talismanic component to the alienation of the individual in modernity and the harbinger of things to come. Unquestionably, the most enigmatic and haunting use of the doll in this period is by Hans Bellmer. He would find his aesthetic equivalence sometimes in film and his inheritance much later in an artist such as Cindy Sherman. Improving on the photorealist/lifelike sculpture of the 1960s, and supported by advancements in filmic effects, at the turn of the millennium, there would rise a new subgenre of sculpture. Artists such as Ron Mueck and Patricia Piccinini toy with realism by purposely making strange: altering size (a too small or too large: Mueck), subverting our expectations of a certain body (e.g., excessive body hair on a girl: Piccinini). Charm returns, but not without the support of the uncanny and the ambivalence that strangeness engenders.

As was already mentioned in the Introduction, the earliest shenanigans of Dada performance by Ball and Hennings were also caught up in references to robots. Indeed, from its earliest beginnings in the early twentieth century, performance art (as it is now called since the 1970s) and experimental theater cannot be extricated, nor the objectification of the body that occurred in art in numerous ways, from Malevich's anonymous automata to Picasso's heavily cubified machine-like bodies in the analytic Cubism between 1911 and 1914. Picasso also designed Cubist theater costumes, and Rodchenko Constructivist clothing, all of which was meant to imbibe the spirit of the machine. It was also at this time, just before the First World War and the birth of Dada, that the Festspielhaus in Dresden-Hellerau, was built; it would house the school of Émile-Jacques Dalcroze, widely understood as the birth of modern theater. Dalcroze's technique was to teach dramatic technique in a highly physicalized manner where musical was used for rhythmic control and for the intuition of abstract relationships. Dealcroze was proceeded by other forms of experimental, formalized theater such Oskar Schlemmer's productions, including *Triadic Ballet* (1922) (Plate 7). In the words of Juliette Koss:

> Bauhaus performances recreated the human body—literally and symbolically, onstage and off—in the shape of the doll, its childlike simplicity combining a comforting and seemingly animate charm with an unnerving absence of human personality. Bauhaus dolls of various kinds maintained a playful ambivalence in the face of shifting models of subjectivity, toying with gender ambiguity and engaging with the notion of abstraction both at the level of the individual subject and as a unified group of creatures, delightfully difficult to differentiate.[5]

Furthermore, the opening of the twentieth century also witnessed the beginnings of a more systematized kind of music, atonal and arranged according to an internal systemic logic, as practiced by Arnold Schoenberg and contemporaries such as Webern and Berg. Just after the First World War, Ferdinand Léger made *Ballet Mécanique* (1924), where, as the title suggests, some bodies are reinterpreted to Cubist-style marionettes, and where the human body is but an agent in mechanical motion. The inordinate emphasis in art on the doll in the early twentieth century suggests a growing consensus with permeability between people and machines in the machine age, and also the possibility of developing forms of expression steeped neither in Romanticism nor humanism.

## Bellmer: The terror of art

Perhaps, for reasons that this book enshrines, there has been a reinvigorated interest in the work of Hand Bellmer, and the work for which he is best known, his photographs of his specially sculpted puppets in states of grotesque misarticulation.[6] This work has become so iconic that it has overshadowed much of his other work, particularly his drawings, which partly prompted the Pompidou in Paris to host the exhibition *Hans Bellmer: Anatomie du Désir* in 2006. This exhibition showed off not only his technical gifts, but also by weight of quantity Bellmer's delightful depravity, which, together with the doll and the fetish, have inevitably led many commentators down the path of attempting to psychoanalyze him. Although not spurred by incarceration, Bellmer's work is to visual art what the Marquis de Sade's is to literature: a tempestuous, vertiginous convulsion of the flesh in which everything is an erogenous surface to be milked, pounded, penetrated, rubbed, squeezed or bitten. That Bellmer executed a portrait of de Sade is hardly surprising. It is an unsavory picture. Wearing a bowler hat like some Weimar pimp, his face a contorted, disfigured mess, like the worst example of a First World War victim of facial shrapnel wounds or of tertiary syphilis. It is not only in this psychic and aesthetic terrain of disfigurement and desire that Bellmer's dolls were conceived, but also in a time when Hitler and the National Socialists came to power in 1933, the same year as Bellmer's first pictures were published in the Surrealist magazine *Minotaure*.

In discussing the *Zeitgeist* of dolls and Bellmer's contemporaries, it is commonplace to mention the 1938 Surrealist exhibition, the Surrealists' general love of dolls, fetishes and uncanny bodies. Bellmer's *œuvre* is also contrasted with the various machine-bodies of twentieth century modernism, from the armored figures of Cubism to Duchamp's various forays into mechanical bodies, prostheses, casts of body parts (notably vaginas) and bodily replicas, culminating in the installation *Étant donnés* (1946–1966). Bellmer was also made aware of Kokoschka's grand fetish by Lotte Pritzel, and the artist also knew about the automata of artists such as George Grosz, Rudolf Wacker and Rudolf Schlichter.[7] He may also have known of the large repertoire of around fifty marionettes by Paul Klee (1916–1925), which the artist began making for his son Felix for his ninth birthday. Such examples comprise the creative climate of Bellmer's contemporaries and peers.

But conspicuously absent in such discussions is the work of the Belgian dramatist Michel de Ghelderode, who was a near exact contemporary of Bellmer,[8] and who shared the same obsession with dolls. To begin with, Ghelderode's penchant for puppets follows an already well-trodden set of preferences and beliefs: the idea that God is the puppet-master, that living actors spoil the playwright's intent with their contingent personalities and that puppets are suggestive because their bodies are after all fake and therefore metaphorical, beliefs he shared with his contemporary, Paul Claudel.[9] Most important, for the purposes of this comparison, Ghelderode preferred the capacity of marionettes for caricature and extremes forms of representation. This was congenial to his style of drama, which was about the darkness of the human condition with its innumerable weaknesses that end in corruption and death.

Ghelderode also took some inspiration from the visual arts. *Les Aveugles* (*The Blind,* 1933), for instance, draws from the Peter Bruegel the Elder's painting *The Parable of the*

*Blind*, in which the misery and loneliness of the figures are used to express the fundamental emptiness of human plight. *Le Siège d'Ostende* (*The Siege of Ostende*), composed the same year, is one of several plays inspired by and in homage to the Belgian painter James Ensor,[10] also a practiced visual exponent of the grisly turpitude of humankind. Gherlderode sought to liberate puppet theater from the perception that it is child's play and to insert it into the formal repertoire, which he achieved with only limited success. Influenced by the brooding Romanticism of Victor Hugo and his theory of the grotesque, Ghelderode has often been placed alongside Antonin Artaud, with respect to the primacy that both give to cruelty. Ghelderode's conception of grotesquerie was to highlight the immanence of death in us all, and ultimately, the vanity of all our pursuits—in the regard that we are all members of the damned. By the late 1930s, Ghelderode was highly sensitive to contemporary events. The outbreak of war only confirmed his acute sense of the disgrace into which humans had fallen. As evidenced in *The School for Bufoons* (*L'École des Bouffons*, 1942), the characters are not only caricatures but are deformed or have presented as debased in some way, symptoms of a depraved world. The members of the inauspicious school are deemed unworthy of baptism. They are of "perverse anatomy," and are the "rejects of heaven and hell." Equally pathetic, "Christ did not die for their kind."[11] Another of his cruel plays, *Hop Signor!*, is written for a cohort of (puppet) dwarfs. We are also in the realms of Jarry's *Ubu roi* (1896), but with a less cynically adolescent, more pessimistically metaphysical gloss.

Naturalism was not to Ghelderode's taste, but rather the imaginary that would show up humans in all their inner depravity and monstrosity. Of a motif in a painting by Hieronymous Bosch, he remarks that he "has depicted very well for us the inscrutable, redoubtable world of things. He shows you a life, for example, and innocent and terrible knife, from which legs have suddenly sprung and which comes toward you hypnotically—today it would be called radio-controlled."[12] The conjunction of mechanical control and spiritual unease resurfaces in the final scene of *The School for Buffoons.* Here, the character Folial, after exclaiming that the secret to art is "CRU-EL_TY," to quote Ghelderode's stage directions, "he flagellates space, his gestures amplifying themselves, he flagellates himself, pitilessly, and not feeling it . . . like an automaton, tragically. The curtains falls, slowly. . . ."[13] Like Bellmer's, Ghelderode's affinity to the doll was not of the Kokoschka kind, except perhaps in the very final stages when Alma was violently ravaged. But for both Bellmer and Ghelderode, dolls were not bodily surrogates in the way of Kokoschka's fetishistic obsession, but rather they were a means of expressing the particularly perverse, disturbed condition of modern human beings. And where there is a certain naïvety to Kokoschka's inclinations, the world of Bellmer, as with contemporaries such as Ghelderode and Artaud, is entirely emptied of innocence.

Bellmer's work is a reaction to Nazism—this is a critically well-established fact.[14] In the same year as they came to power in 1933, his daughter was born to his first wife Margerete, who would die in 1938. But even if these factors all contributed to the direction in his work, they are not entirely reducible, nor do they explain the swiftness of the change that his work took. The intensity and quantity of his work on dolls has the air of predestiny and singular purpose. It also appears that, like his contemporaries, Bellmer was also riven with a deep feeling of despair about the direction of society, believing "the world is a

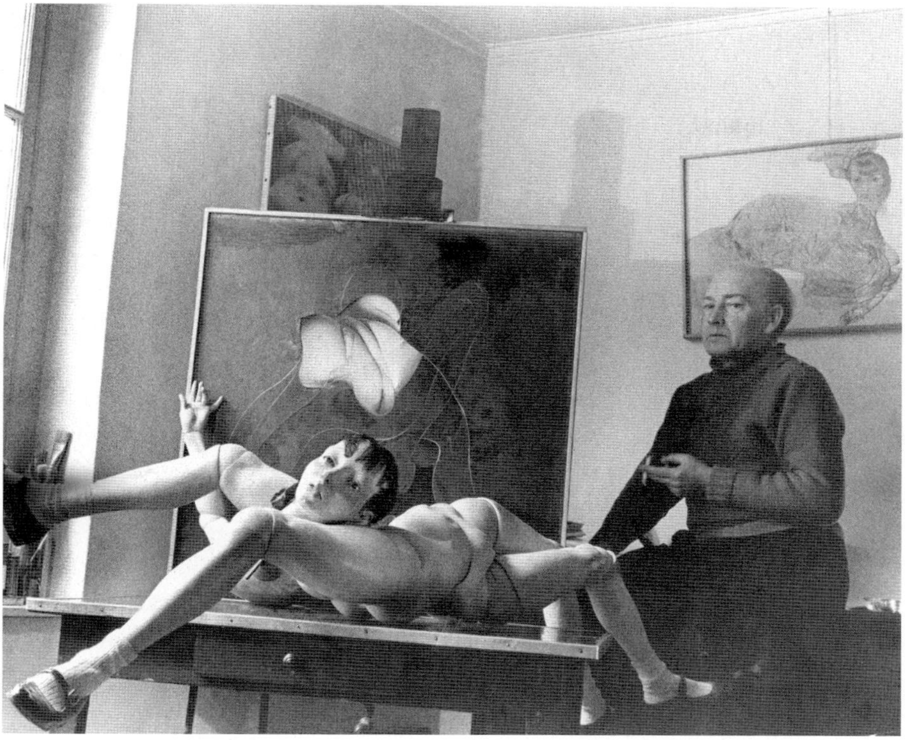

**Figure 4.3** Hans Bellmer in his house, 1963. Photo by Mau/ullstein bild via Getty Images.

scandal."[15] Throughout his career, the appearance of Bellmer's dolls remain relatively consistent: They are all of adolescent girls. Understandably, this has incited its own small industry of feminist criticism followed by its apologists. Like Balthus and Nabokov, one cannot have devoted so much energy and time to a motif and a body type without some form of interest in it, but at the same time, it is glib to point too readily to misogyny or love of young girls. For there is a solid argument to suggest that the body of the adolescent girl is the symbolic site of deflowering, and of transgression; it is the most vulnerable of sexualized bodies and also the most desired because the most forbidden. This makes Bellmer's dolls not only figures of shock and disgust, but also figures of mourning, of something indelibly, unerringly lost. The sadness that suffuses the images is palpable. Therese Lichtenstein argues that Bellmer's work evinces "an ambivalence toward femininity,"[16] yet to this should also be added that this ambivalence was not wholly his own, but rather one that stalks the social constructs of gender roles as a whole.

The first doll was made of papier mâché and plaster that had been shaped over a wood and metal armature. Around 135 centimeters (c. 4′6″) tall, it could be disassembled for the sake of playing out the bodily permutations for which the artist is known. It resulted in a series of photographs that were assembled into a limited-edition book simply titled *Die Puppe* (*The Doll*) a year later. The second doll, made in 1935, was more shapely and painted a flesh tint. It was more flexible than the first and subject to an enormous amount of modifications; Bellmer made around a thousand photographs. What is significant is that he did not begin with a complete doll, but instead worked continually from fragments. This meant that Bellmer did not have anything like a figurally whole starting point that he broke down into abjection; it was a fractured body from the very outset, never complete, and therefore, never subject to the anthropomorphic identification that is normal for dolls. Rather, it appears that these dolls were geared toward misindentification. For since they did not begin as whole bodies, they are to be read as robots whose concern about the loss of an appendage is only how long it can be repaired or replaced.

Alternatively, taking a cue from Bellmer's own writings, the arranging and rearranging of body parts has been compared to anagrams. As Lichtenstein observes, "As a plastic anagram, the doll in the book [*The Doll*] invites the viewer to decipher a secret or hidden meaning by which its changing appearance is symptomatic of unconscious psychosexual and emotional states."[17] The anagram is not an interpretative conceit, but rather a logic of articulation, of making. When mentioning the anagram, Bellmer also contends that "the body is like a sentence that invites us to rearrange it."[18] The body exists for the sake of its permutation, its confusion. Thus, it is also important that the final diagnosis, or message, remains undisclosed, hidden and in remaining so gives leverage for further disruptive constructions that entrench rather than resolve the "problem." In Bellmer's words, "the anagram is born from a violent and paradoxical conflict."[19] And conflict is at the center of the "resolved" and "whole" human subject. Hence, the Lacanian realization that subjecthood is a series of components, as material and as idea, whose wholeness is arbitrary, but nonetheless a "resolved" order, is only constituted by the way they circulate around the void of the Real.

It is also this fragmentation that also accounts for the fictive wholeness of sex and gender. The precariousness of gender may also account again for why the dolls are adolescent girls. By being the most unmistakable objects of desire, this unmistakability and this desire are stretched to their outer limits. In her examination of gender and language, Luce Irigaray proposes that we are an "enunciating machine" that exists together, but also external from that of gender:

> While she might be of a sex, this should not exclude other kinds of properties and hence competencies, She, this machine, also has a nose, lips, eyes, ears, hands, for example. She is composed of a variety of possible points of *entry* and *exit*, uses that are substitutable, contiguous, concurrent, interfering, implicating, excluding, etc.[20]

There are two orders of language, the putatively neutral language of society and the language of the mother. It is with the assumption of the former that we search for the latter, which is impossible since it is subject to an entirely different order. In *Die Puppe*, Bellmer yearns to return to "the enchanted garden" of his childhood.[21]

But unlike the more conventional attempts at such a return, a dream-like image in the style of Gérard de Nerval, or else something akin to a children's book, Bellmer confronts the very impossibility of such a return and the traumatic rupture of castration. At the same time, if this return is "successful," it is achieved with results that are imponderable, and instead of comforting, catastrophic to the adult mind. "If we see the dolls as sadistic," writes Hal Foster, "then the object of this sadism is clear" woman. But if we see the dolls as representations of sadism, then the object becomes less obvious."[22] The first kind of sadism associated with Bellmer is that of Nazism, but there is another that is the sadism of fate's inexorability. The kind of terror that the dolls portend is expressive of melancholy of loss, and thus, of castration. The fantasy of the loss of childhood is here not a wistful retrospection, but something more terrible and horrifying, to be read as castration. Castration, writes Foster elsewhere, is here mercilessly ritualized, for

> not only are the *pouppées* broken up rather than made whole, but they are also posed in fantasmic scenes suggestive of rape rather than sightings of castration. In short, castration is not disavowed here; on the contrary, it is staged again and again. Indeed, it often appears punished, with the 'horror at the mutilated creature or triumphant contempt for her.' And yet is it strictly the fantasm of a castrative woman that is avenged in the dolls, or does the figure of the castrative father lurk behind?[23]

One would have to answer that it was both, but also seated back in the disorder of the pre-Oedipal mind.

The traumatic element does not however rule out pleasure, for it seems that the dolls were sites where sadism and masochism were enacted simultaneously. Bellmer commented toward the end of his life that the dolls "represented an attempt to reject the horrors of adult life as it was, in favour of a return to the wonder of childhood, but the eroticism was all-important, they became an erotic liberation for me."[24] Presumably, the liberation comes at the cost of immersion in violence that, because carried out on an inanimate body, is celebrated rather than proscribed. Like Ghelderode, it is satisfaction that comes at the considerable cost of humiliation and pain, if only on an ersatz body.

## Cindy Sherman and the evaporated self

No artist in history has devoted herself so solidly to the range of possibilities involving dolls, disguise and masquerade than Cindy Sherman. From her very earliest work in the 1970s after she abandoned painting for photography, Sherman's principal model is herself. In straddling both art history and mainstream culture, Sherman's work explores the multivalent role of self as both observer and participant. Inevitably, her work also charts the shifting meanings and possibilities of the model as a vehicle for meaning, the model as a base frame on which meanings and assumptions are imposed. In the respect of her emotional detachment to her subjects, she is an incarnation of Craig's "Übermarionette." In commenting about herself after her series in 1990, in which she appropriated a selection of Renaissance and Baroque paintings (known as the "History Portrait" series),[25] Sherman stated, "I feel I'm anonymous in my work. When I look at the pictures I never see myself; they aren't self-portraits. Sometimes I disappear."[26] While it is tempting to examine this dynamic in detail and the role of the model and the mannequin, to be dealt with in the following chapter, this section confines itself to the work with inanimate dolls. While no doubt both animate and inanimate are conceptually linked, the works using dolls and body parts are important ripostes and complements to Bellmer's work in light not only of Sherman as a woman, but also in the growing popularity of body modification and the increasing presence of pornography at the end of the twentieth century.

These bodies of work, begun not long after the art historical works, are ones that understandably received the most mixed reception. But it is also these works that secure Sherman as an artist of singular sophistication. For while the *Untitled Film Stills 1977–80*—her first major body of work—follow a strong and convincing feminist line, the works using body parts are a challenge to conventional feminism in not only reducing the body to objective parts, but also their recourse to pornography. Or let us say that with her mature work, Sherman opens up a plurality of feminisms. The earlier photographs of herself in simulated film stills expose particular stereotypes of vulnerability in the representation of women. By savage contrast, there is nothing vulnerable in these works except for the effect wrought on viewers, who are made to feel like witnesses to some unspoken atrocity. They share in Bellmer's lewd masturbatory fantasy, but differ for the way in which their grimness is also infused with humor and irony. Amelia Jones "reads her work as strategically failing to cohere the (female) subject and, in so doing, assisting in the production of a new eye." Is this one way of saying that Sherman's work is neither complicit with the "male gaze" nor conventionally allied to the feminist task of reorienting or discrediting this gaze? It certainly opens up a destabilized space in which pat presumptions about gender and power cannot be countenanced.

In his analysis of the abject and the obscene in Sherman's work, Foster divides Sherman's work into three groups as he sees it having evolved at his time of writing (1996). The first involves the film stills and is "the subject under the gaze, the subject-as-picture."[27] The second is the color photography of 1983–1990, ranging from fashion photographs to art history and the aftermath violence. Thus, "Sherman moves to the image-screen, to the repertoire of representation."[28] In the third phase, with its serial abjection and objectionable subject matter, as opposed to "the middle work, where it [the subject] is invaded by the gaze," in the work that follows, "it is obliterated by the gaze."[29] In this regard, they are worth mentioning alongside Robert Gober's work, also of the early 1990s, of body parts, usually legs fantastically extruding from a wall, another form of obliteration and emasculation. These are images of a similar genus of abandonment to Bellmer's dolls, but male agency, and by extension the male gaze, is cast adrift. In some cases, it is abruptly annulled.

One problem with Foster's attractively neat topology is that the work involving "objectionable subject matter" intervenes in the more decorous and more easily-theorizable work of Sherman-as-female victim or hysteric or Sherman in art historical masquerade. The so-called "Disasters" series begin as early as 1986, and are the first in which the artist's own body is absent, but as a result begging a series of questions about motivation and content, especially in how they fit with the more legibly coherent other suites of work. Photographed using eerie colored filters (or "gels"), these pictures can be roughly divided in two: the ones of detritus and putrescence, and those artificial bodies in various states of deformation, distention and grotesque reassembly. In one work (*Untitled #184*, 1988) (Plate 8), a child's doll of the modern-day toy-shop variety lies dejected in a landscape of junk, its face mostly in shadow. It is a work that tells of the disarray of posttechnological society and an allegory of isolation, but an isolation shorn of all romantic connotations. These works were also very important in prompting the theoretical and artistic reinvention of Georges Bataille's notion of the *informe* or "formless," and in reintroducing abjection as an important form of transgressive feminism, but also using formlessness to think beyond the anthropological framework, and eventually, toward the "posthuman."[30] As Rudolphe Gasché remarks on Bataille's *informe*, it is the invocation of something perversely deprived of order and categories and "The human being that this formless universe creates is described as a 'useless product' supposedly different from everything else."[31] This "useless product" is what eventuates from an excess of different identities. After so much costuming, the self becomes redundant. It is a conclusion, if it be called that, of countless reshaped surface identities: The ritual refashioning of self finally devolves to the life of the objective surface. The thing can speak as well in the absence of the body. Or better: The object-body is more effective expression than the "real" biological body.

Another way that Sherman's doll works to thwart the conventional feminist critique is that it is unclear to whom or why the violence is enacted, nor is it certain as to what gender they are. Atop figures with large breasts are faces that are decidedly male. In one (*Untitled #187*, 1989), we stare upward at what appears to be a replica of a pregnant woman's torso, the nipples a bright crimson in the shape of miniature Celtic shields. The face is a sad male clown, and the feet below are unmistakably that of an infant. Any trace of tenderness that these may evoke is swiftly dispelled with the tip of a nose peeking out of the belly button and a small accent of dark pubic hair at the base of the image.

Sherman's manipulations of masks, doll parts and prosthetics would reach a more erotic pitch a few years later. In her own studio notes to herself, Sherman wrote:

> (2/2/92), <u>Sex pix</u>: funny become cute and doesn't work—should move more towards terror.
>
> Shouldn't be merely about sex per se as shock element. The shock (or terror) should come from what the sexual elements are really standing for—death, power, aggression, beauty, sadness, etc.
>
> It's too easy to make a funny or shocking picture based solely on the appearance or revelations of the sexual organs (especially <u>those</u> organs). The difficulty is making <u>poignant</u> yet explicit imagery.
>
> But I also want to explore the abstract use of the body parts—a more formal (traditional) approach.[32]

With knowledge of the images, we balk at the last line and the conjunction of "abstract use of the body parts" and "a more formal (traditional) approach." What Sherman does achieve is to show the extent to which human identification is caught up in sexual identification, and therefore, the impossibility of seeing "just" a hole when it is located in an erogenous zone, for instance. In *Untitled #258*, 1992, we are shown a doll presenting its rear end, the two hands on the buttock cheeks in invitation. The most startling and disconcerting part of all is what stands for the anal passage; a wide cavity leading into the void. The cavity is purposefully crafted with two layers of material, so that we can only

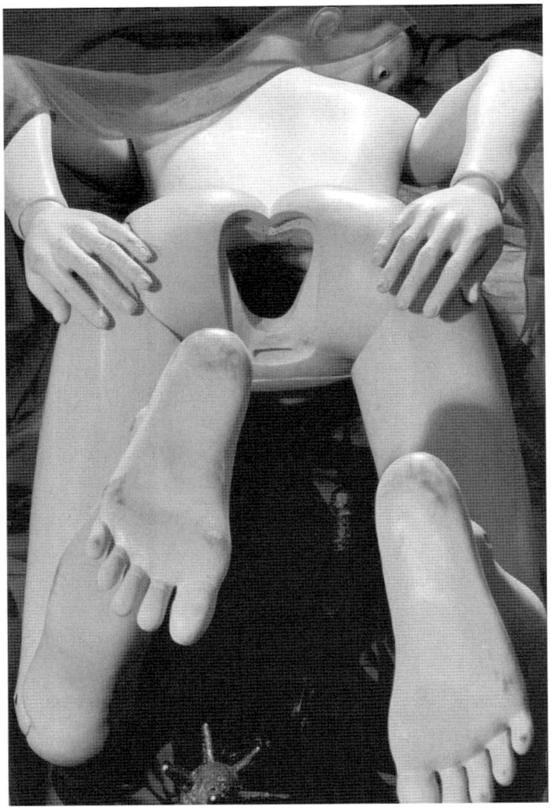

**Figure 4.4** Cindy Sherman, *Untitled #258*, 1992. Courtesy of Metro Pictures, New York, and the artist.

surmise that it is a sex toy with the washable or disposable attachment removed. At the top left of the image is some thin blue material as if to cover the head, but still we detect an impassive doll's eye. Its very muteness and generic neutrality quickly pass to mournfulness. In this work, the artist achieved her goal of making sexually explicit imagery poignant.

Sherman would continue to explore the path of sexual violence through the encounter of the natural and the artificial body, and in 1994, more literally when real and fake come conjoined, confounding both. *Untitled #302*, 1994 (Plate 10) depicts a doll in heavy makeup and tousled auburn hair with a red smear down her left cheek; the chin is stippled with the same red, probably lipstick but connoting a vampiric bout, a suspicion that is only hardened by the most astonishing part of the picture, a cavity crudely carved in the torso (which is the back region; there are no breasts), containing an up-ended dolls head, the eye makeup more crudely applied in the visual language of the archetypal two-dollar whore. Two long legs, the artist's, in silver pants emerge from a black dress; the doll's arms are in the same larger disproportion to the head. The background is a draped fabric of patterned gold silk or faux silk of the sleazy boudoir variety. Again, this work is highly ambiguous in where it stands with regard to gender as the female has not eaten a man in the manner of a Salomé or a Judith, but has devoured another woman. It is a work that evokes a powerfully rapacious self-hatred, but also remorseless violence, the doll's imperturbably factual stare defying the viewers to reflect on their own judgment of it all.

In a similar vein is the work from a year later, *Untitled #315*: three pink dolls of different sizes and sex, all facing out at viewers. The "baby," with a strap-on penis, looks either wistful or forlorn with its head to one side, while the "mother" has her eyes covered, but bears a disconcertingly uneven set of teeth. A naked male dwarf behind her gazes over his shoulder; his penetrating blue eyes solemnly fixated and interrogative. This work suggests the artist's menagerie and storehouse of macabre materials come to life in some travesty of *Toy Story* or revealing the travesty in all popular imagery of dolls, that radically disavow their inherent uncanniness, and by extension the obscene social repression of both child sexuality and the strong instincts if children are to grasp the darker side of life.

## The vulnerability of fake flesh: The hyperrealist dolls of Jinks, Mueck and Piccinini

Hyperrealism in sculpture occurred at about the same time as photorealistic painting in the 1960s. It enjoyed a revival in the 1990s, spurred along by advances in film effects. The term *hyperrealism* instead of *realism* addresses an issue that all of the principle exponents of this genre have in common, namely, they use the spectator's habitual reaction to literal reality to shock or disorient. The works play a double game of identification and estrangement. The attention to detail only heightens this friction. With digital and digitally assisted technologies, the effects can reach startling proportions.

How these works of artists working in this field—here, the focus is on Sam Jinks, Ron Mueck and Patricia Piccinini—differ from the traditional waxwork or related figures, such as those by George Stuart mentioned above, is that historical anecdote is either suspended or it is manipulated for the sake of making new associations. When we stare at the two heads on spikes of Louis XVI and Marie Antoinette in Madame Tussaud's or the motley gang of murderers in the Chamber of Horrors, we are also in the harness of historical fact and anecdote, driven by facts and the fictions spun from them. We are also in thrall with the pluck and audacity of Tussaud herself, not to mention her very strong stomach. While both the conventional waxwork and the hyperrealist sculpture share the same capacity for drama and wonder, the works of the main artistic exponents are of anonymous types, and visual literalness plays a central part in the way in which other components, such as size or deformity, are introduced with fascinatingly jarring effects.

In tracing a rough genealogy of such work, the principal figure from the 1960s is Duane Hanson, who used fiberglass and vinyl to compose scenic tableaux or single figures. The figures in groups are usually shocking as the titles suggest: *Riot* (1967) and *Vietnam Scene* (1969). His single figures are similarly motivated by social commentary, being of indigents or the plainest kinds of people, that is, the least likely to make into the waxwork sideshow hall of fame. As a poet of the prosaic, Hanson made great strategic use of the matching of verisimilitude with the inanimately artificial. For the viewer is able to gaze indefinitely at these figures without fear of feeling rude or intrusive, or of the figure faltering and moving. Hanson presents the mundane (such as *The Surfer*, 1987) with a poised dispassion that is all the stronger for how it goads viewers into a realm of speculation. Curators typically place Hanson's single figures around corners and in places where viewers may chance on them without warning.

The surprise operating in the more recent generation of artists has deeper social causes and implications. Just as Bellmer's work is linked closely to the rise of Nazism; or Sherman's work, to the rise of second wave feminism (which she, in many ways, also subverts), the work of an artist such as Mueck is attributable to the global culture of hyperrealism, not only in the form of mass imaging, but also in the way in which personality and celebrity have infected everyday life. In effect, contemporary life enlists humans to a comparison with an endless stream of examples in the form of celebrity and style that exhorts us always to be clothed and comported in a certain way. Fashion and popular culture are the drivers of the identity that we assume and who we should emulate. Contrastingly, Mueck's figures are presented in multivalent nudity, that is, not just naked (although not exclusively), but in states of vulnerability, be it death, illness or pregnancy. When they are clothed, they are humble, unspectacular. The vulnerability of Mueck's figures differs from that of Bellmer insofar as they do not aspire to the same kind of darkness, guilt, anger and melancholy, but instead reach to the fundamentals of humanness: sentient flesh requiring love and affirmation that is nonetheless alone, and which grows old and dies. Bellmer's purgatory is inflicted and comes with its own compulsion, whereas Mueck's purgatory is the very substance of life.

Ron Mueck began his career as the creative director of a children's television show aired out of Melbourne, Australia, where he also made, operated and did the voices of a number of puppets. Subsequently, Mueck was a puppet maker for Bill Henson. He entered into art by chance, invited by his mother-in-law Paula Rego to fabricate a set of small figures for a tableau as part of an exhibition at the Hayward Gallery. With the patronage of Charles Saatchi, Mueck formed complement of the "yBas" ("young British artists") in exhibiting in the enormously popular *Sensation* exhibition with *Dead Dad* (1996–1997), a highly reduced facsimile of his father lying naked on a white plinth, in which the artist used his own hair. As Kelly Grovier notes, its size renders it "disturbingly between mannequin and diminutive toy, its awkward stature somehow heightening, as it were, the discomforting effect." Mueck apparently had a troubled relationship with his father.[33]

A regular strategy is making his figures either inhumanly small or impossibly large. On rare occasions he resorts to the supernatural, as in the early work of a small glumly contemplative naked man on life-size stool with outstretched wings (1997) or gruesome hairless dog with the face of a bald elderly man. These are exceptions, for by and large, Mueck's people are unremarkable in their body shape or in the facial appearance. The effectiveness of the size difference locates an important trait in the human relation to the artificial body. For unlike the waxwork, which enlists the material reinvocation of lifelike appearance, together with clothes and maybe props for the sake of creating an imaginative space that pretends to bring history back to life, the undersize figure, the doll or the figurine, has less of a spell to cast and exists for the sake of what we bring to it. With the

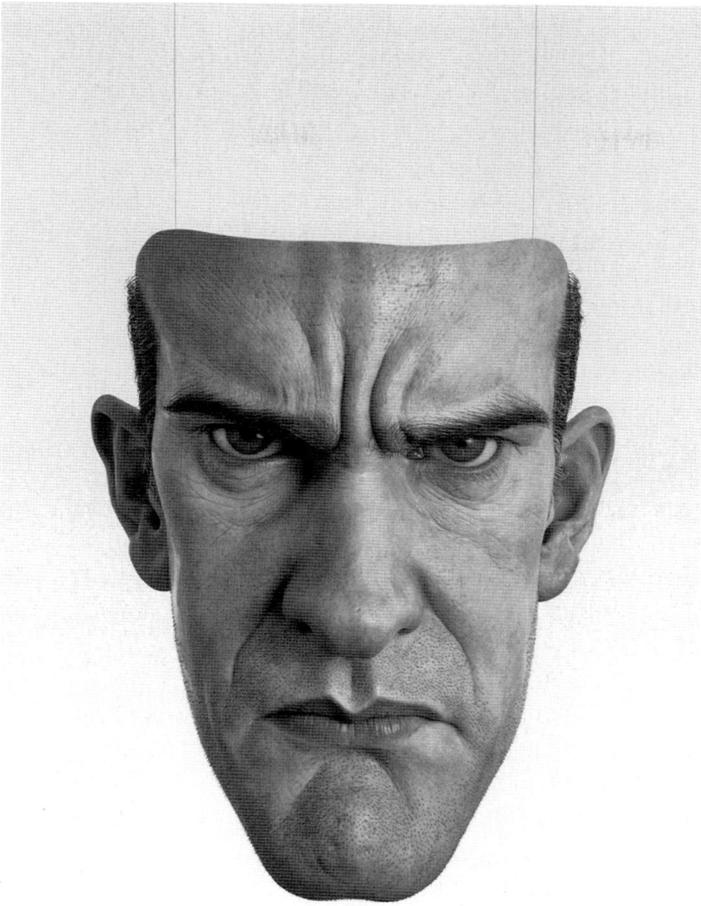

**Figure 4.5** Ron Mueck, *Mask (Self Portrait)*, 1997, polyester resin and mixed media, 158 cm × 153 cm × 124 cm. Photo by Alain Benainous/Gamma-Rapho via Getty Images.

exception, perhaps, of his mildly menacing, frowning face (*Mask [Self Portrait]*, 1997), Mueck's oversize figures are, indeed, exclusively psychologically, as it were, undersized: the self-portrait that is a hollowed out shell of a face, on its side, with eyes closed (*Mask II*, 2001–2002); *Big Baby II* and *Big Baby III* (1997), or a naked pregnant woman some 2.5 meters tall with her arms raised (*Pregnant Woman*, 2002).

Two sculptures are popular centerpieces for the collection that house them. One is *Boy* (1999), a crouching boy wearing only a pair of shorts, 5 meters high, peeping over his shoulder as if cowering or startled (ARoS art museum, Aarhus, Denmark). Another is a massive bald, thick-set man crouched in a corner (*Untitled [Big Man]*, 2000, Hirschhorn Museum, Washington, USA). If his face is menacing, it is also disturbed as if forlorn or afraid, similar in vein to the tightly apprehensive bearded, 9-foot man on a stool (*Wild Man*, 2005), whose aggression is entirely defensive. The smaller works have the same disarming, empathetic stillness, such as a couple sleeping in a spooning configuration (*Spooning*

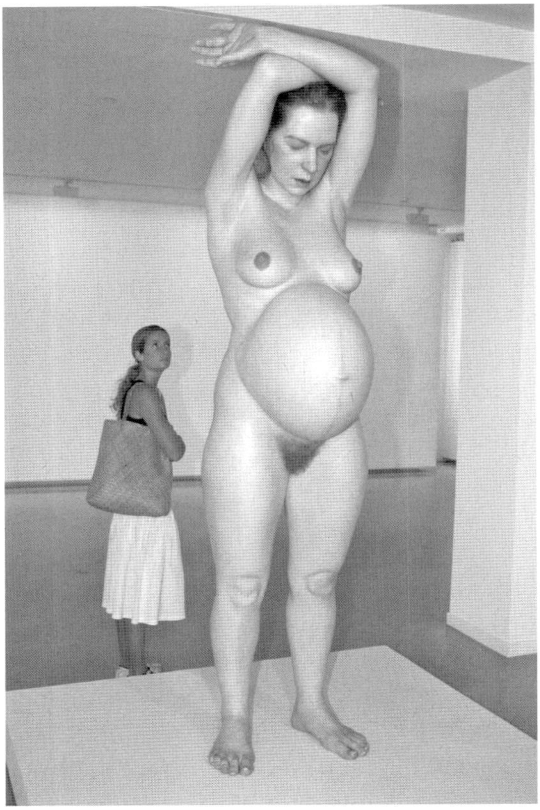

**Figure 4.6** Ron Mueck, *Pregnant Woman*, 2002, polyester resin and mixed media, over 250 cm. Photo by Olivier Chouchana/Gamma-Rapho via Getty Images.

*Couple*, 2005), or a recent work (*Youth*, 2009), a negro boy of only 65 centimeters high, holding up a T-shirt to inspect a gash under his ribs. The poet Craig Raine emphasizes the understated nature of Mueck's work and its lack of sentimentality and that "the emotion is as accurate as the physical detail."[34]

If it still has qualities of Mueck's harsh physical pragmatism, the work of Sam Jinks moves subtly in the direction of the macabre. His work does step into the outlandish, such as the prone thin naked man with the head of a dog (*Doghead*, 2008), but like Mueck, these are extremes that express more explicitly the malleability, mutability and mortality of all flesh—and yet it takes simulated flesh with none of these qualities to convey this. *Hanging Man* (2007) is an undersized, emaciated middle-aged man with short, evenly cut hair, his face ruddy and downcast, suspended from under his shoulders by two rods of metal dowel affixed to the wall. Rather than slumped, the fingertips of both hands press against the wall, arching his body slightly, suggesting some undisclosed intent. Musing of this work, the art critic Robert Nelson remarks:

> The scary thing . . . is not what might be happening to the pictures—though this is sinister—but rather the comprehensive level of detail. The verisimilitude in the treatment

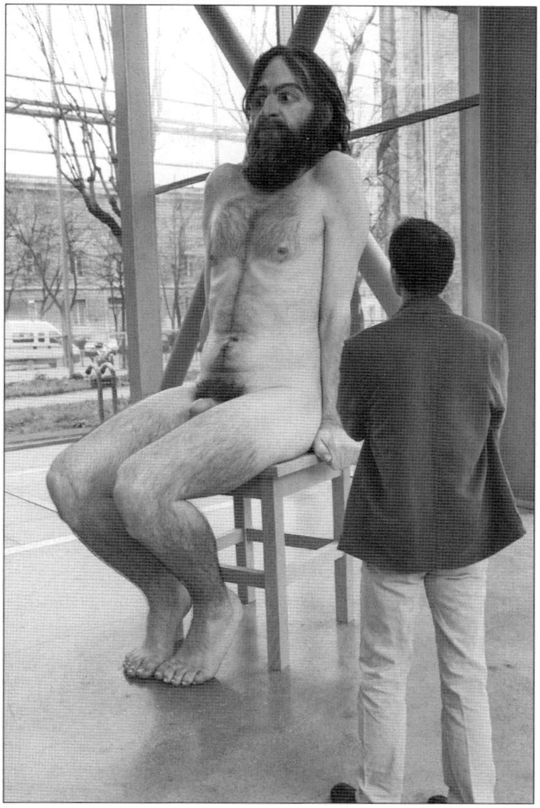

**Figure 4.7** Ron Mueck, *Wild Man*, 2005, polyester resin and mixed media, over 250 cm. Photo by Olivier Chouchana/Gamma-Rapho via Getty Images.

> removes you from the comfort of analogous images in the history of art. In the tradition of figurative sculpture, the agonized figure—from Ghiberti to Kollwitz—is bathed in aesthetic heroism.

Nelson concludes that it is "a figure that oscillates between being aft and being man; a stripped down sign of a tortured spiritual history."[35] But it is also worth adding that this history is inscribed in the inevitability of suffering that occurs with biological degradation.

Jinks's *Still Life (Pietà)*, 2007, achieves this with singular intensity. A life-size, somberly and conservatively dressed man of middle age with downcast eyes holds the dead body of a very old man, held up slightly and resting on the younger man's knees, which are covered by gray drapery. Immediately evocative of Michelangelo's *Pietà* (1498–1499) as well as innumerable other works in this iconographic convention, the artist captures the same profound sorrow, yet the figures are deprived of anything heroic. The old man lies limp and shows every sign of the helplessness and depletion that old age delivers. Such deaths, if they are slow, are usually met with as much relief as sorrow. The son holding his father evinces the blankness that comes from mental exhaustion and facing the ineffable. This work finds its complement in *Woman and Child*, 2010, (Plate 12) where an aged

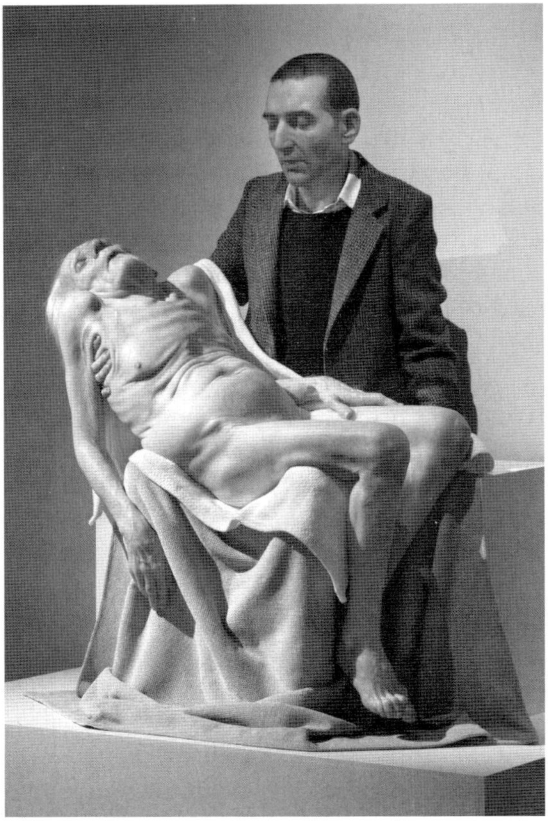

**Figure 4.8** Sam Jinks, *Still Life (Pietà)*, 2007, silicone, pigment, resin, human hair and mixed media. Courtesy of Sullivan+Strumpf and the artist.

woman in a white slip holds a newly born child, nestling patiently on her chest. Her chin gently touches the crown of the infant's head, and the eyes are closed in a state of devotion, of love and also in contemplation of the life's inexorable evanescence. And as if elaborating on this mute dialogue with death, Jinks more recently produced *Untitled (Standing Pieta),* 2014 (Plate 13), redolent of Pontormo, in which a white-haired man holds a younger man by the shoulders, the poses beautifully discordant.

Children and parenting are also a preponderant theme in the work of Patricia Piccinini, who also explores the horizon line of human frailty and compassion, but with figures that are fictional, or that have animal traits and sometimes bordering on the gruesome. Yet, with Piccinini, gruesomeness is always constrained and displaced. For example, in a work that also alludes to an historical work of art, *Doubting Thomas* (2008) (Plate 14), a sweet-looking boy of five or so, dressed in casual clothing, leans forward to touch the moist cavity of an appalling amorphous lump of a creature with no discernible appendages that sits (or rests) on a chair. The work is a pastiche of the scene recreated in several Renaissance and Baroque paintings of the episode when the apostle Thomas sought assurance of Christ's resurrection by touching his wounds. Specifically, Piccinini's work is inspired after the most famous of these, Caravaggio's *Incredulity of St. Thomas* (1601–1602), in which Christ invites the apostle to dig his finger into the wound on his torso. In Piccinini's words, Caravaggio's work has a "really unselfconscious corporeality. No metaphors here."[36] The tension that she recreates is through the interplay between the innocence of the boy and the unfathomable ugliness of the thing, with its pink, mucusy orifice, wrinkled skin, skin spots and hair, and large tuft of which is gathered on its "back." The reference to Christ and his apostle immediately downplays the revulsion and undermines the fear of injury.

In an extraordinary work from a few years later, *The Welcome Guest* (2011) (Plate 15), a small girl in a gray marle top, blue patterned dress and pink tights stands on an antique bed on whose bedhead a peacock is perched. She is staring at the most startling aspect of the work, which is an indescribable creature with large tapering blunt tusks for hands and feet, poised precariously on the bedclothes, its claws closed on the girl's shoulders in some kind of embrace, with the girl, her hands forward, appearing to approve of the welcome. The creature's torso, which is that of a conventionally athletic youth, leads to a head of a simian or Down syndrome shape with a low-slumped forehead and widely spaced eyes. Yet, the look it gives the girl is vaguely intelligent and attentive—and benign. It is a benevolence that is at loggerheads with the first visual cues: from the peacock, conventionally a bird of ill omen (over-weaning vanity) to the miserable homunculus, everything of which spells violence. The fact that the girl is the artist's daughter, only adds to the compelling nature of the work, for aside from its imaginary force and the aesthetic charge generated from its deliberate visual contradictions, it can also be read a moral corrective. For as children's fairytales repeatedly demonstrate, the book should not be judged by its cover, and real virtue lies in the soul who penetrates to the other's goodness to see past beauty and riches.

But there is also another philosophical narrative that is timely, and that fits also into a key tenet of this book. Unlike Mueck and Jinks, Piccinini presents us with a distinctly posthuman universe. "Piccinini's clones," notes Kim Toffoletti, "are emblematic of our current cultural condition where the status of the human, identity and the body are no longer fixed."[37] This interest was already present at the beginning of her career in the early 1990s as an artist in which she fabricated what she called a "Lump" from pig's skin (which explains the kind of skin that her creatures frequently have, including the one in *Doubting Thomas*), an amorphous thing accompanied by a primitive website in which the user could customize his or her lumps from a small number of options. Piccinini has devoted her career, which also encompasses painting, video and photography, to examining the many worlds of biological manipulation. Hers is a world where, in the marriage of technology and imagination, almost everything is possible, everything is credible, and therefore, to be taken seriously—if only still, at the moment in the real world, hypothetically. Writing on the work of Ron Mueck, Robert Rosenblum asserts that it belongs "to a growing progeny of synthetic human beings spawned by artists who seem to be responding to a contemporary world in which perfect replications—whether electronic or biological, a computer print-out or a cloned lamb—are saturating our experience and blurring distinctions between originals and copies."[38] But this observation only applies to a certain point because Mueck's replicants are static and have a particular sensibility. On

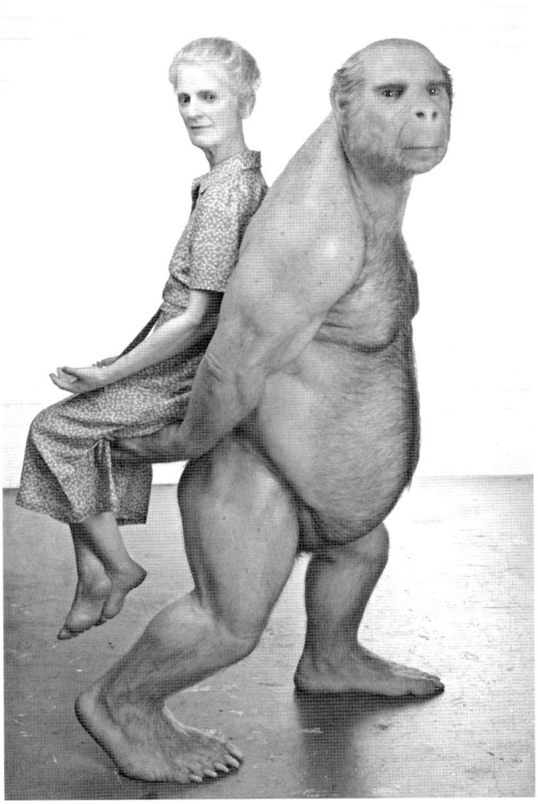

**Figure 4.9** Patricia Piccinini. *The Carrier*, 2012. Silicone, fiberglass, human hair, clothing. 170 cm × 115 cm × 75 cm. Courtesy the artist.

the other hand, Piccinini's work is about a world in which clones and new creations live seamlessly (and harmoniously is seems, for the most part) in human society such that the very concept of "human society" has become an anachronism.

We might conclude that Piccinini is posthumanist, whereas Jinks and Mueck are humanist. For example, if we juxtapose Jinks's *Untitled (Kneeling Woman)*, 2015, with *The Carrier,* 2012, the differences are plain to see. Jinks's work is a deeply moving portrait of tender, again naked, supplication—*mon cœur mise à nu* ("my heart laid bare"). Kneeling with the torso prostrate on them, the clasped hands make it hard not to see this in terms of a numinous experience that we then share. Piccinini's "carrier" is out of science fiction, and Dr. Seuss: a muscular humanoid with a charming bald head and benign snout carries a slight old woman, the quintessential sweet grandmother in a floral dress. This newfangled creature is presumably doing his life duty, and in a Seussian vein, his name is the same as his function. Piccinini's work can be said to be humane in that it retains qualities of moral responsibility, the extensiveness of sentiment, but it also gestures to a reconsideration of normalcy. This is not to make any qualitative claim about the value of these two approaches, however, only to emphasize that with Mueck and Jinks, the work is irrepressibly human, poignantly so, while Piccinini distends to the idea to admit of a different definition.

In his thorough examination of posthumanism, Stefan Herbrechter rightly observes how in science fiction the artificial or new animal intelligence undergoes a "humanization" either at the hands of humans, or it can even be process that humans themselves must undergo themselves as a realization or rite of passage. *Planet of the Apes* (1968), for instance, "never breaks out of its anthropocentrism, however, in first projecting human 'evil' onto the animal other and in the end presupposing the need for atonement and humility within 'the animal'."[39] While, to some extent, this anthropocentrism can be seen to be active in the work of Piccinini, it is also true that her human-to-nonhuman relationships occur in a space after conflict, or where no conflict has ever occurred. In this respect, she is heavily Spinozist, Spinoza being one of the incipient posthumanist thinkers. Spinoza advised that animals that could cause harm such as spiders or snakes were not inherently evil, but rather had "expressions" that were inhospitable to our own particular "substance." Or as Deleuze puts in his study of Spinoza, "there is no Good or Evil [*de Bien ni de Mal*] in nature in general, but *there is goodness and bad* [*du bon et du mauvais*], useful and harmful for each existing modality. Evil and bad come from the point of view of one or another mode. Being human, we judge what is bad from our point of view".[40] Goodness and also beauty are therefore highly contingent qualities. Piccinini's work exhorts us to consider that there are more than just a few more standards of measure than those of our own or our neighbor. The monstrous may not be monstrous after all; perhaps the monstrous lies in overexaggerating, overemphasizing, hypertrophying the "human" in both body and concept. Maybe it is humans who are the monsters.

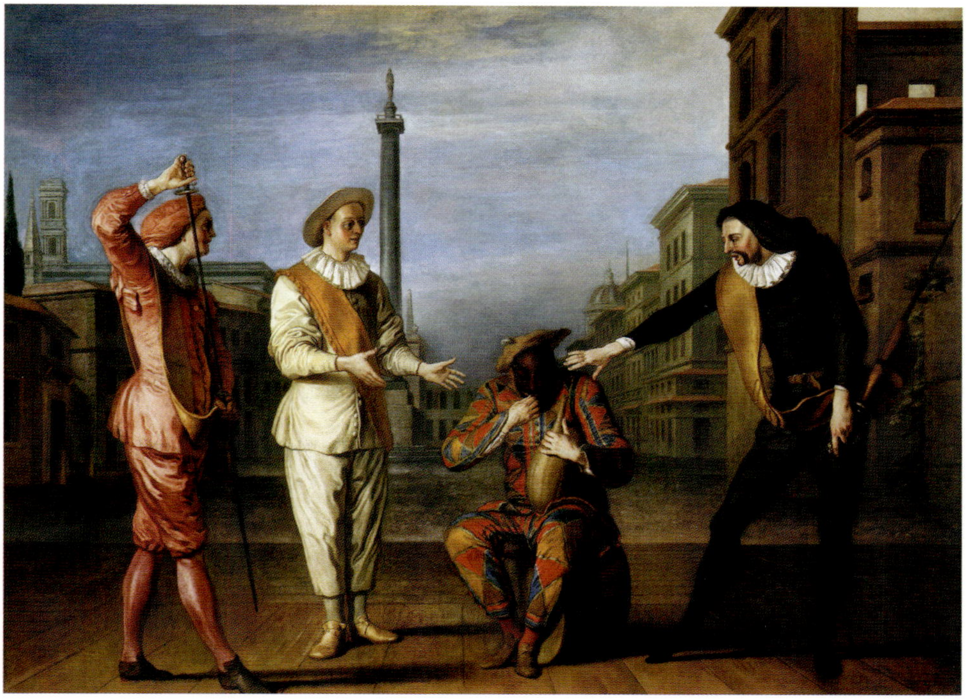

**Plate 1** Claude Gillot, *Tombeaux de Maitre André*, scene from Commedia dell'arte, eighteenth century. Paris, Musée Du Louvre. Photo by DeAgostini/Getty Images

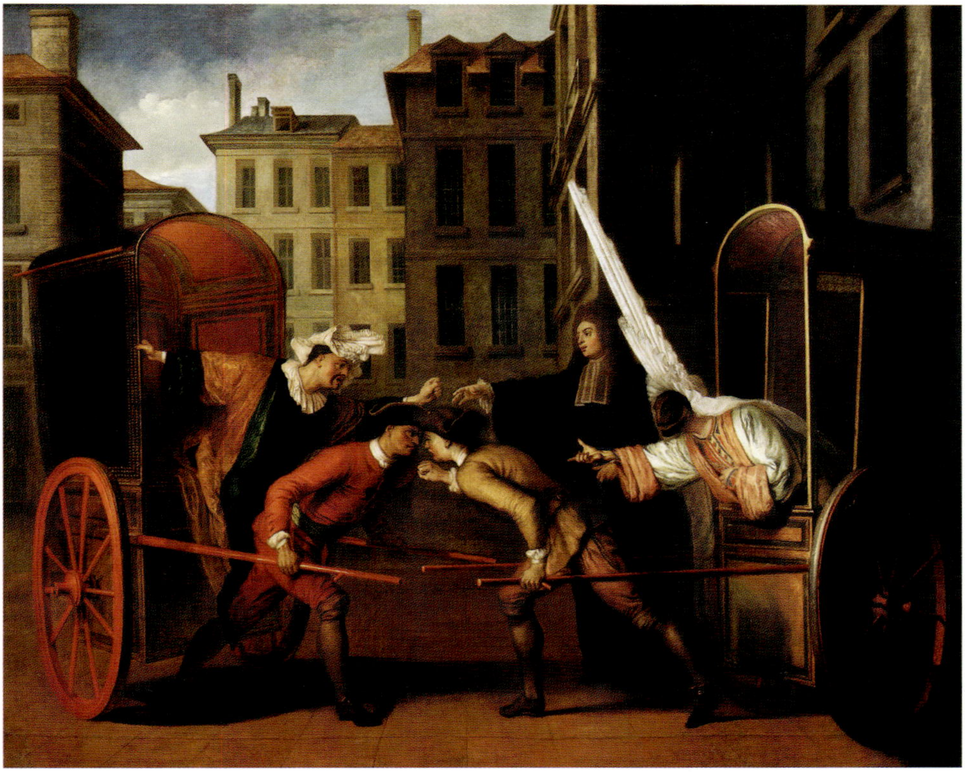

**Plate 2** Claude Gillot, *Sedan Chair*, scene from Commedia dell'arte, eighteenth century. Paris, Musée Du Louvre. Photo by DeAgostini/Getty Images

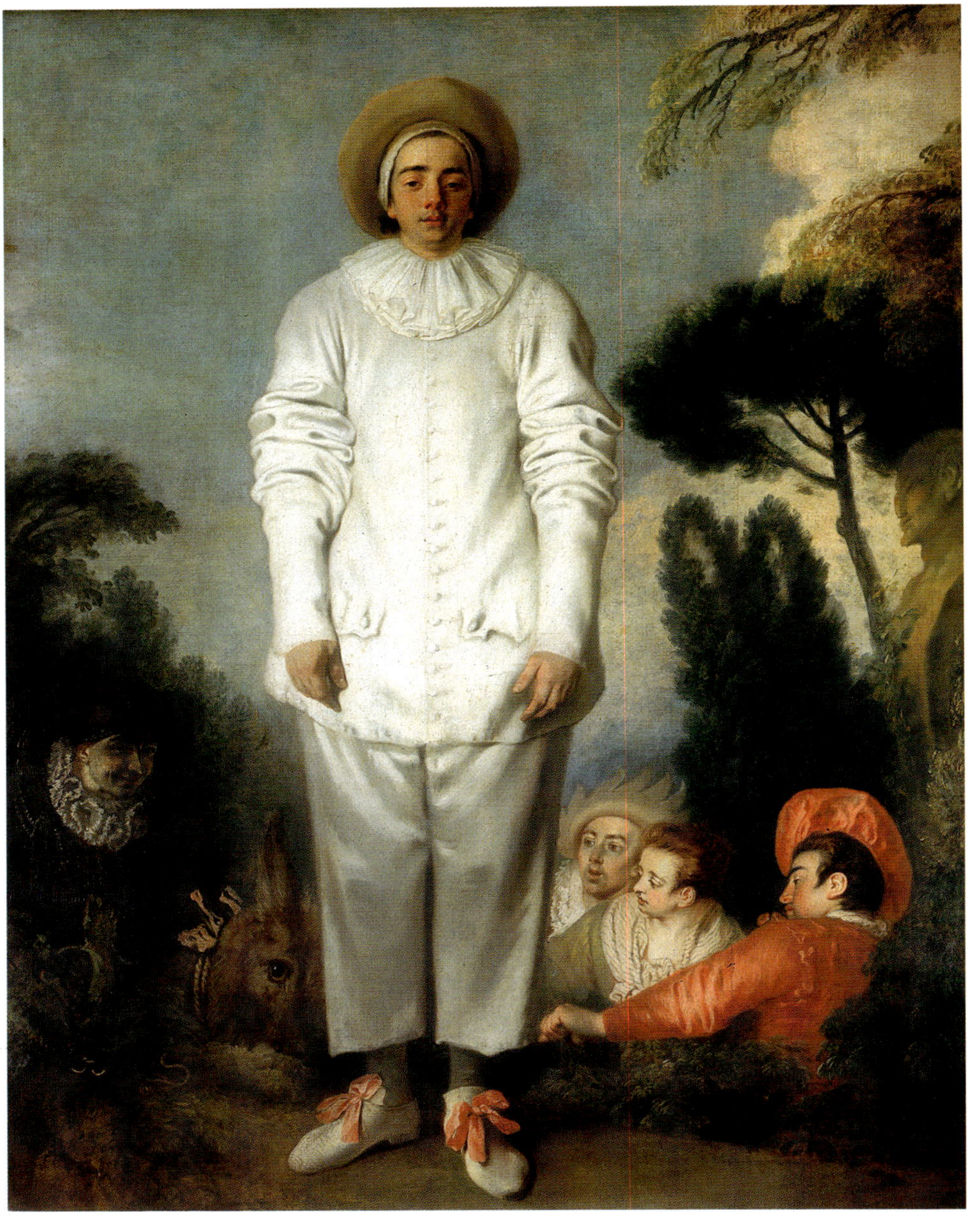

**Plate 3** Antoine Watteau, *Gilles—Pierrot*, 1718–1719. Photo by Art Media/Print Collector/Getty Images

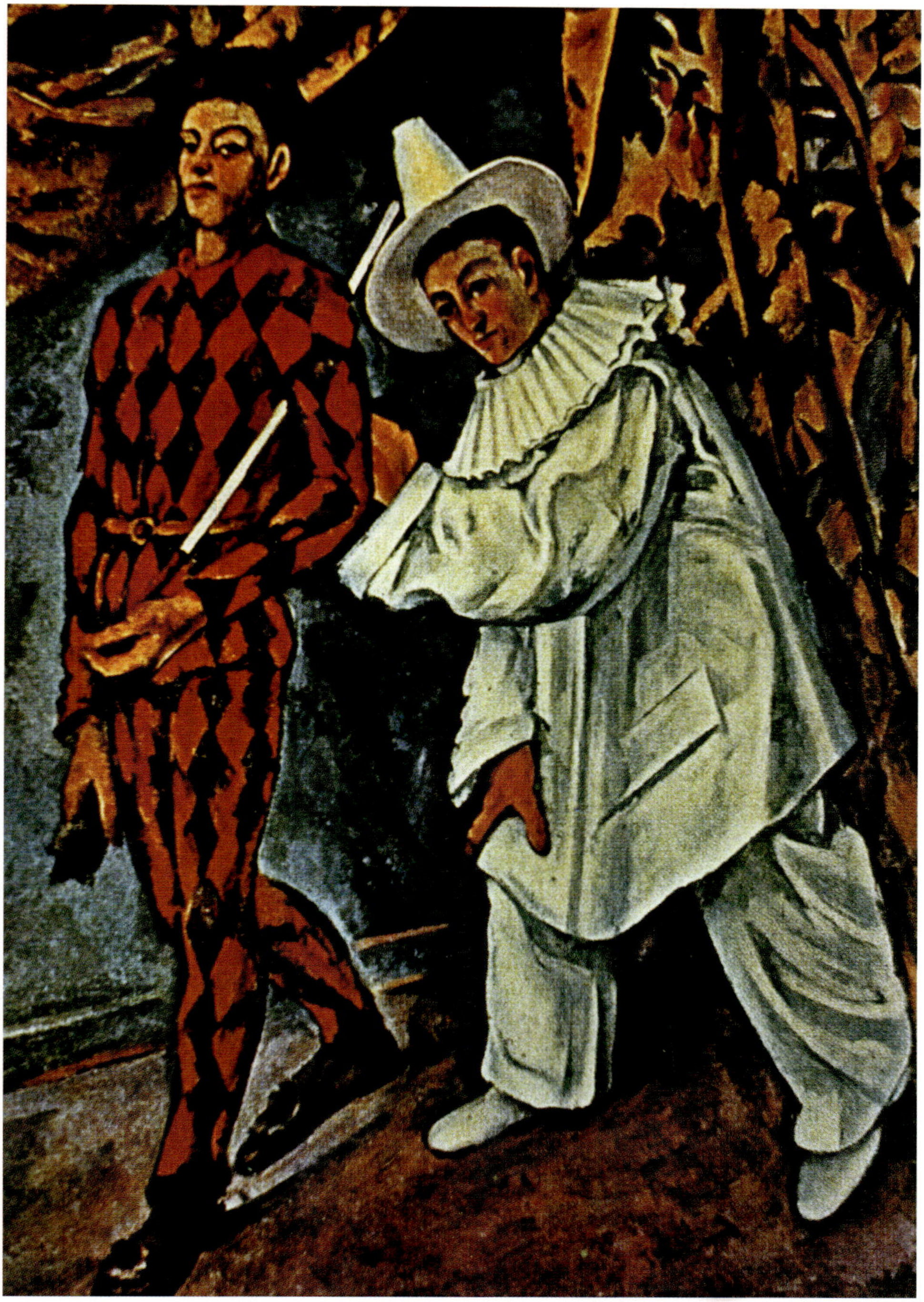

**Plate 4** Paul Cézanne, *Mardi Gras*, 1888. Oil on cavas. Photo by Universal History Archive/Getty Images

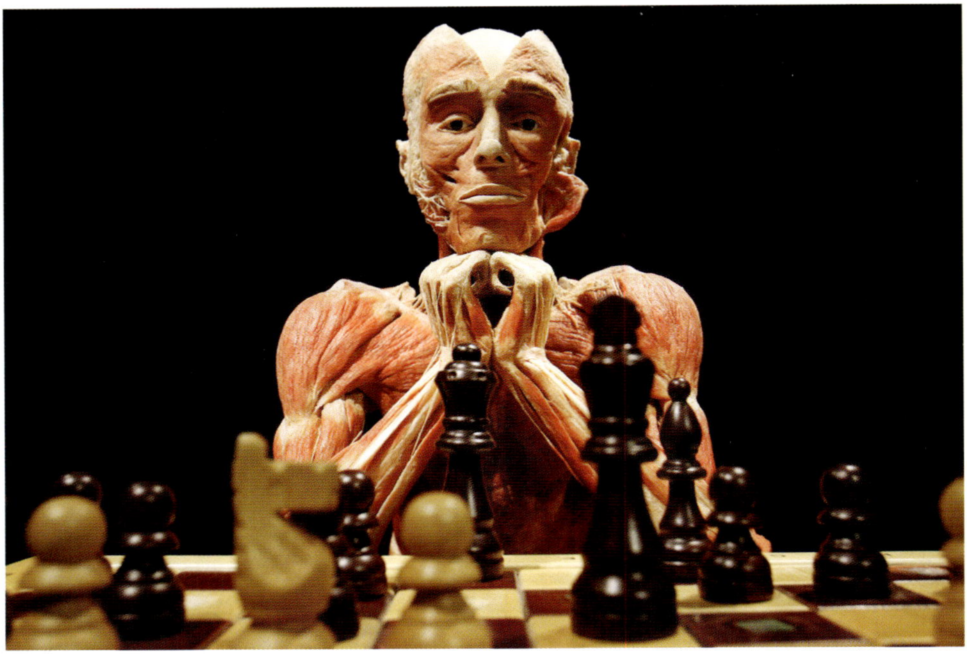

**Plate 5** A "plastinated" cadaver. Photo by John MacDougall/AFP/Getty Images

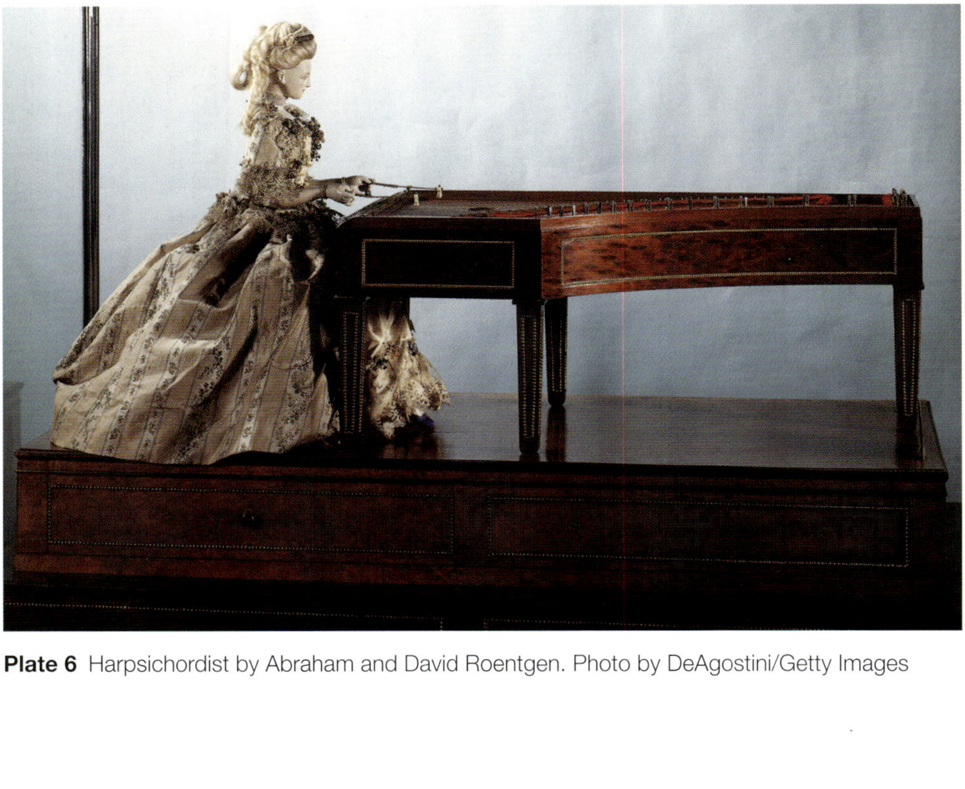

**Plate 6** Harpsichordist by Abraham and David Roentgen. Photo by DeAgostini/Getty Images

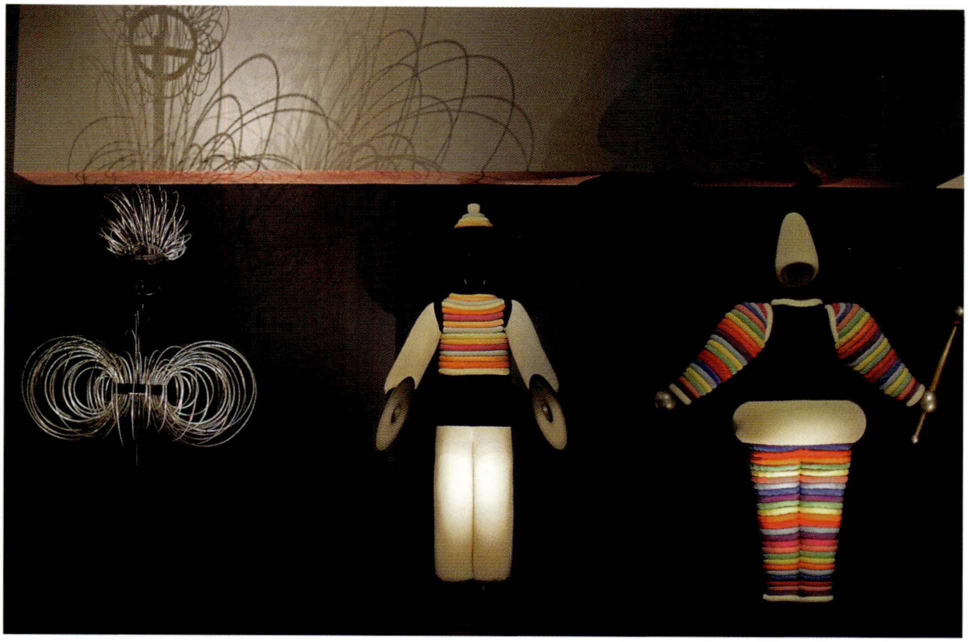

**Plate 7** Costumes from Oskar Schlemmer's Triadic Ballet. Photo by Peter Macdiarmid/Getty Images

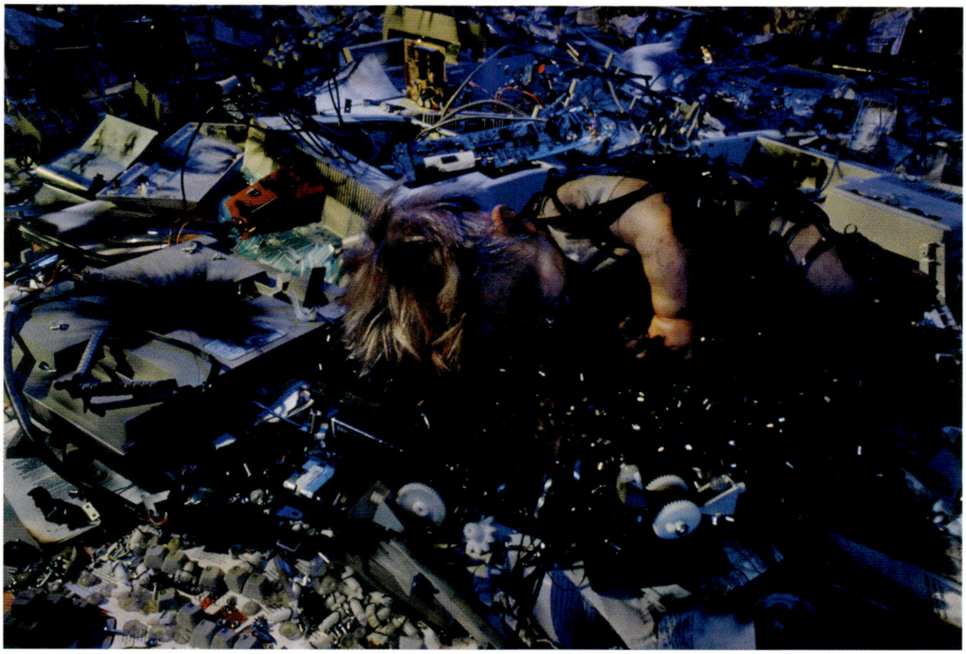

**Plate 8** Cindy Sherman, *Untitled #184*, 1988. Courtesy of Metro Pictures, New York, and the artist

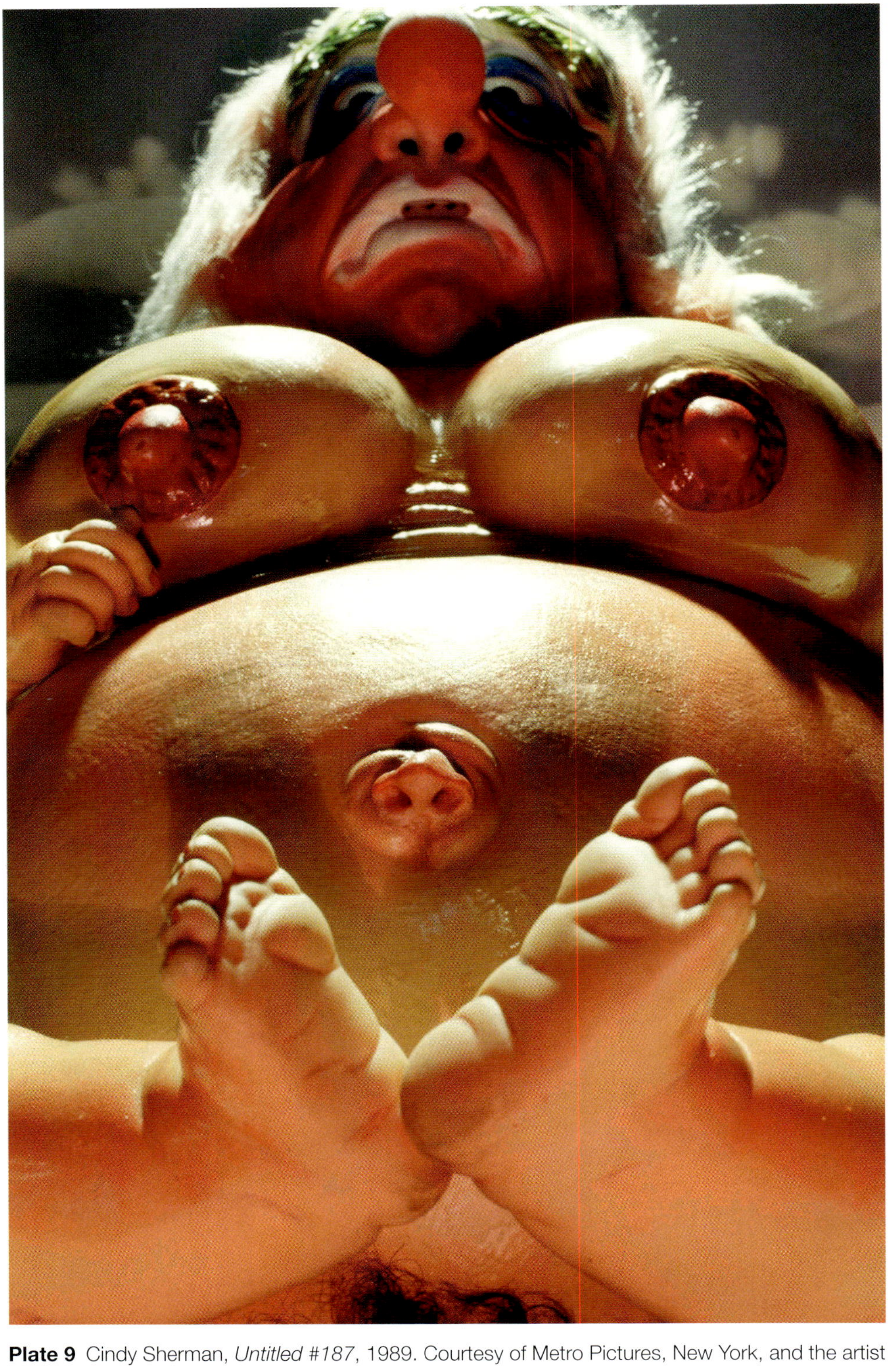

**Plate 9** Cindy Sherman, *Untitled #187*, 1989. Courtesy of Metro Pictures, New York, and the artist

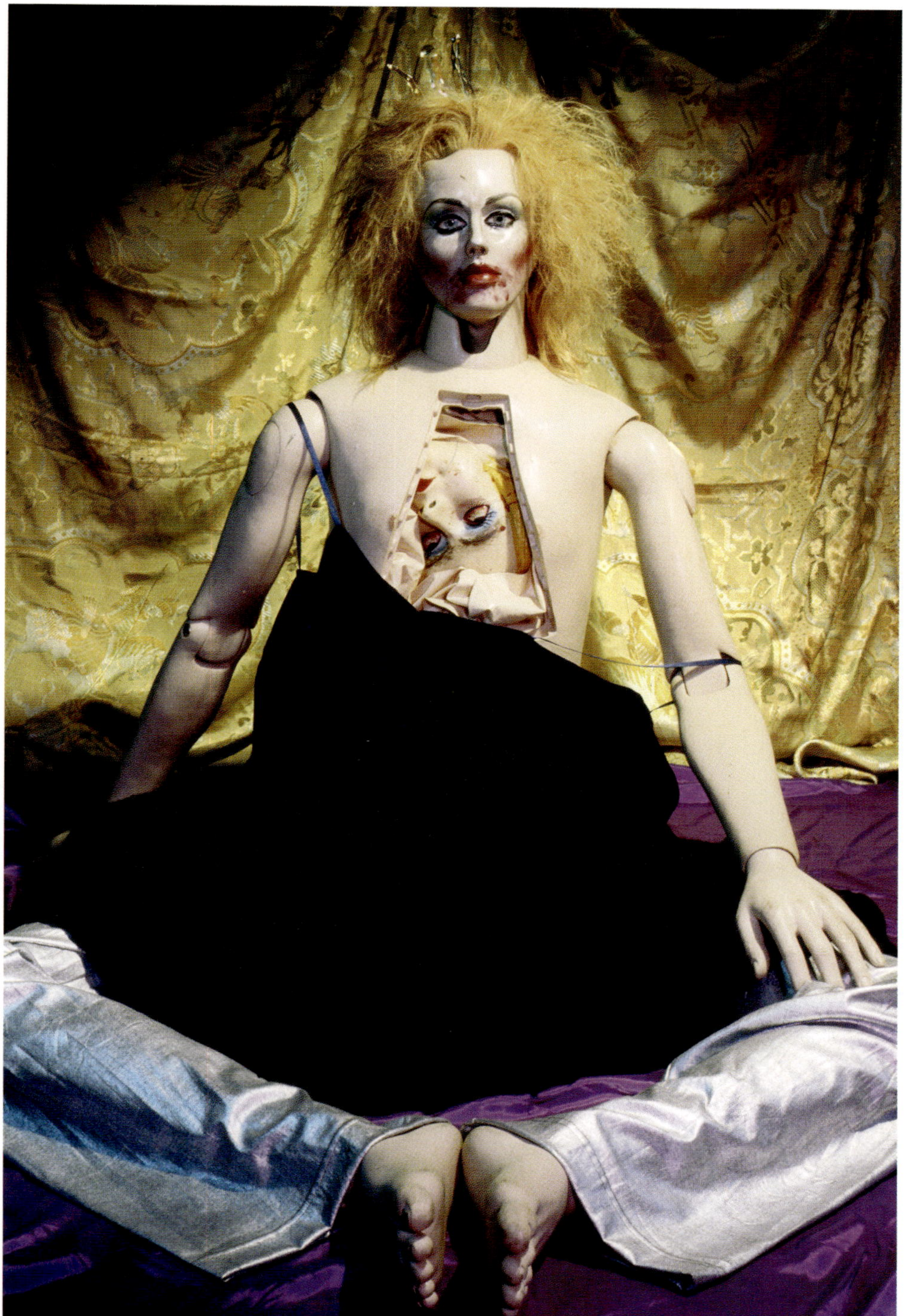

**Plate 10** Cindy Sherman, *Untitled #302*. Courtesy of Metro Pictures, New York, and the artist

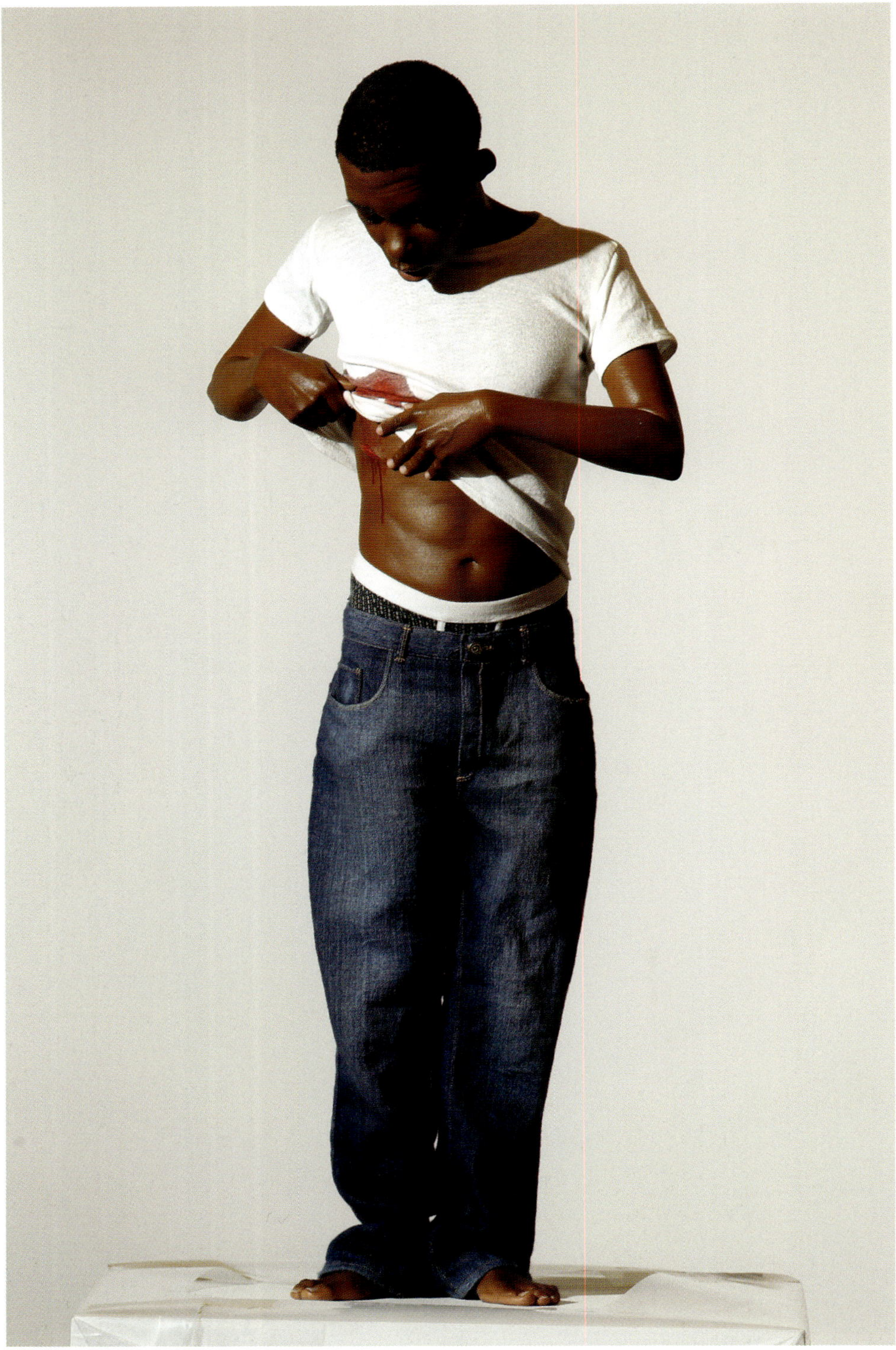

**Plate 11** Ron Mueck, *Youth*, 2009. Photo by Dan Kitwood/Getty Images

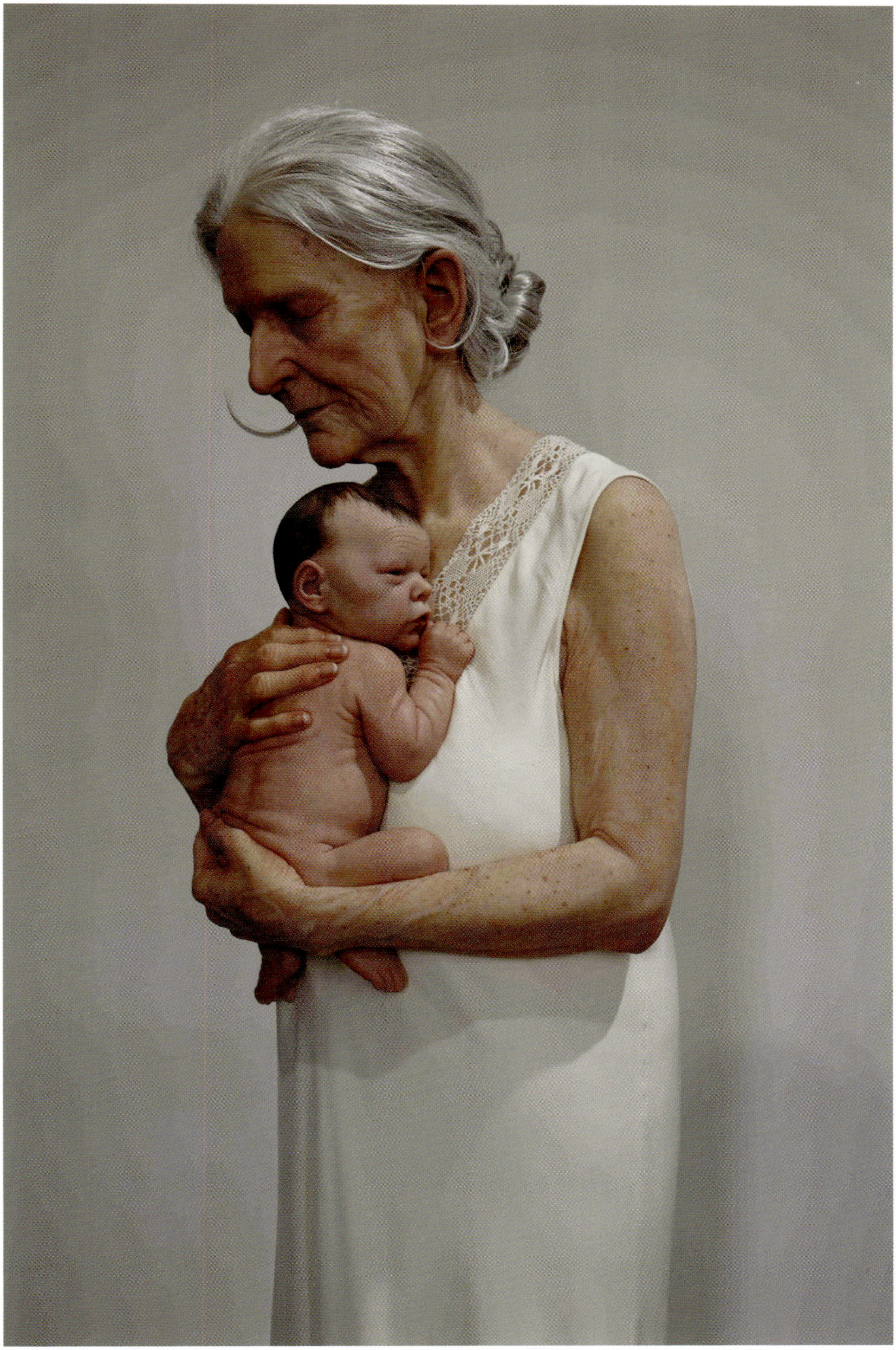

**Plate 12** Sam Jinks, *Woman and Child*, 2010. Silicone, pigment, resin, human hair. 145 cm x 40 cm x 40 cm. Courtesy of Sullivan+Strumpf and the artist

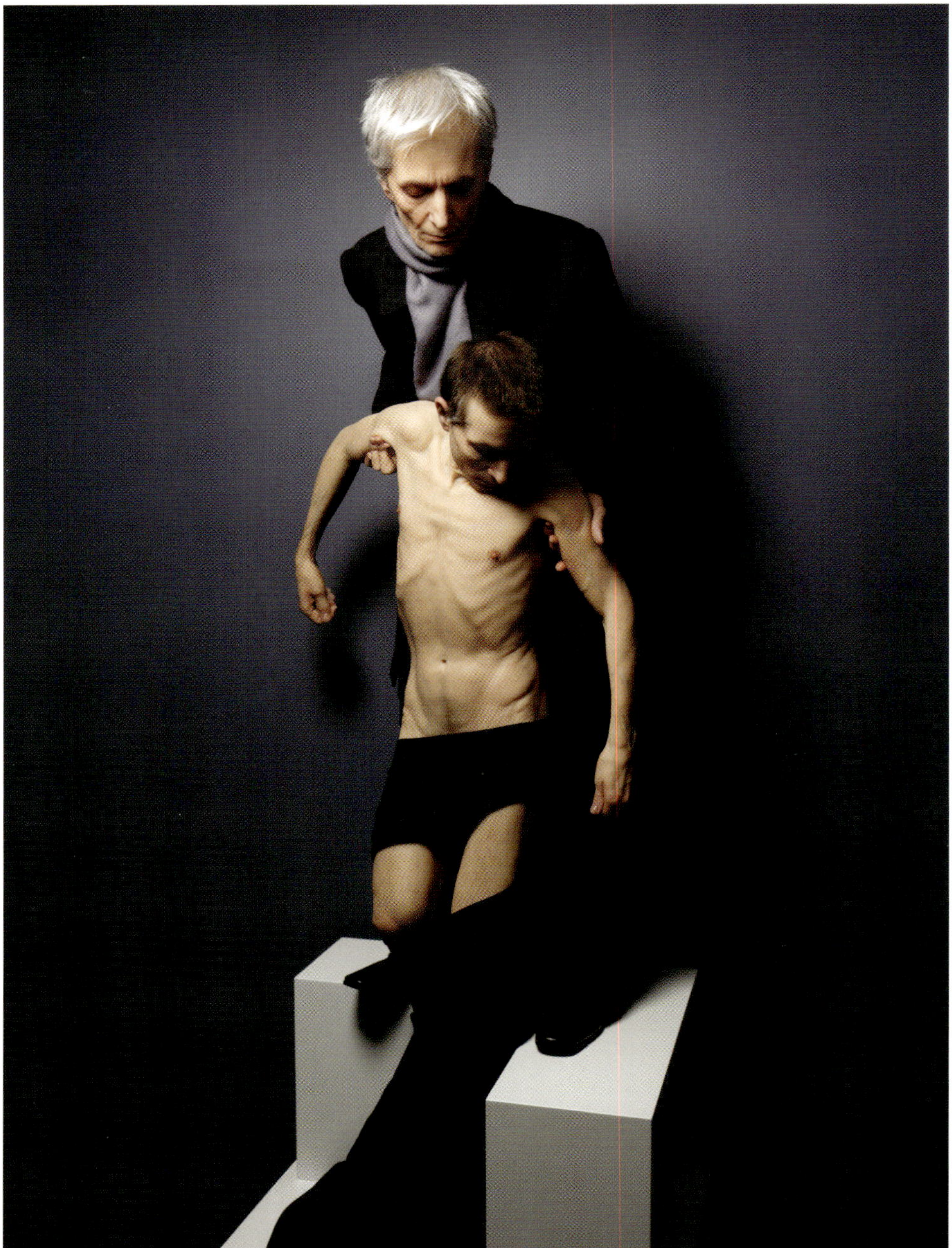

**Plate 13** Sam Jinks, *Untitled (Standing Pieta)*, 2014. Silicone, pigment, resin, human hair. 240 cm x 66 cm x 59 cm. Courtesy of Sullivan+Strumpf and the artist

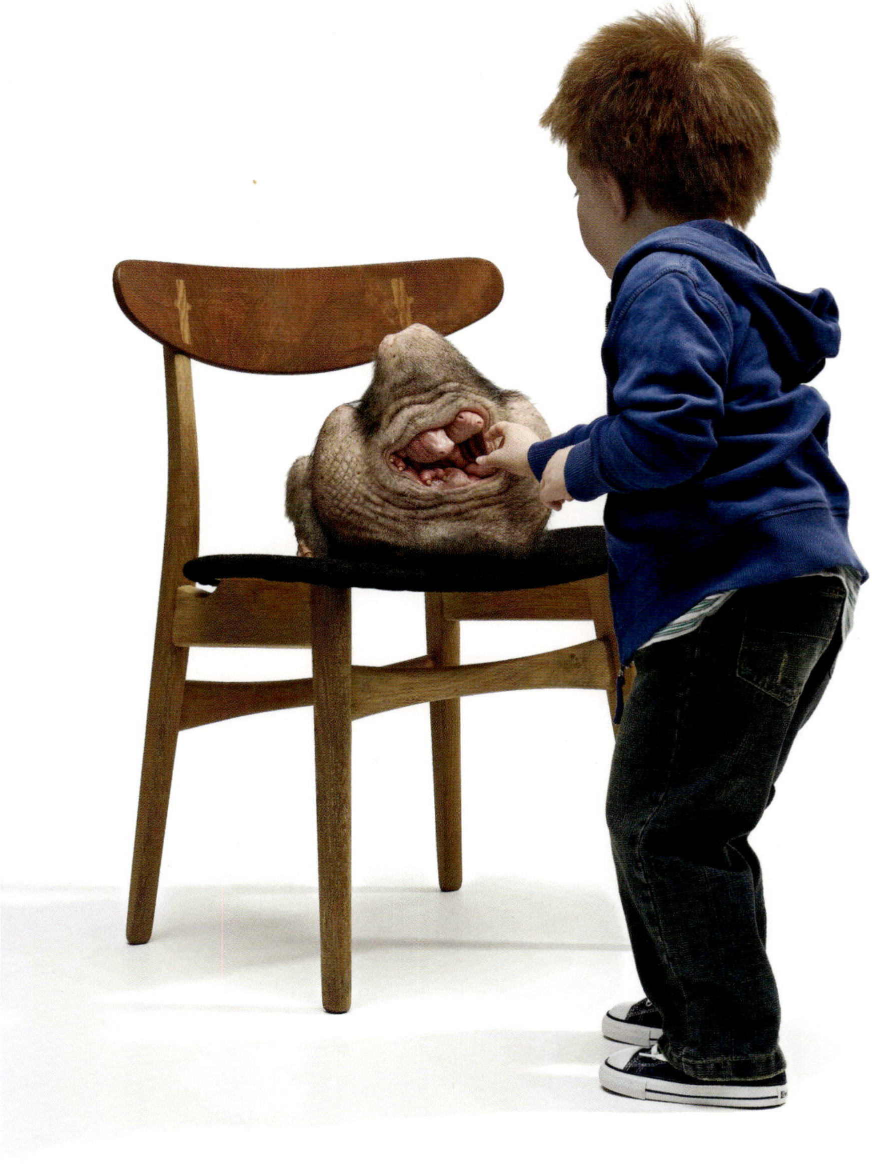

**Plate 14** Patricia Piccinini. *Doubting Thomas*, 2008. Silicone, fiberglass, human hair, clothing, chair. 90 cm high x 100 cm x 53 cm. Courtesy of the artist

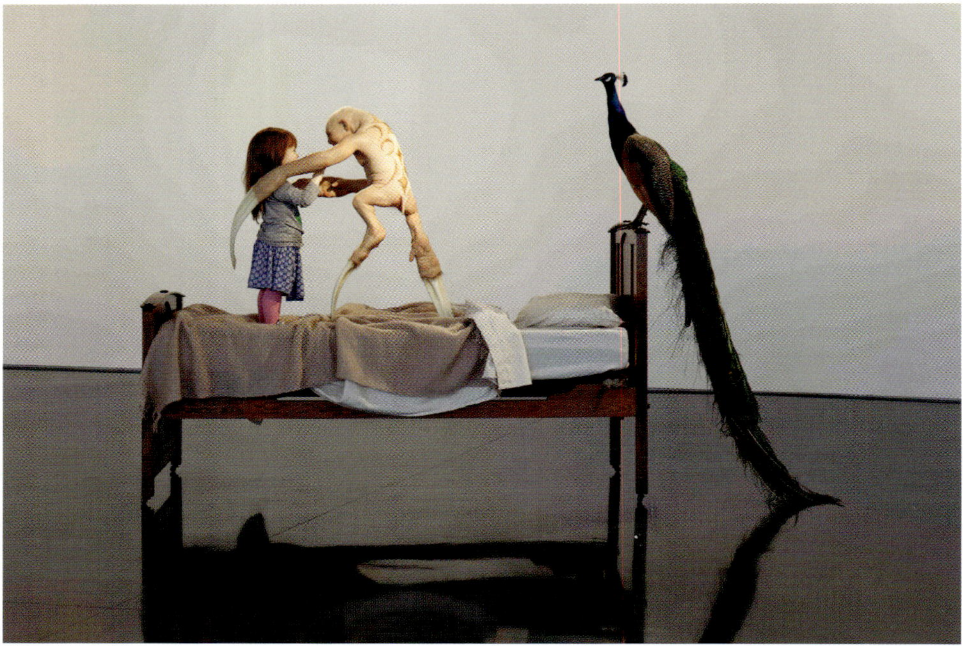

**Plate 15** Patricia Piccinini. *The Welcome Guest*, 2011. Silicone, fiberglass, human hair, clothing, taxidermied peacock, timber bed, bed clothes. Courtesy of the artist

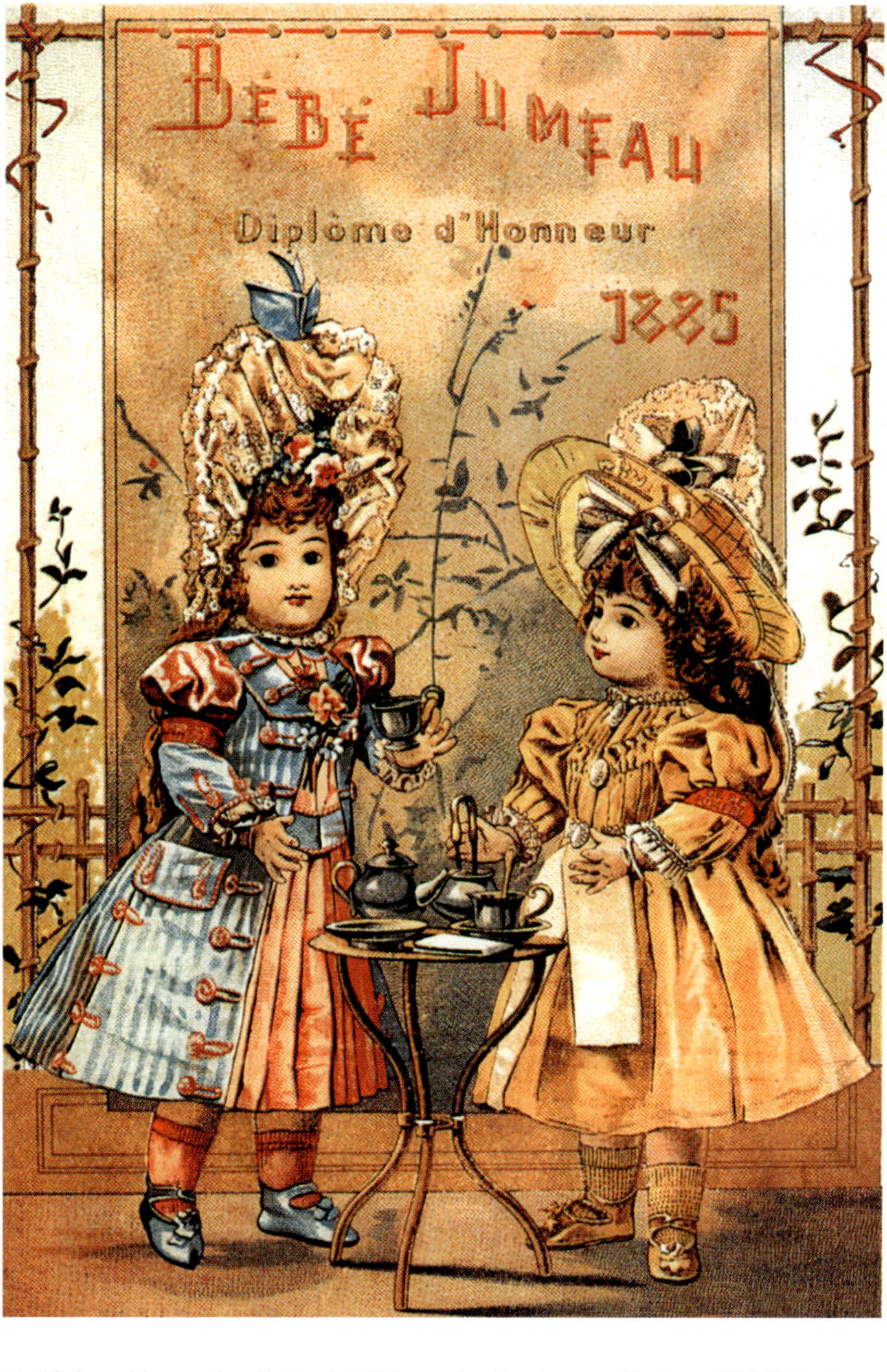


**Plate 16** A card for a national lottery in 1885 organized by Jumeau. Photo by APIC/Getty Images

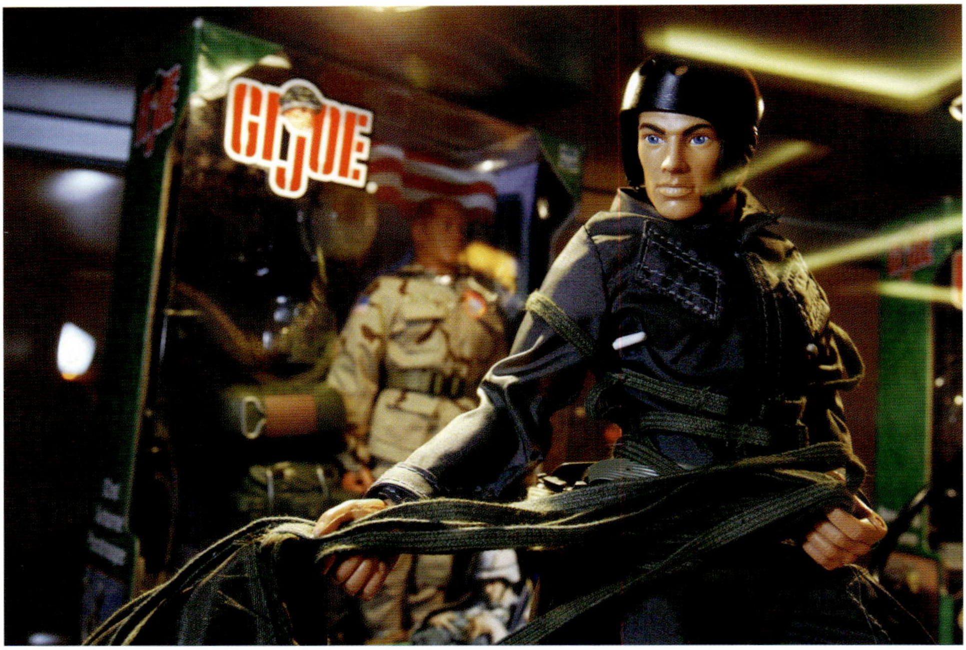


**Plate 17** Joe Paratrooper action figure. Photo by Justin Sullivan/Getty Images

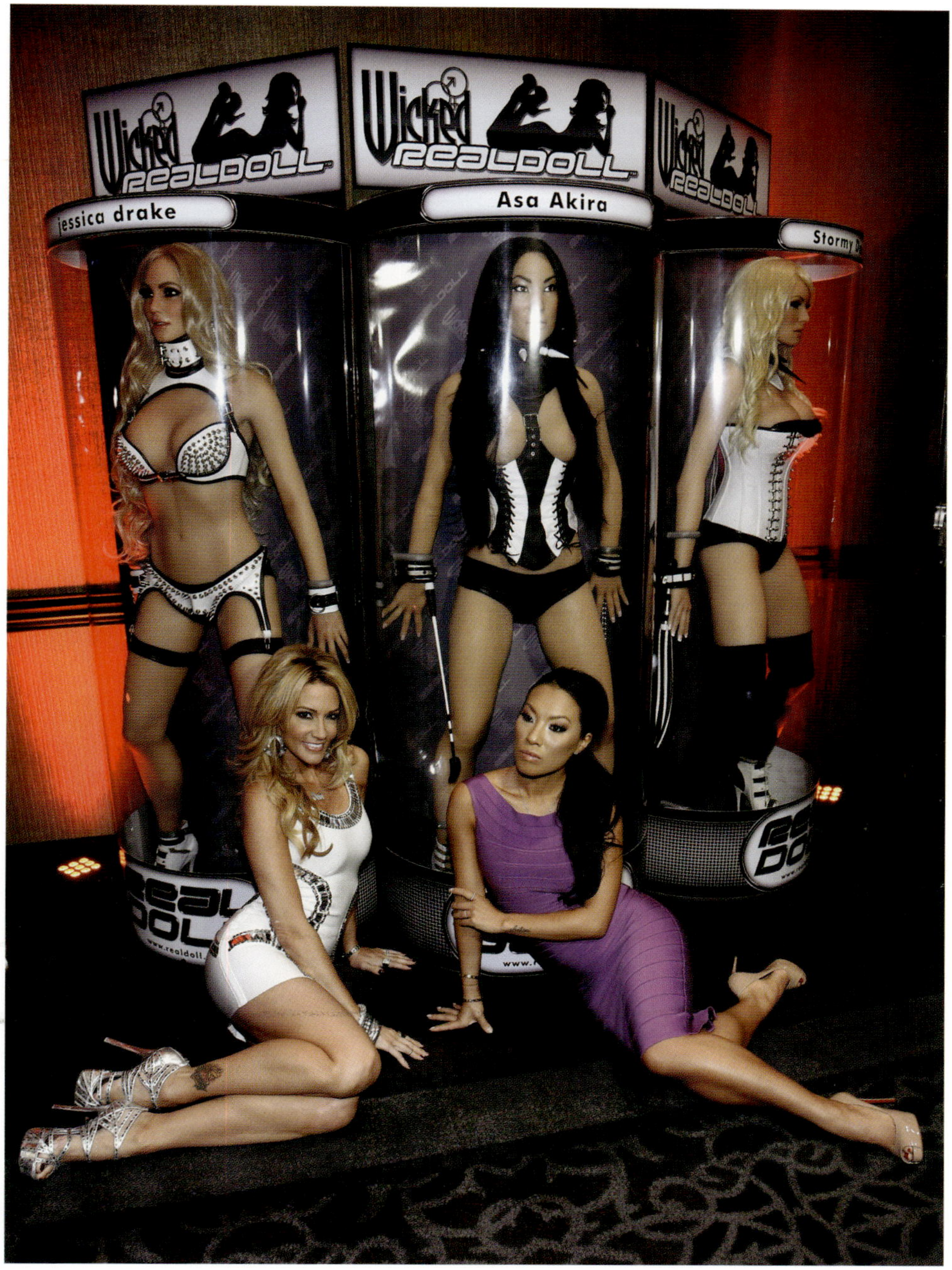


**Plate 18** Adult film actresses/directors Jessica Drake (left) and Asa Akira (right). Photo by Ethan Miller/Getty Images

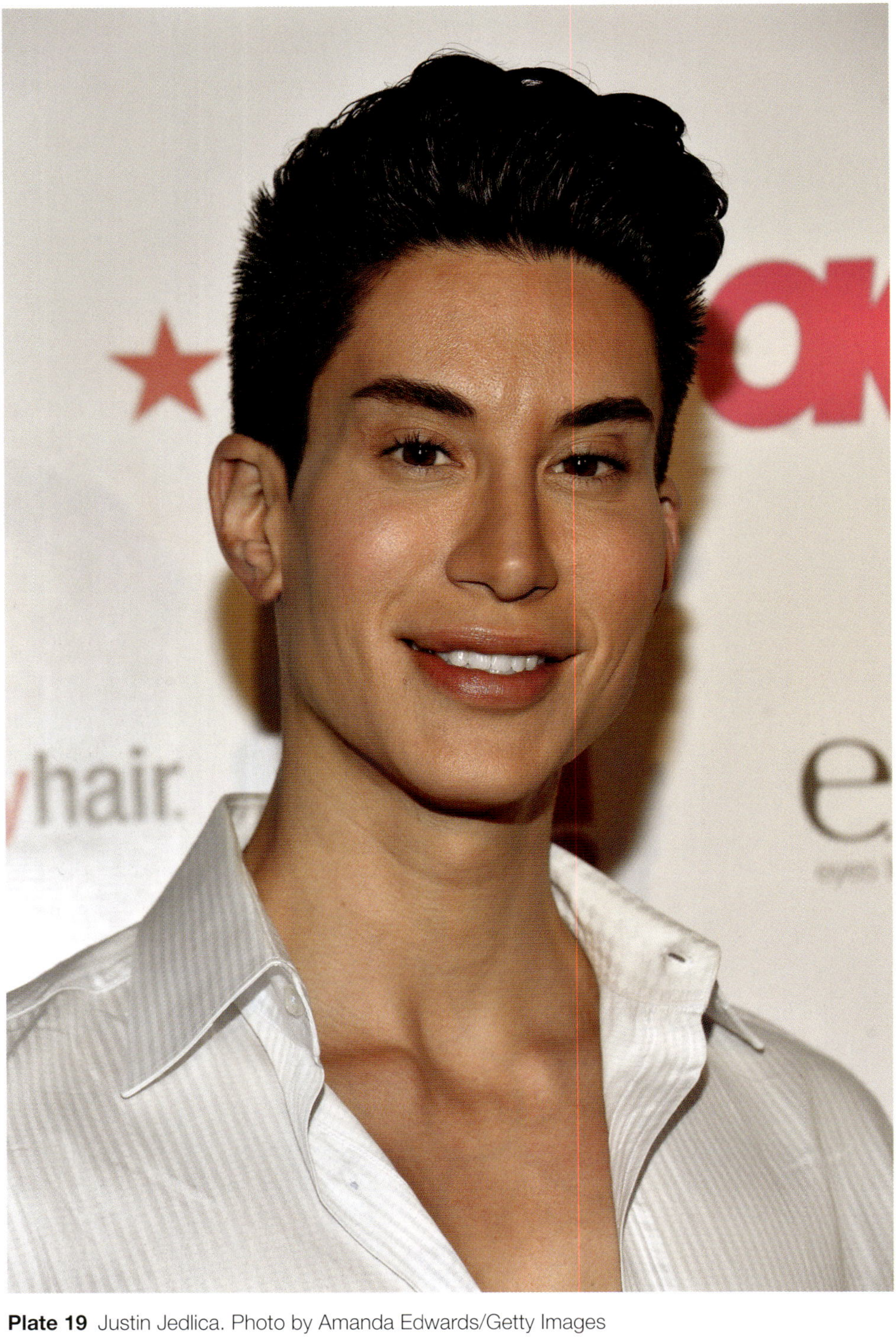

**Plate 19** Justin Jedlica. Photo by Amanda Edwards/Getty Images

# 5

# A MODEL SUBJECT: THE WINDOW DUMMY, THE FASHION DOLL AND THE DOUBLE[1]

*Nevertheless, it is a fact that I have not failed at times to play men certain tricks not altogether unworthy to be compared to your own work; as, for example, boring men's ears, or lips, or noses, and lacerating them with the trinkets which I place therein; or scorching their bodies with hot irons, which I persuade them to apply to their persons by way of improving their beauty. Then again, I sometimes squeeze the heads of their children with ligatures and other appliances, rendering it obligatory that all the inhabitants of a country should have heads of the same shape, as I have ere now accomplished in America and Asia. I also cripple mankind with shoes too small for their feet, and stifle their respiration, and make their eyes nearly start out of their heads with tightly laced corsets, and many more follies of this kind. In short, I contrive to persuade the more ambitious of mortals daily to endure countless inconveniences, sometimes torture and mutilation, aye, and even death itself, for the love they bear toward me.*

—GIACOMO LEOPARDI[2]

From the outset, the first fashion models were dolls, which may explain the French word for fashion model, *mannequin*. But it is a detail that creates more problems than it solves since it suggests that the model, the prototype, the aesthetic imperative, for fashion begins with an inanimate copy of a human. Hence, Leopardi's satirical "Dialogue Between Fashion and Death," in which "Fashion" declares her ability to make people mold themselves to an improbable shape and to conform to sundry "follies." The prophetic nature of this arrives when contemplating the fact that Barbie first entered the market as a fashion doll for adults. After decades of children's consumption, Barbie returns in the shape of a human, with a string of women since the 1990s willingly endure "torture and mutilation."

From her earliest days before the fashion model was known as a mannequin, she was a *sosie*, another word for "double."[3] The earliest models were generic, characterless and object-like, and in the beginning of the twentieth century, when on tour and not dressed in designer garments, they were expected to dress the same. Charles Frederick Worth, one of the first to use fashion models, considered himself an artist; his models were armatures of his artistic creations, much as a frame operates for a painting, except the frame is on the inside. And so opens up another conundrum: Fashion begins with a doll, then a body-cipher that carries the "creation." Fashion begins with a series of inhuman objects that precede the human subject. With this in mind, the contemporary desire to become Barbie may seem understandable or historically accountable, albeit still perverse. But this genealogy is far from a smooth one, for an abrupt change is observable after the 1980s, in which ideology of the fashion garment begins to dissolve in favor of the ideology of the body. With the malleable, alterable, perfectible body, one effectively *wears* a body, a relationship between biology and technology that I have elsewhere called the "natrificial."[4]

The spectacle of the modern body is specific to the commodity, in the respect that consumers were expected to see themselves in terms of representations and imaged aliases. While the mid-eighteenth century reveled in the possibilities offered by the classical ideal, it was also beset by a growing number of publications—the *affiches* and *feuilletons*—that were circulated in cities, especially Paris. While these contained discussions of what high society was wearing, its visual representations were all imaginary and hypothetical. This is another example instance of the inversion immanent to the fashion system, namely, that the person would forever be a copy of the model, a dilemma on which scholars, such as Nancy Troy in her study of Poiret, have deliberated.[5] If the images offered from antiquity were sufficiently remote to allow for improvisation, which it well and truly did, the fashion image offered a tacit mandate, a blueprint, for people to follow. From doll to "doll" (in the sense of the designation for a girl), there remains one constant: nonchalance. If the actual doll was unaware of what it was wearing through the obvious fact of not being sensate, a consistent factor in fashion modeling would always be an aloofness to the point of the mindlessness, a key to glamor being the indifference to no matter how expensive and impressive the clothes she is wearing.[6]

## Fashion dolls

Well before the inception of the living mannequin, a popular means of circulating fashion styles was through dolls. No scholar has probed so deeply into the fashion model as Caroline Evans who states that largely

> the fashion model has much more to do with the doll than with the artist's model who most people assume to be her immediate predecessor. Indeed the first fashion models *were* dolls: they were models for models, if you like. And, like her predecessor, the fashion model exists on the cusp of the organic and the inorganic, between the animate and the inanimate, bridging the worlds of the living and the dead.[7]

The earliest surviving examples of this date from the mid-eighteenth century. Although cruder types in wood are also extant, the best are made of wax. In some cases, the fashion doll and the child's toy were used interchangeably, but the delicacy and fragility of several of these dolls can only mean that they were intended for specialized display.[8]

From what can be gleaned from portraits and diplomatic reports, dolls were used for circulating examples of foreign dress since the early Renaissance. Among the earliest surviving documents is from accounts from Charles VI of France in 1396 recording payment to Robert de Varennes, embroiderer and valet to Isabeau of Bavaria, for "dolls and their wardrobes for the Queen of England."[9] Another early, notable case is a detailed letter from 1515 by Frederico Gonzaga, who requests on behalf of François I a doll from his mother Isabelle d'Este.[10] The part in question reads:

> The King wishes My Lady to send him a doll dressed in the fashions that suit you of shirts, sleeves, undergarments, outer garments, dresses, headdresses, and hairstyles that you wear; sending various headdress styles would better satisfy his Majesty, for he intends to have some of the garments made to give to the women of France. Therefore, would you be so kind as to send this and as soon as possible.[11]

Isabella was an early equivalent of today's *fashionista* or perhaps a royal fashion icon such as Lady Diana Spencer. In the absence of photography, dolls were the most serviceable way of communicating matters of taste in dress and styling. Yassana Croizat speculates that the Frederico's omission of specifications as to the doll's appearance suggests that such a request was not out of the ordinary. For Isabella also received a similar request from her younger son Ferrante, residing at the court of François I's rival, Charles V.[12] From all of this, we may surmise that dolls were used as pawns by which sartorial style was traded, observed and brokered for the assurance of courtly image. Dolls and fashion dolls differ for the way the latter were offered as diplomatic gifts.[13] In François's case, ensuring that his female courtiers were well dressed was an important component to the expression of the glory of his reign, by the end of which more money was spent on clothing than on building.[14]

As in the Renaissance, and indicative in the quality of most that have survived, dolls in the eighteenth century were not only toys, but also indicators of class. They were expensive, and with clothing considerably more so. Leslie Reinhardt asserts that the bodies of dolls of this time "were relatively uniform, and the same doll could have different clothes to characterize it as a man. Doll bodies displayed the ideal body shape of the eighteenth century, with straight spine, shoulders held back, and wide chest; even undressed they reflected the fashionable standards of the period."[15] These served also as important measures by which fashion could continue to be communicated and imported overseas, including to America and the colonies. Inevitably, such dolls raised the ire of the more modest colonies that saw them as examples of British or French cupidity.[16] It also appears that the dolls that were important made no distinction between fashion dolls and play items.[17] Nonetheless, Reinhardt remarks that "Dolls were such important markers of fashion that Shippen [writing from England in 1787] joked that he was afraid woman would imitate his gift doll's lopsided, badly painted mouth."[18]

Of the best dolls from the eighteenth century, their high level of detail, especially of the wax dolls, suggests that they were readapted dolls of the religious caste, where discarded sacred figures were "repurposed" as hedonistic secular figures. But by early sixteenth century, there were already specialized craftsmen, the *poupetier* or *poupelier*, who specialized in making dolls as well as masks and theatrical paraphernalia. By the reign of Louis XIV, they were also given special names above and beyond *poupée* such as *La grande Pandora* and *La petite pandora*, which were dressed in lavishly detailed miniaturizations of court dress (*grande toilette*) and fashionable dress (*negligée*).[19] The highly intricate way with which eighteenth-century dolls were dressed suggests that while they may have been play things, they would also have been decorative diversions for grown women, including communicating matters of dress among each other. "By directly encouraging demand for the textile industry," notes Karen de Perthuis, fashion dolls served a commercial purpose, but in their uniqueness and exquisite quality, they served as a less easily definable purpose of reinstating cultural supremacy."[20] It was a common practice of French dressmakers to communicate their ideas to people abroad using dolls, a diminutive form of advertisement whose persuasion was predicated on the draftsmanship of the doll and the clothing. Given the limited mobility of women, and with the exception of the Grand Tour, given that traveling and tourism were not yet fashionable pastimes, they were important drivers of trade and taste.

Many of the few surviving dolls are breathtaking in their detail. They are clothed in silk and are in ensembles that include chokers, mittens, aprons, bracelets and other accessories. There are even a number of dolls with detailed genitals intact.[21] Using human hair, if not made of wax, the faces and hands were of biscuit, or unglazed porcelain, which has a seductively low luster. From the fact that these figures were adult women to the relatively isolated case of their sexualization forces the return to the beginning of the book: the use of dolls as examples of exemplary gender roles, and the lineage that has been drawn to these and the contemporary phenomenon of the Barbie doll. But in her detailed study of this cross-relation, Juliette Peers asserts that the line between inanimate doll and woman-as-doll becomes blurred after the eighteenth century, with the explosion of the commodity culture in the nineteenth century and women as the prime carriers of these commodities:

> The doll not only frequently looks like a woman, sometimes she *is* a woman; in fact she is a clear, unmistakable sign of women's limited intellect, passivity, frivolity. In opera, operetta, ballet and short stories women may even be confused with dolls, so closely does one symbolize the other.[22]

In the earliest critical examinations of fashion, such as those by Georg Simmel, women are descried for their superficiality, which lends themselves to be fashion objects.[23] In fact, the superficiality of fashion and the superficiality of women renders the two interchangeable—whence the ongoing perception that fashion is art's poorer intellectual cousin. The fashion system, that is, the idea that one is either in or out of fashion, is an irrepressibly modern animal, which is tightly associated with the mobility and agency of the modern subject. Fashion is the surface on which such mobility is rendered, as achievement or as possibility, but with distinct configurations according to whether a person is man or woman. As Peers argues:

> Ironically essentialism's key stereotype is that woman is neither fixed not stable but false and empty, constantly shifting, a chimerical illusion, a performance of carefully judged and confected surfaces and maquillage: so woman in post-Enlightenment, modernist legend is primarily a doll. . . . When the male edits and re-orders the world he is an artist, when the female edits and re-orders—principally herself—she is a doll.[24]

The rise of modern fashion sees the imbrication of woman and doll becomes not only more complex but also more pervasive. For in antiquity identification with the doll was meant to have salutary effect on instructing basic codes of appearance and deportment, in modern times, this was taken to a new level that implied a paring down of action and will. This was also present in the use of corsets so that the body was forcibly shaped to resemble something similar to the window dummy, forcing an almost seamless correspondence between fashion doll, fashion model (mannequin) and shop dummy.[25] The living woman had to insert herself somewhere within this artificial universe.

To anyone who has looked on with skepticism and bewilderment at the battery of dolls of an obsessive doll collector, what is also remarkable is not only quantity, but the variation and loving detail devoted to the best of these. The dolls that were made in ever increasing amounts from the mid-1800s were deployed as part of the fashion industry to educate and to disseminate what was proper and desirable. They were, to use Peers's words, a "fashion interlocutor," for the French fashion doll became an indispensable integer in growth and development of haute couture. While the origins of this relationship remain uncertain, these dolls depicted various ages, including the "bébé," the child doll which was essentially the stand-in for the living model of child fashions.[26]

One of the most successful doll makers was Pierre Jumeau, who in 1849 already had fifty women in his employ making dolls. They were celebrated for their attention to detail, and Peers observes that such dolls had a critical effect in "bringing a new sense of mystique and power to the designer/supplier." The dolls of Jumeau and others such as Adelaide Huret anticipated Worth for pushing a sense of individuality and style associated with their makers.[27] (Another irony in this history of dolls and doubles is that Jumeau is almost the same spelling and the homonym in French for "twins.") (See also Plate 16). Such examples were later no doubt helped along by periodicals such as *La Poupée modèle*. Founded in 1863 and still alive into the early 1900s, it was the doll equivalent to the fashion magazine. By the early 1900s, publications like these featured not only images and advertisements of dolls, but also paper cutouts and their attendant clothing. They allowed women imaginary participation in both the actual world and in fantasy.

What is perhaps a climax in the history of the fashion doll occurred at the end of the Second World War. By 1944, the world was not only starved physically, but culturally as well, and Parisian couture found itself in the doldrums, its lucrative U.S. market having dwindled to near nothing. To breathe life back into the industry, Parisian couture resorted to an old concept. Couturiers would clothe fashion dolls, which would be meticulously made and placed against the Parisian setting of leisure designed by known talents in

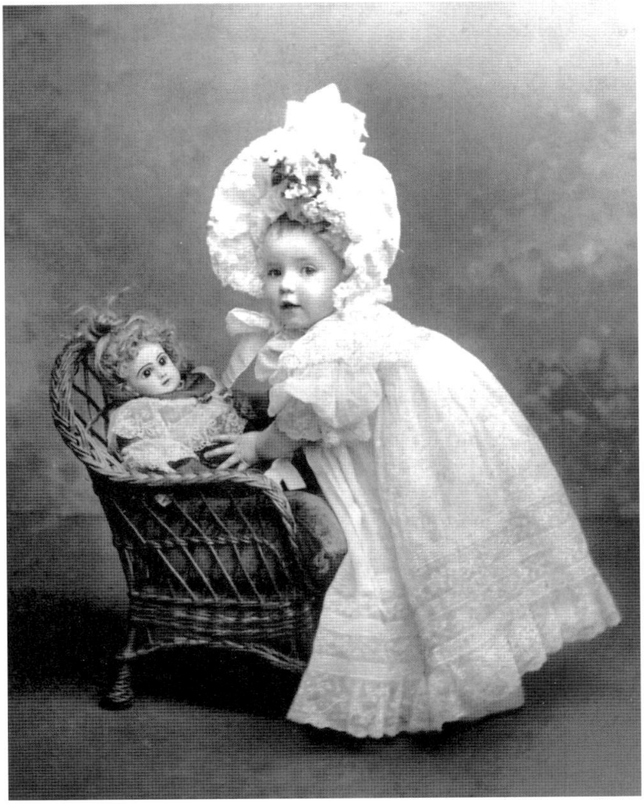

**Figure 5.1** A little girl with a lace suit playing with a doll, c. 1900. Photo by APIC/Getty Images.

drama and art. With their bodies made of wire, of which there was no shortage, their heads were made of plaster by the Catalan sculptor Joan Rebull. The settings were entrusted to the likes of Jean Cocteau, Boris Koschno and Emilio Grau-Sala.[28] Some 240 *poupées* were produced, and Paris couture showed off its skill in clothing of meticulous detail. The dolls were exhibited in March 1945 with uproarious, and clearly cathartic fanfare, attracting 100,000 visitors in a matter of weeks. The exhibition then toured throughout Europe, ending in New York in 1946, and revived in 1990.[29] In many respects, the enthusiasm lavished on these dolls had the added effect of lifting the spirits of French couturiers, who quickly embarked on bringing life back to their houses in the spirit of postwar optimism and relief. Elsa Schiaparelli, for instance, embarked on a tireless campaign of bringing her own house back to prominence, including publicity stunts such as attending a charity ball with a birdcage with a live canary tied to her neck,[30] reminiscent of the mannequins from the 1938 Surrealist exhibition.

Inspired no doubt by the doll exhibition in 1946, the U.S. firm Effanbee commissioned Schiaparelli in the early 1950s to design a line of dolls to be known as “Honey.” These were followed by other lines for another company, Virga, named “Go-Go,” “Chi-Chi” and “Tu-Tu,” names that were as cute as they were conceivably inspired by Dadaist babble to which she had been intimately acquainted in the inter-war years.[31] Hers is an early case of the niche market for fashion dolls that would try, in the longer term unsuccessfully, to compete with Barbie's widening popular appeal.

In some circles, the fashion doll has made a contemporary comeback, particularly if one casts an eye to the work of Viktor & Rolf in several exhibitions since 2008. Instead of using the conventional mannequin or dummy, they chose to make miniaturized copies of their major pieces worn by handmade porcelain-faced dolls and papier mâché bodies, recalling the classic Jumeau bébés of yesteryear. Rather than be nostalgic, however, V&R's motley battery of dolls appear to straddle past and present, giving the scaled down garments an emblematic, timeless quality. Since this period dolls are distinguished inhabitants of the V&R universe, recalling perhaps Edvard Munch's justification of his paintings in woodblock prints because he could not bear to be without his "babies." As the designers themselves comment about their now extensive progeny of avatars:

> We wanted to create a new world. Using dolls is like taking control. When we had just started out we created a series of miniature installations visualizing our strongest ambitions: a doll on the catwalk, a doll in a photo studio, and the scenes they enacted showed a life we desired by dared only dream of. Looking at that life from a distance, fantasizing about it in a suggestion of play—as serious as these adult toys were—instead of really living it, seemed to be the closest we could get to the realization of our dreams.[32]

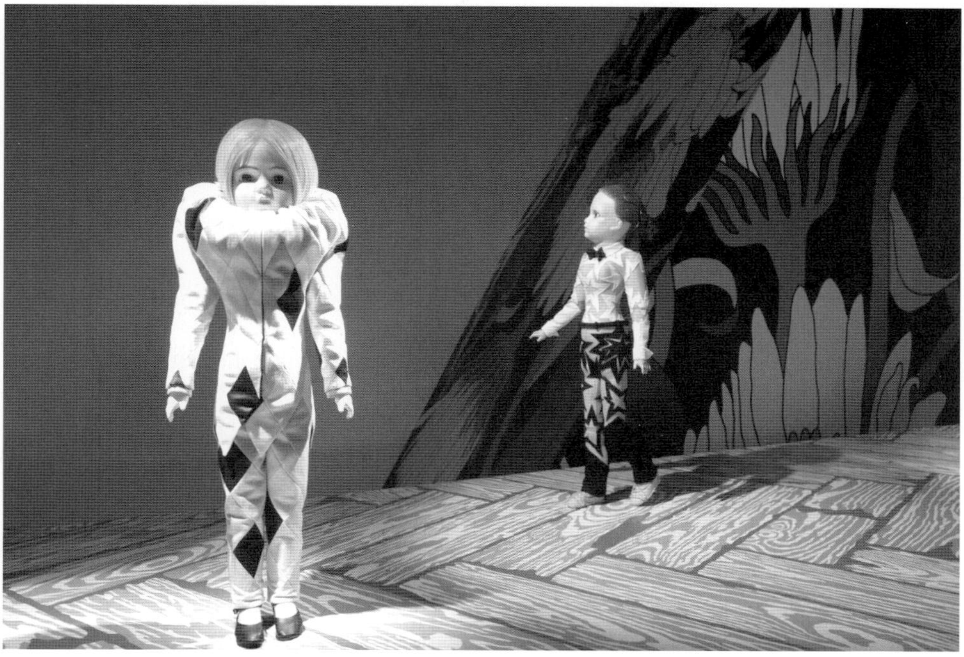

**Figure 5.2** Viktor and Rolf, installation at the Ontario Museum, 2014. Courtesy of Ontario Museum and the artists. Photographer © Team Peter Stigter.

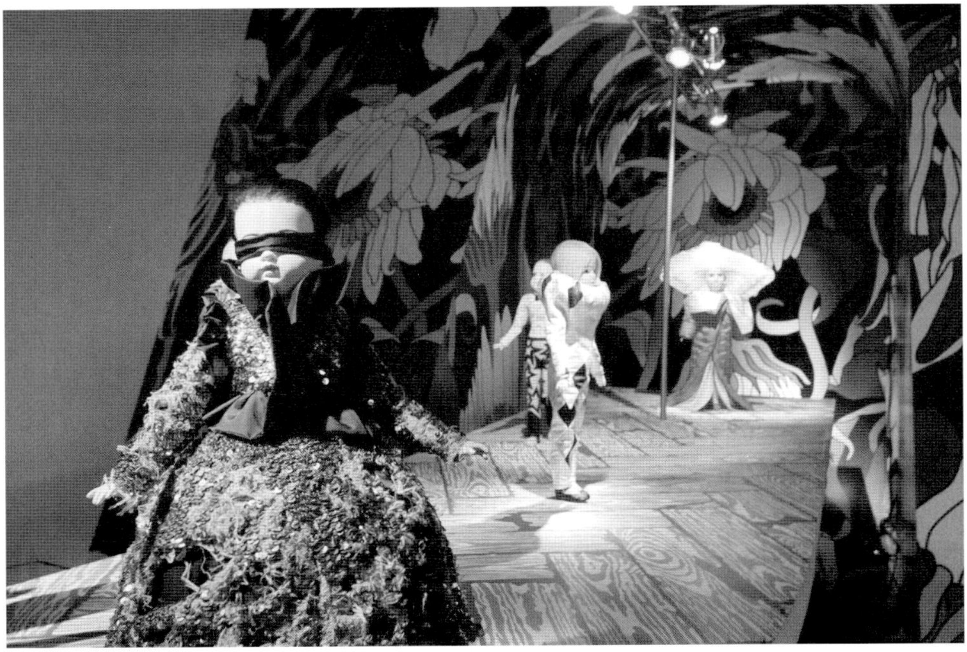

**Figure 5.3** Viktor and Rolf, installation at the Ontario Museum, 2014. Courtesy of Ontario Museum and the artists. Photographer © Team Peter Stigter.

This short meditation is also one easily conferred to fashion itself since to be fashionable is also to attempt to assume possession of an image for the sake of power and desire, but whose effect is always intangible and fleeting. V&R's dolls are talismans to the dreams of fashion, and while present are also symbols of their ultimate elusiveness. This elusiveness is also because, to look at things more simply, the first "person" to wear the fashion garment is not a real person—and when they were, they were, at least in the earlier days of the fashion model, meant to mimic artificial bodies.

## The birth of the mannequin

If Worth used *sosies*, the practice only became standardized and integrated into fashion houses at the beginning of the next century with Poiret, Patou and Chanel. But while the genesis of the fashion model is disproportionately female, and associated with twentieth-century modernism, the first fashion models in Paris were not women, but men. Alison Matthews David shows how tailors hired attractive men to be their "mannequins" to inhabit places like the races or exhibitions that were dense with fashionable people and prospective clients.[33] (We might also recall that *mannequin* means "little man.") A source from 1814 describes how tailors employed these young men when the shape of the suit was renewed, which occurred every three months. The new clothing worn by the male mannequins was propositional: "If it is judged divine, then it is unanimously adopted."[34] The men who performed these tasks were far from gentlemen, yet they did have their admirers. David even asserts that when Worth had his models frequent the races, he was feminizing something that had been province of men.[35]

Worth was a voracious vampire of influence and also an arch-simulator, lifting ideas from paintings of masters such as van Dyck and Titian, while taking great pains to simulate in his own house the salons and ballrooms of the rich, the aristocratic and the hopeful. His immaculately groomed and perfumed models would perambulate in a dazzlingly lit salon. Worth's talent for spectacle intuited that it was best to create an imaginary vision that people would gather to watch, as opposed to the common practice of dressmakers to visit the home. As Evans notes, fashion modeling only became widespread after the 1870s when people made the visit to the couturier's "house." By the end of the century, to visit the rooms of Redfern, Lafferière, Rouff, Fred, Callot Sœurs, Worth and Doucet was an afternoon pastime.[36] The fashion model, then, was the mute and anonymous play actor in the newfangled stage-play of fashion. Despite the model's male roots, as with the history of the painted nude after the 1500s, by the end of the nineteenth century, modeling had become a wholly female business.

Evans points out that in 1886, at the very time when fashion models had begun to appear in fashion magazines, the Symbolist writer Auguste Villiers de l'Isle-Adam published his novel *L'Eve Future* (The Future Eve) about a fictional Thomas Edison who builds an android for an English nobleman, Lord Ewald, to compensate for the deficiencies of his mistress, who has a troublesome personality. Named Hadaly, she is an "Andréide"—hence, "android"—and she is made of "female armour, of brilliant silver leaves," her hands are gauntlets adorned with "rings of different jewels," which connect her to the electricity that powers her.[37] Edison reminds Ewald that it is not to be taken as a person "in the ordinary sense of the word," then begins to boast about the superiority of his ingenuity over his illustrious predecessors:

> These unfortunates, for lack of sufficient means of execution, produced only ridiculous monsters. Albertus Magnus, Vaucanson, Maelzel, Horner, etc., etc., were, barely, the scarecrow manufacturers for birds. Their controllers are worthy of inclusion in the most hideous wax salons, as objects of disgust coming from a strong smell of wood, oil rancid and gutta-percha. These works, formless sycophants, instead of giving the man a sense of power, can only induce him to head down to the god Chaos. Remember this set of jerky and Baroque movements, like those Nuremberg dolls—this absurdity of line and colour! these tunes from wigmakers storefronts! the noise of the key mechanism! this feeling of emptiness! Everything, finally, in these abominable masks, exasperates and shames. It's the laughter and horror amalgamated into a grotesque solemnity. One could say that these manitous from Australian archipelagos, or these fetishes from the tribes of equatorial Africa: these models [*mannequins*] are but outrageous caricature of our species. Yes, these were the first drafts of Andréidiens.[38]

But his patron hesitates, that it is still a doll, whereupon Edison rejoins that "it is the living that resemble a doll." Hadaly's speech and physical appearance have been meticulously modeled on the woman she is supposed to surpass, Alicia Clary. When Edison finally perfects and completes the android, he introduces her as Alicia to Ewald, who mistakes her for the real thing, but notices that his original irritations at her personality have disappeared. The android eventually not only reveals who she really is, but also explains that she has also absorbed some spiritual essence of Edison's assistant, Sowana. Ewald leaves on a voyage that is ill-fated, and they drown.

Eccentric and troubled as Villiers's tale is, it is still very much of its time. From the outset, fashion mannequins intrigued novelists and journalists because of their borderline status between subject and object, since an important aspect of their job was the erasure of their status as sentient subjects and to simply to be the support for cleverly designed things. As Evans observes of fashion journalism contemporary with Villiers's strange novel:

> Their reflections created a parallel to the repetitious nature of the task, indifferently modeling the same garment ten times a day to ten different clients, each time as if it were the first. All these features combine to make the fashion model something a little less than human: mechanical or doll-like in her smooth performance, her body as always svelte, her step rhythmic and her movements gliding, qualities that, again, contribute to her slightly unnatural, even uncanny appearance.[39]

Modern fashion would attempt to sanitize the fashion model's inherent uncanniness, but it is a quality that haunts her until the entry of the celebrity supermodel who was by definition allowed to have a personality and so stand for something human together with performing her function as embodiment of beauty and clothes horse.

## Early modern modeling

Chanel is given the credit for the modern revolution in fashion over Poiret—who dispensed with the corset before her and lifted the anxiety caused by women wearing pants by introducing an Orientalist twist—Vionnet and Patou because of her charisma and personal celebrity, thereby adding narratives of personality and lifestyle to her design image. Chanel's clothing and its subsequent imitations allowed women to dress quickly, without assistance, and to dispense with the corset. But as her biographer Rhonda Garelick also advises, Chanel's clothing did not admit for one, unsympathetic jersey fabric that would have made a corset visible, and slender lines of the designs would have drawn attention to the folds of skin corsets caused.[40] This was because, to a greater degree, Chanel designed for herself and in the shadow of her own silhouette, which was svelte and narrow-hipped. In turn, in order to show off the clothes in the best possible light, models had to comply with the same shape. These details reveal that when feminist criticism descries the wearing of manly, austere and suit-oriented clothes by women in the workplace, or the pressure on models to be thin and near androgynous, it was indeed a woman, Chanel, who stands accused.

An important forerunner of the modern notion of the fashion model is with the English couturier Lucile, who rose from humble origins to find success in not only London but Paris and New York. Lucile's gowns were worn by the royal family and such social eminences as Lady Duff Gordon, wife of the diplomat, and various other high-profile actresses and *demi-mondaines*. At the end of the nineteenth century, when clothing was not displayed on wood or wax figures, it was modeled by women wearing a *maillot*, a black sheath and long boots, the all-body covering that gave her a strikingly doll-like effect,[41] ensuring that the garment would remain unsoiled and that the model's modesty untarnished. Lucile did away with these measures of austerity, and dispensed with the sheath to reveal the natural skin. (Vionnet presented uncorseted, unsheathed and barefoot mannequins while working for Doucet between 1907 and 1914.) Her models were drawn from the lower classes, but subjected to a rigorous reeducation in deportment, a refashioning that places Henry Higgins's reeducation of Eliza Doolittle in Bernard Shaw's *Pygmalion* into sharper relief. Each of these models were given an exotic name, and as a cohort, they were announced as "Lucile's mysterious beauties."[42] (Evans equates such renaming with the way prostitutes were given new aliases upon entry into a brothel.[43]) Like all opportunistic marketers, Lucile likes to lay claim to having instigated the fashion parade. She, at least, contributed to the status of the fashion show as a popular spectacle entertainment for the wealthy and fashionable. Presaging the theatrical pageants of Gaultier and McQueen, in 1909, Lucile designed a fashion parade as a seven-act drama entitled *The Seven Stages of Woman*. It had snippets from Shakespeare, and the gowns were named after certain female archetypes that they were designed to typify or denote,

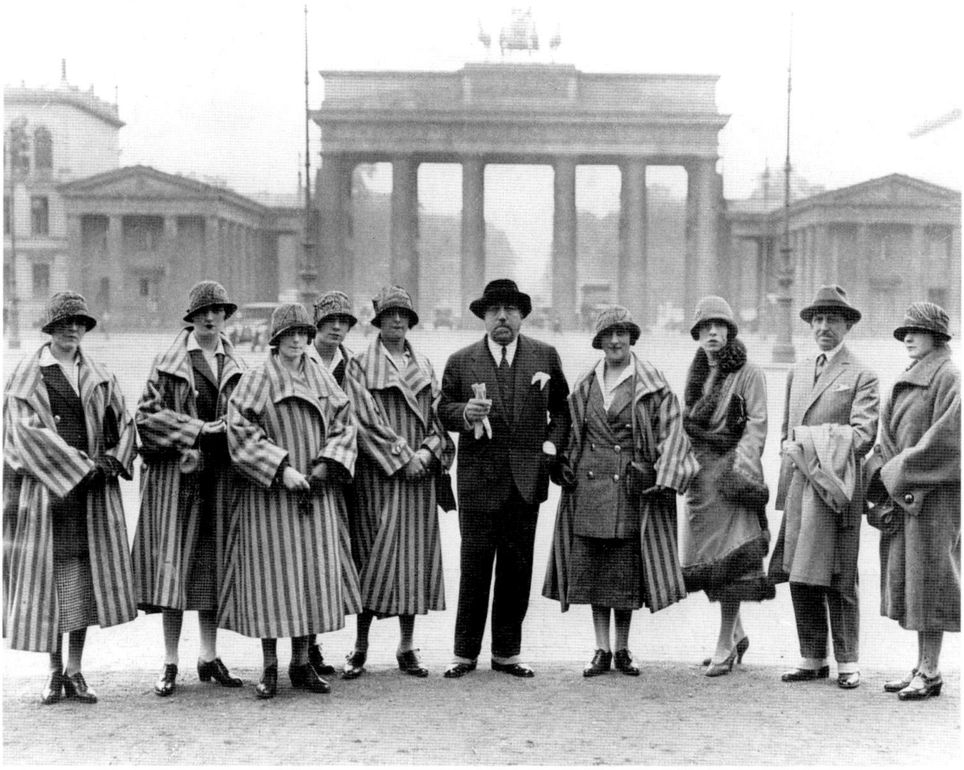

**Figure 5.4** Paul Poiret and models before the Brandenburg Gate on their Berlin tour, 1933. Photo by ullstein bild/ullstein bild via Getty Images.

such as "The Schoolgirl" or "The Fiancée" or "The Dowager." In 1916 her fashion show in New York was a series of *tableaux vivants* under the banner *Fleurette's Dream at Peronne*, which led to Florenz Ziegfield inviting Lucile to design for his *Follies*, which itself was the beginning of the modern showgirl.[44] With a few of Lucile's models attaining celebrity status in the United States (such as Dolores who went on to be beauty of the *Ziegfield Follies*), there was much journalistic talk and street gossip generated around the mannequin of the turn of the century, which became another breed of femme fatale that corrupted the married, killed lovers or married into wealth.[45]

Lucile's success in generating spectacle and in spectacle-generating sales was not lost on her French contemporaries, who were quick to send mannequins on tour to the United States. Both Paquin and Poiret made successful tours before the First World War. In Poiret's second tour after the war, he advertised a beauty contest of American girls, which he invited to return to Paris with him along with his French models. Patou did a similar thing in 1924, a publicity stunt that had the added prestige of being associated with *Vogue*. Such examples are isolated ones among a growing climate of fashion spectacles whose only lull in its acceleration came as a result of the war. The model was at the epicenter of moving spectacles of entertainment and consumption. The model had evolved from somatic support to the actor in an invented and highly choreographed fantasy.[46] Similarly, Chanel's love of show drew her naturally to theater and art, and she along with distinguished members of the artistic avant-garde, including Picasso and

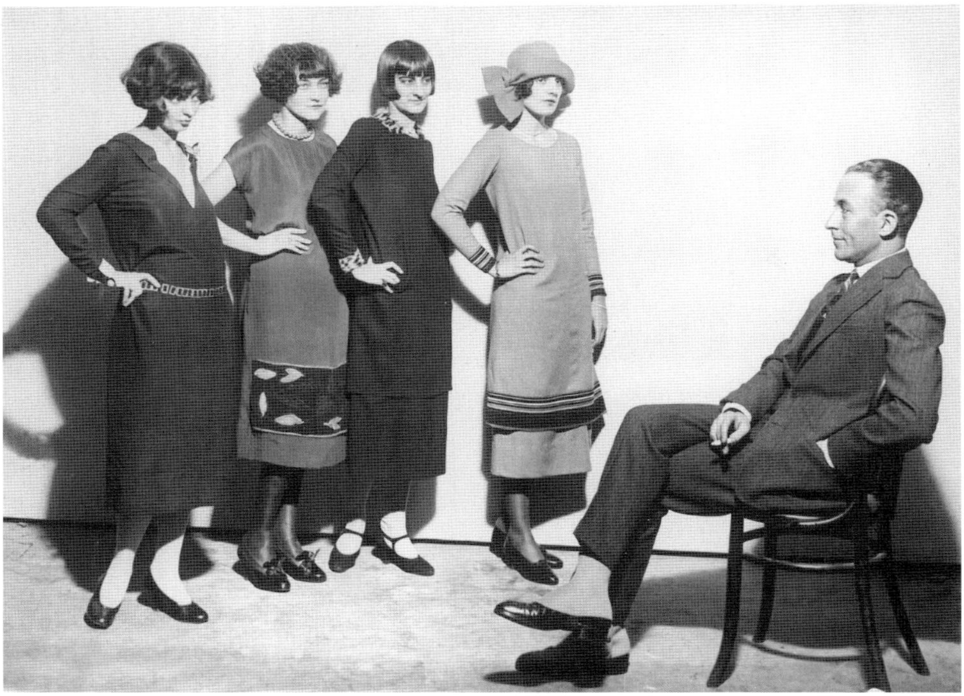

**Figure 5.5** Jean Patou choosing models in the United States for his French atelier. Photo by Keystone-France/Gamma-Keystone via Getty Images.

Matisse, designed for Diaghilev and his troupe. She was accustomed to turn her showroom at the rue Cambon into a theater, styling her fashion shows like miniature plays.[47]

## The doll standard and the modern body

The modernist body[48] that Chanel, Vionnet and Patou helped to shape and institute is, according to Evans in her detailed study of the fashion show of this period, a "rationalization of the body," which she aligns to Taylorism, leisure and popular culture, from cinema to dance crazes, and to the mechanical bent in art as evidenced in the work of Duchamp and the Futurists.[49] She makes a distinction between Worth's shows in which the models also walked about, with the fashion shows of the beginning of the twentieth century, which has much more to do with the march of modern life, the integration of technology and the celebration of the active, sporting body. She even goes so far as to say that the stylization of the fashion mannequin, and the codes that surrounded the way she walked, posed and gestured, were definably modernist.[50] The fashion show and the models who performed within them were a combination of old-world conservatism combined with the adventurousness percolated down from the artistic avant-garde. The Paris 1900 Exposition Universelle is also central to such considerations, as was the phenomenon that was the Ballets Russes.[51]

The growth of modern production, even before the more recent prêt-à-porter concept, meant that couturiers had to anticipate their clients and their clients' bodies, which at remote distance from Worth, who would not only make unique objects that (supposedly) reflected their wearers, but also if needed, were voluminous enough to cover any bodily deficiencies. It was therefore in the interests of couturiers to devise a standard type of body, not only simply one that was deemed beautiful, but one that would anticipate the majority type of wearers, either in terms of the body they had or by dictating the body they should have. In 1913, Doucet describes the optimal type of model (using the word *modèle*) as having to be beautiful and "neither fat not thin."[52] Evans reports how a year earlier, the *Boston Daily Globe* published a fierce criticism of French models in which "the tape measure becomes the judge."[53] But really, this standardization of the body has to be understood together with standards of architecture and design such as the standard size of a bed, to that of the width of a door, and so on. Modernist design occurs with an imaginary ideal type in mind. While there were houses at the beginning of the twentieth century that catered to a variety of body types, and while there are periodic concessions to this day with the now formally but still euphemistically named "plus-sized model," the ideal female body that emerges after the Second World War is one that ultimately coalesces into that of Barbie: long legs, small waist and pronounced, improbably (before plastic surgery) horizontal-tending breasts.

An instance in Chanel's later career illustrates this. When she exhibited her collection in 1954, her signature pared-down simplicity, she met with resistance to the point of hostility. It may have been novel in the 1920s and in keeping with the fashions of the time, but by the 1950s, fashion had retained the rudimentary practicability for which she was known, but had also favored a different, more buxom and more fecund body. So, for her collection of 1954, in the words of Garelick, "the models looked as they always had—like Coco; lithe brunettes all. . . . They presented the clothes as Chanel models always had, walking with hands in pockets and pelvises tilted forward, in deliberate, tutored imitation of Chanel's own gait."[54] But critics were indignant. *Le Monde* expressed its distaste at the lack of femininity in the suppression of "breast, waist, or hips . . . a melancholy retrospective." Another critic chimed in with the same complaint: "Chanel takes us back to yesteryear . . . no breasts, no waist, no hips."[55] Breasts, waist, hips. Add to this: long hair, no hair anywhere else—and white.

## Barbie, beauty, queer

The 1950s was not so much the birth as the sedimentation of an ideal body type that drew from an artificial source. Barbie was launched in 1959 and first intended by the company Mattel to be a fashion doll, before it became de rigueur for every self-respecting, upwardly mobile middle class girl in the developed world. Her inventor, Ruth Handler, drew direct inspiration from the Bild Lilli doll that arrived on the market in 1955, which was based on a

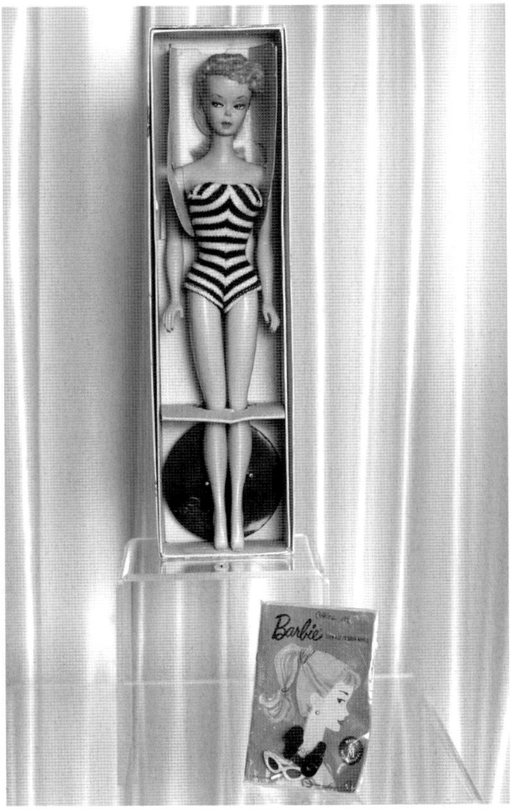


**Figure 5.6** The first Barbie doll in 1959 in her original box displayed during the exhibition "Berbie Retro Chic" at the Musée de la Poupée on February 13, 2014, in Paris. Photo by Chesnot/Getty Images.

German cartoon character by Reinhard Beuthien for *Bild-Zeitung* in Hamburg. Unlike Chanel's epicene bodies, Lilli's body, with her long legs, high heels and perky, protuberant breasts, reflected the newly confident woman of the postwar era and is an early historical marker in female sexual expression, with many risqué clothing accessories, including a sheer bikini. But in anticipation of Barbie, her embodiment of femininity had a divided audience. M. G. Lord in *Forever Barbie* witheringly describes the Lilli doll as "a lascivious plaything for adult men . . . marketed as a sort of three-dimensional pinup."[56] It is a valid statement when considering the way that the modern love/sex doll was soon to become emotionally integrated into the lives of desperate men. Lilli's production ceased in 1964 when the company was purchased by Mattel in order to draw all the focus to its own product, Barbie. Barbie's own appearance was debuted to great fanfare at the American International Toy Fair. The date, March 9, 1959, is celebrated by venerating fans as her official birthday. This makes her, at the time of writing this book, well past the stages of menopause.

To quote some of Mary Rogers's opening words in *Barbie Culture*, "Barbie has a great deal to show us about how we are, who we want to be, and who we fear we might be or might become."[57] As opposed to cultural icons, which are, or were, existing people

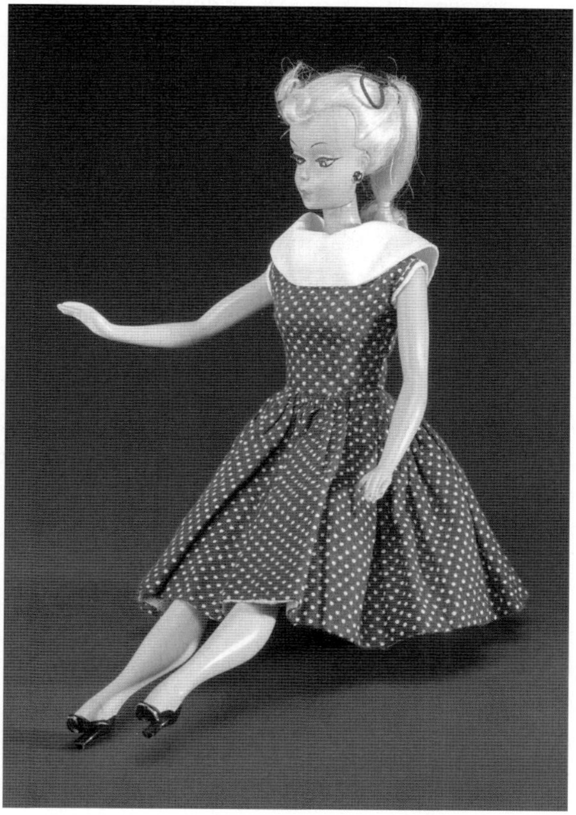

**Figure 5.7** The Bild Lilli doll. Photo by SSPL/Getty Images.

(Michael Jackson, Elvis Presley, Marilyn Monroe), Barbie is a fictive and *fantastic icon* in the same grouping as superheroes who help to galvanize or thirst for enchantment, nostalgia and escape, and that can "burst cognitive and emotional limits on consciousness."[58] Barbie evolved from her German cousin Lilli, who was an object of male delectation, a "comical gift,"[59] to become a paragon of cultural styling and female identity. At the end of the twentieth century, Handler, her "mother," is reported to have stated that "Barbie is an institution, and has been copyrighted as a work of art."[60]

In Barbie, we find encoded a series of highly pronounced and recognizable traits of femininity that are anchored in a signature prettiness and daintiness. If she is dressed as something more butch, such as a cowgirl (1981), her suit is in white satin and has silver trimmings,[61] and any other ensembles with trousers are off-set with one or more visual cues associated with decorative and delightful womanliness, whose underpinnings are in leisure and luxury. Barbie does not work, and if she is in working apparel, it is more for the sake of the clothing and the look than the activity. She is thus what working women could become should they become rich or marry "well," although Barbie "herself" has never married; her counterpart, Ken, who came about in 1961, is her occasional companion. But it is this unresolved state that Barbie inhabits that have led to speculations that she is more of an adolescent than a woman, a doll-dream of "every" adolescent girl who wants to be and do all things. Marketed to girls pre-adolescent and adolescent alike, a child idol, Barbie occupies what Catherine Driscoll calls a "tween space."[62]

As such, Barbie, who paradoxically touches on every facet of life, with every guise imaginable, is always in some kind of vacuum. She is the quintessential cipher, which is always necessary for a fashion model, who ultimately must serve the clothing, the scenario, the image, the theater fashionability. Barbie would therefore never quit her original "role" as fashion doll: Oscar de la Renta designed a line for her in 1984, while a year later, a Barbie with a distinctly anime face was released wearing clothing designed by Kansai Yamomoto. In 1994, a year after Barbie sales had climbed to close to a billion dollars,[63] Bloomingdales commissioned from Nicole Miller a Barbie that they called the "Savvy Shopper," while in 1999, Paris staged two exhibitions to celebrate her fortieth birthday, which were later featured in Monaco, including the Barbies owned by Princesses Caroline and Stephanie.[64] Since this period, there have been prestige lines of Barbies wearing high-end clothing, such as by Dior, Givenchy or Escada.[65]

Barbie's manifold and close attachment to the fashion industry also serves to exemplify another point, which has to do with the complementarity if not the inextricability between body and dress. For it is also haute couture's taste for outrageousness at its most experimental and indulgent that also necessitates equally outrageous body types. As Rogers declares, "Barbie's style might be called *emphatic femininity*. It takes feminine appearances and demeanor to unsustainable extremes."[66] The use of the word *unsustainable* has many trajectories, in particular, the way in which some commentators have inverted the rather consistent querulousness and outrage over her feminine stereotyping. Erica Rand, for example, argues that these traits and trappings are so unsustainable, so emphatic, that they stretch the limits of plausibility such that she retreats from being a fully-blown woman to enter the terrain of the drag queen. This observations takes its cue from Judith Butler's influential idea of gender performativity. While all gender

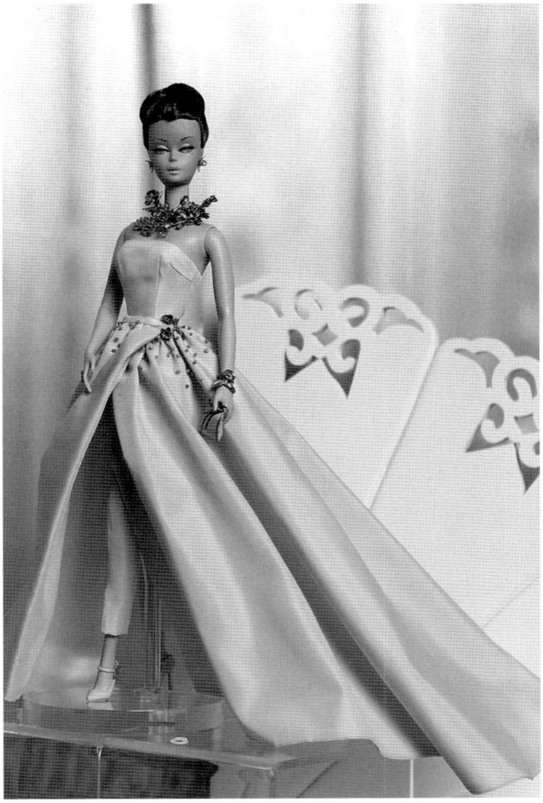

**Figure 5.8** A Barbie doll created by Maggia (unique model) displayed during the exhibition "Barbie Retro Chic" at the Musée de la Poupée on February 13, 2014, in Paris. Photo by Chesnot/Getty Images.

is performed, its status as performed is confirmed in dragging, when attributed and emphasized and writ large. As Butler states:

> As much as drag creates a unified picture of "woman" (what its critics often oppose), it also reveals the distinctness of those aspects of gendered experience that are falsely naturalized as a unity through the regulatory fiction of heterosexual coherence. *In imitating gender, drag implicitly reveals the imitative structure of gender itself—as well as its contingency.*[67]

Rand sees in Barbie a regular playing out of this configuration through the re-instatement, overstatement and parody that is found in male drag queens. Meanwhile, Ken is inscribed with a gay identity. In interviews with gay and lesbian adults, Rand also shows how Barbie was significant to their own identity building.[68] One factor in all of this is that gay and lesbian identity in not buttressed by the rational fiction of heteronormativity, that it is rational and right. Queer identity is constructed and artificial,[69] so it would follow that Barbie, also heavily constructed and artificial *avant la lettre*, would play a starring role. Rand recounts how

Barbie has participated in the identity of femme lesbians, who are not necessarily complicit in imposed norms, but rather are conscious of its construction.[70] She discusses the way in which Barbie was treated or refitted by girls who became lesbians, such as being "rolled in dirt or dressed like the hot baby-sitter next door."[71] It precisely Barbie's pronounced femininity that makes her so liable for subversion and desecration, a perfect sexual object ready to be spoiled and messed up.[72] It is her perfection that makes her prone to be the site of children's, and adult's, frustrations and left-of-field desires.

In considering Barbie's longevity and pervasiveness, it is also worth reflecting on the way that she retains her dual status as both toy and fashion doll. A visual survey of her passage through time is also to chart the evolution of fashion from the 1960s to the present. The Barbie industry employs hundreds of people to ensure that she is continually reinvented.[73] In her maximal and extraordinary mutability, Barbie is also the ultimate cipher of identity: She is at once astronaut and nurse, and plays any sport, does anything.[74]A marriage of artifice and eternal mutability, she is the embodiment of fashion itself, palpable in her plasticity, but elusively outside and unreal. She is as restless as her male counterpart, the bodybuilder.

# 6

# EXTREME HELLENE: SPORT, SUPERHEROES AND THE MODERN *ÜBERMENSCH*

*I am my own marionette*

—KARL LAGERFELD[1]

*Their mirror image, which incessantly snaps at the bodybuilder, always burdens him with the shadow of the impossible.*

—BODO KIRSCHOFF[2]

In our contemporary world, exercise and sport are commonplaces, part of our social lives, our leisure and our everyday well-being. Those for whom sport is not part of their lives, stand in its shadow, know it to be there, like nutrition facts about food groups, additives and the like. But what it is to have a healthy body and the means to arrive at it are only made possible by technology. The ethos of "98%"' natural, "fat free" and "organic" are all ideologies made possible by the technologized body. Sport is a modern phenomenon, and bodybuilding is the ultimate modern or postmodern practice of a body that shows the signs of immeasurable toil without having performed an iota of productive labor. Metaphors about bodybuilding armor crop up again and again. For just as armor is a composite of different components, to "work the body" in the most effective, that is, additive manner, is to subdivide it into parts. These are assisted by special food supplements of isolated compounds for accelerating muscle growth. No surprise, then, that one of the greatest bodybuilders of all time, Frank Zane, was nicknamed "The Chemist" for having a science degree and consuming large doses of amino acids. The most prestigious competition for bodybuilders to win is Mr. Olympia, which is not only based on mass, but proportion, proportions based on the Hellenic ideal. This is, however, a techno-Hellenism, an ideal state of nature made possible through depersonalizing discipline, interaction with machines, and by ingesting highly mediated substance, and by replicating eight mandatory poses.[3]

Perhaps, the closest thing to approximate the discipline and rigors of bodybuilding would be classical ballet. To this it is worth returning to Kleist and Hoffmann; and in the words of Lucia Ruprecht:

> Kleist's and Hoffmann's union of the beautiful and the mechanical does not only point towards the paradoxical tension between nature and art, it also teases out myth of omnipotence and invincibility that underlie the neoclassicist imagination. Classical ballet, then, also represents a form of self-empowerment entailed by the deliberate production of the superior "natural" body through technique. This process actually resounds with the eighteenth-century dream of the automaton that elevates man to the position of divine creator, reinstalls redemption by the transcending of flesh, and seeks to secure a form of artificially created immorality. It betrays a desire for the mythically refashioning the human body, outside and beyond its biological limits. In this sense, the idealization of the *homme machine* and the perfect proportions of the sculpted body are but two sides of the same coin.[4]

Ruprecht isolates again the strange conceptual interplay between naturalness and the way this naturalness is modulated and mediated, hence artificially realized. Looking at the paradox that Kleist and others set up with regard to the natural and artificial body, it would seem that since the idea of naturalness took shape in the eighteenth century, two natures have emerged, the first the ethos of let be, the other articulated and subject to scrutiny and alteration. While the optimal female body is governed by the image of a doll, the optimal male physique is impossible to attain without reducing the body into parts and submitting it to a regimen that, when at extremes, is unhealthy and uncomfortable.

## From the "normal" body to the sport body

To a large extent, the nineteenth century maintained this division between the imaginary ideal of classicism and the "normal" body of living people, with the exception of the entry, toward the end of the nineteenth century, of the ephebe. The beautiful little boy, as exemplified by the famous Hellenic sculpture of a boy pulling a thorn from his toe (*Boy with Thorn*, also known as *Fidele* or *Spinario*), was one of the highest ideals of beauty since antiquity and was revived in the early Renaissance with such sculptures of David by Verrocchio and Donatello. To some extent the ephebic body was emulated through keeping slim, but the body was suggested, not shown. Nor had the shape of the body much to do with health or athleticism.

However, at roughly the same time the image of the ideal body was undergoing some changes, especially with the formalization of sport and its international popularization with the first Olympic Games in 1896 staged appropriately in Athens. The Olympics did much to turn attitudes and actions to the age of Periclean Athens where nakedness was a sign of strength as opposed to vulnerability or weakness; it was also a mark of civilization.[5] Thucydides remarks at one point how the Spartans played their games naked while the *barbaroi* (whence "barbarian") persisted with genitals covered. The connotation was that naked body was a subject of pride and confidence.[6] In the words of Sennett in his book *Flesh and Stone*, "The civilized Greek had made his exposed body into an object of admiration."[7] Modern codes of decency and modesty precluded this level of nudity, except for in private homoerotic parties where Hellenism was popular and Adonia festivals

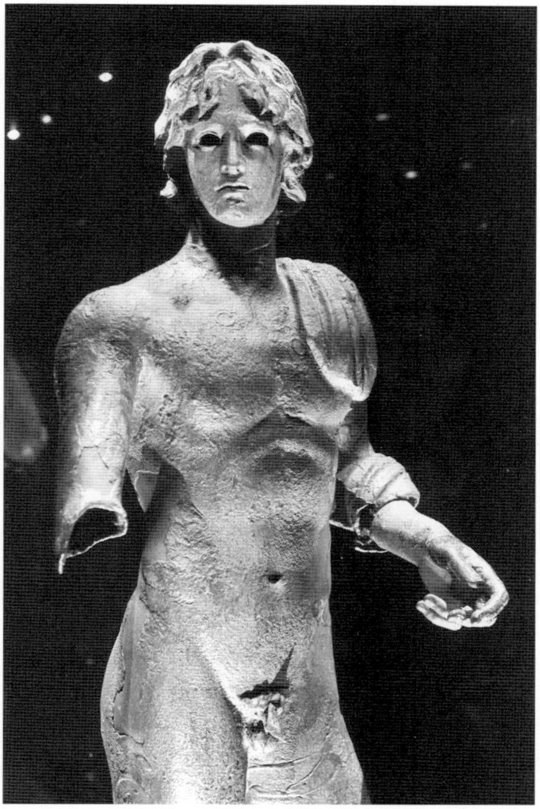

**Figure 6.1** Picture taken April 21, 2010, at the Ephebe Museum in the French southwestern city of Cap d'Agde depicting a Hellenistic bronze sculpture found in the waters of the Hérault river in 1964 dating back to the fourth century BCE, probably depicting Alexander the Great. AFP Photo/Pascal Guyot. © Getty Images.

a subject of extravagant nostalgia. But by the end of the nineteenth century, the growing popularity of sport, and sport's infiltration into social life, as well as the attendant consciousness of health and well-being, meant that societies in Europe and America began to have a more self-conscious attitude to their bodies. Sport as a socioeconomic institution meant that it permeated codes of dress and self; how people socialized, dressed and organized their time. Having a good body underneath the clothes became increasingly of issue, eventuating in a gradual change in what people wore.

The strong man of antiquity, as with the Japanese sumo wrestler, was not valued for his physique so much as strength alone. This changed dramatically at the end of the nineteenth century when the cult of Hellenism ran parallel with much larger social urges related to personal improvement and economic success. The cult of the body as it came to be known had three main points of interest. Interconnected, one was aesthetic, the other biological, and finally, ritualistic. It was expected that the inner health of the body be reflected on the outside—although this would be far from the case in contemporary bodybuilding. The characteristics of health would then ally us better access to human instinct and to a wider more abstract grasp of life and living. As we see in some of the paintings by the German Expressionists of figures cavorting naked in forests and near streams, in the years before the First World War, it became popular in Europe for people to participate in their own version of Bacchanalian rites. Here, the body would participate in its own "naturing."

It was another German, Eugen Sandow, who is credited with being the first bodybuilder, that is, a man of heavy and sculpted musculature who performed various moves on stage. He is said to having invented early forms of specialized equipment associated with bodybuilding, coming to be known as nautilus machines. A popular performer in the 1890s, Sandow organized the first bodybuilding competition ironically in the same year as

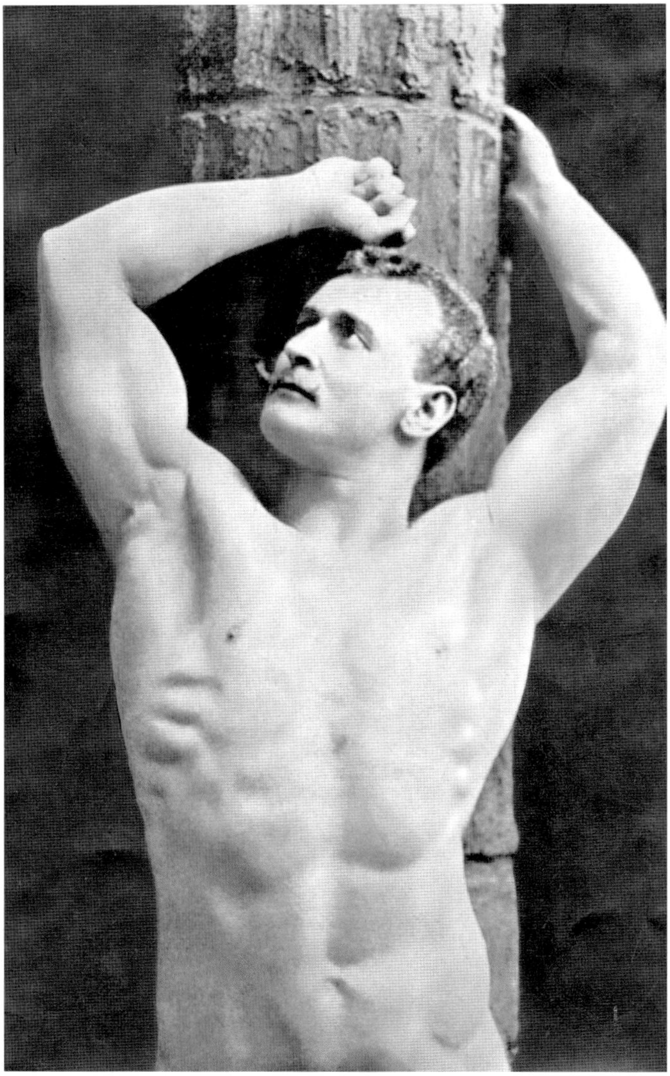

**Figure 6.2** Eugen Sandow in 1910. Photo by ullstein bild/ullstein bild via Getty Images.

the first Olympiad, in 1901. It was held at the Royal Albert Hall, with himself and Sir Arthur Conan Doyle among the judges. From 1968 to this day, the winner of Mr. Olympia is presented with the same statuette of Sandow, similar to what he presented to the winner in the inaugural competition. The doll is again imbricated in message of the best living body. Before we return to the bodybuilding culture that became fashionable and even hyperbolic from the 1980s onward, it is worth first discussing the male action dolls that preceded it.

## Male doll culture and superheroes

It might be good to begin with a few dates in charting the itinerary of male role models, which are either superhuman, or perpetuate the stereotype of the hyper-masculinized physique. Although created in 1933, Superman first appeared in *Action Comics* #1 in June 1938, Batman a year later (*Detective Comics* #27, May 1939). Captain America was born in 1941, while Spiderman took a little longer to arrive in 1962, coinciding with the Hulk, and Thor, and with Iron Man coming a year after that. These would eventually incarnate into action figures, but not before G.I. Joe, who appeared on the market in 1964.

Responding to the extraordinary sales of Barbie, the only woman on the planning team of the firm Hasbro, Janet Downing, suggested that they could make dolls appeal to boys if they were suitably masculine, which meant making G.I. Joe a soldier an obvious choice. Influenced from the television show *The Lieutenant*, G.I. Joe was a reticulated figure that was accompanied with a large range of costumes, weapons and tools. The figure produced by Sears a year later, Johnny Hero, was still referred to as a "boy's doll." "Action hero," the convenient sanitization of "doll" began to stick as a term along with the descriptor of G.I. Joe as "America's Mobile Fighting Man of Action."[8] When his popularity dwindled due to the disapproval of the Vietnam War, G.I. Joe increasingly became painted as a "Man of Action" and a member of an "Adventure Team" (Plate 17). Mego, the company that created Action Jackson to compete with G.I. Joe in 1971, made its greatest success in 1972 with "World's Greatest Super Heroes," a line of figures licensed from DC and Marvel Comics.

At around the same time, Mattel produced its highly successful Big Jim line that lasted until 1986. When not having superhuman powers, all of these figures fitted an unequivocally masculine stereotype, and despite their inherent immobility, their trappings and accessories bespoke every kind of dynamic and dangerous activity ("action"). Big Jim was the nodal point from which came a litter of countless variants and offshoots. His off-sider was Big Jack, perhaps the first benign, nonderogatory Afro-American doll; Big Josh (a bearded version of Jim); Big Jeff (an extreme Aryanized version of Jim); Dr. Steel (with Kojak bald head, a steel right hand a dragon tattoo on his chest); and Chief Tanuka, an American Indian. Successive releases sometimes had the same figure renamed, but continued the penchant for outlandish names that merged military codenames with the futuristic and supernatural: Double Trouble Big Jim, Torpedo Fist or Zorak Ruler of the Underworld. Big Jim figures could also be outfitted with a helicopter, safari truck or jet airplane. Strength and prowess were of the essence: tellingly Big Jim initially began its concept as "Mark

Strong," which was marketed together a karate board, a dumbbell and a belt that tested strength. These lines were occasionally interspersed with female counterparts, such as G.I. Jane, and later, Wonder Woman, and it is open to argument whether they were examples of the capable and assertive woman, or just a woman in the shadow of a man's role, in drag, as it were. With these dolls, boys could partake in a world of racial tolerance but where the default was comfortingly white, and in secure masculine play, where the default was sport, wealth and war, thus mirroring the commercial films produced in the United States from the 1960s onward, and picturing a stable, if one-dimensional model of what real men were like. Such figures, also largely more movable as dolls than stiff Barbie, perpetuated the cliché that women were passive and men active.[9]

Dolls, figurines and action figures have become a ubiquitous component of every major television and movie franchise. All the major horror creatures, from Dracula to Frankenstein have a range of figures by a number of companies; there are Star Wars figures as there are X-men figures. As witnessed by the highly successful *Lord of the Rings* then *Hobbit* trilogies, both articulated and nonarticulated figures amassed a tidy profit, the latter style boasting itself to be a high quality collectable, like Meissen figures, but made of resin and trophy piece all rolled into one.

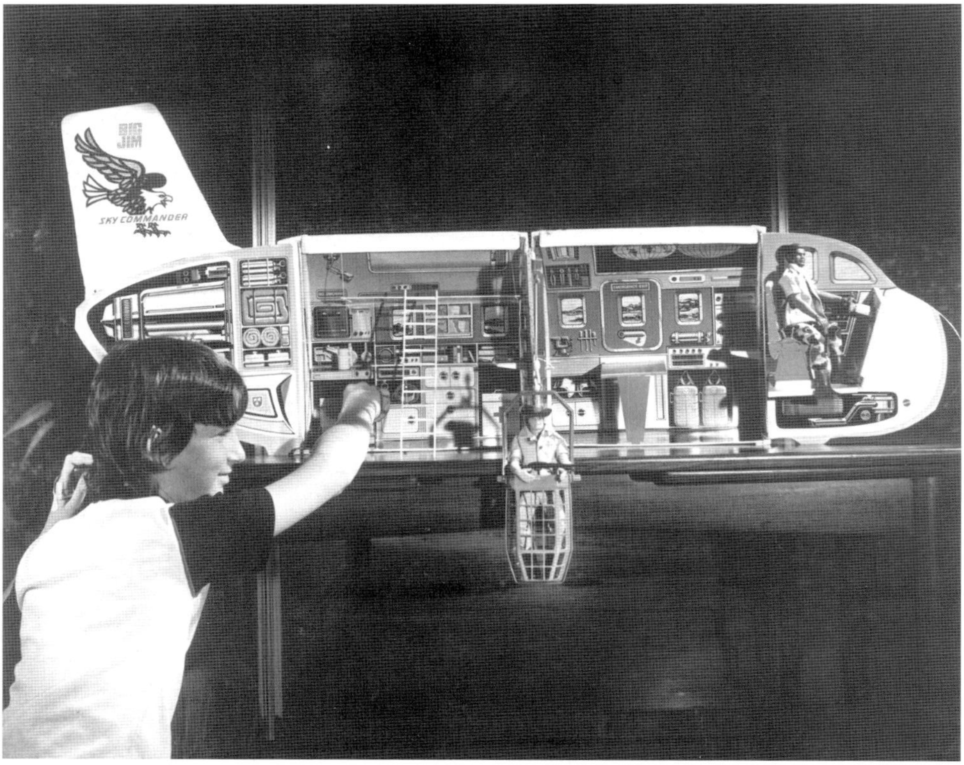


**Figure 6.3** A boy plays with a Big Jim Sky Commander jet toy with male action figures, 1970s. Photo by Hulton Archive/Getty Images.

In the early 1980s, people dressed up as their favorite fantasy figure became more numerous and conspicuous at comic and science fiction conventions. Impressed by the quality of these dress-ups, upon returning to Japan from attending World-Con in Los Angeles, Takahashi Nobuyuki, founder of an anime publishing company Studio Hand, coined the word *cosplay*. This was favorable to *masquerade*, whose Japanese translation is "aristocratic costume party."[10] Cosplaying parties and competitions are the masquerade of global culture, with thousands of members, and practice that has become highly encoded and specialized.

## Pumping iron and building a body (a)part

Before the 1970s, bodybuilding was still a specialized niche sport practiced by hapless, morbidly obsessed people. It entered into the popular mainstream with the documentary *Pumping Iron* (1977), which catapulted Arnold Schwarzenegger to celebrity status, also assuring some screen fame for Franco Columbu and Lou Ferrigno, who would go on to play the Hulk in the televisions series in the 1980s. Directed by George Butler, the documentary tells of the 100 days before the Mr. Olympia and Mr. Universe competitions in Pretoria in 1975. Still watched today, the film offers a penetrating and personal insight into a sport, and an obsession, which had previously been treated with skepticism, and to some extent, feared. And the influence of this film and the "Arnie phenomenon" that followed it was inestimable. As the follow-up documentary *Iron and Beyond* states, where once bodybuilding was reserved for the backs of comic books and the activity of "freaks and fools," it led to the multi-billion dollar fitness revolution of the 1980s.[11] A spin-off "sister" version involving women, *Pumping Iron II: The Women*, was produced in 1985.

*Pumping Iron* was followed by a small flurry of film and telemovies, including *The Hustler of Muscle Beach* (dir. Jonathan Kaplan, 1980), about a competition at the muscle mecca, Muscle Beach in Venice California, and which included appearances from Columbu again and Frank Zane. Somewhat eclipsed by the stellar career of Schwarzenegger (who in the muscle world is affectionately referred to as just "Arnold"), Zane preceded him as Mr. Olympia, and is one of only three to have beaten him in a contest (1968). Zane was instrumental in ushering in the distinction in bodybuilding between considerations of proportion and beauty over basic mass. He would also author numerous self-promoting books about the virtues of bodybuilding. But in the words of Sylvester Stallone, Schwarzenegger's "place is secure as the father of the new wave of pumpology."[12]

After the sequel to *Pumping Iron*, *The Comeback* (1980), Schwarzenegger began his film career as *Conan the Barbarian* (1982). Deriving from the comic book series, what distinguishes this more from other films of this ilk until this time was, to put it plainly, Arnold's body. Although he had appeared in film before, such as the ill-fated *Hercules in New York* (1969), the historical fantasy element to *Conan*, while never pretending to be a Visconti masterpiece, lent the main actor, who grunted his few lines, an air of mystery and otherworldliness. Early films such as *Hercules* (Pietro Francisci, 1958) had involved men of muscle, but they were not assisted by steroids and other weight-gaining supplements.

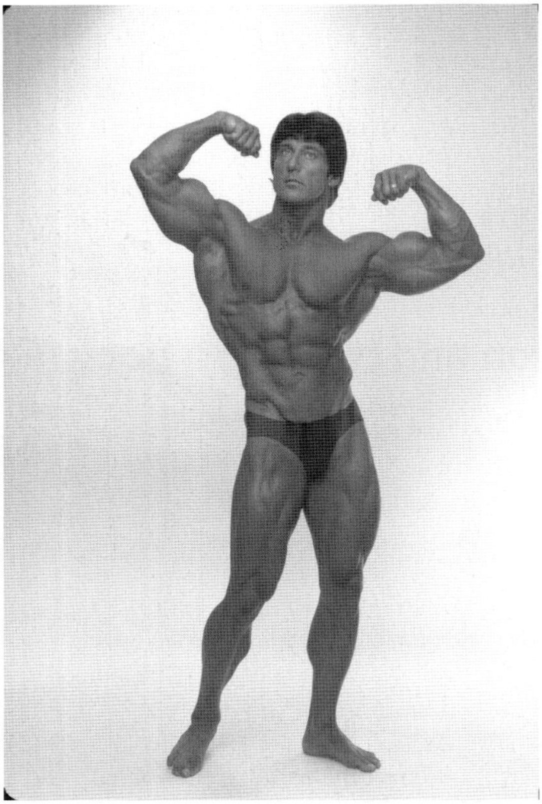

**Figure 6.4** Frank Zane in 1979. Photo by Jack Mitchell/Getty Images.

The maximalized, hypertrophied body that would come to be identified with the brashness of the 1980s was definitely of a different order and has come to define benchmarks in film ever since. One only needs to compare the still muscular but now comparatively scrawny body of Charlton Heston in *Ben Hur* (1959) or Kirk Douglas in *Spartacus* (1960) with that of Gerard Butler in an antiquity flick of more recent vintage *300* (2006). The implausibly high level of buff-to-fat ration of such a film is the result of nutritional technology and sophisticated training techniques.

The frenetic rise in popularity of bodybuilding in the 1980s—which also saw the first female bodybuilders and bodybuilding contests—is also attributable to the age of economic rationalism and aggressive foreign policy, the Reagan era. In *Hard Bodies: Hollywood Masculinity in the Reagan Era*, Susan Jeffords makes the strong case that the kinds of films produced in the 1980s were a clear reflection of a culture that had grown uneasy and impatient with what was widely considered the emasculating pacifism of the Carter era. Schwarzenegger's films such as *Terminator* (1984) and Sylvester Stallone's acclaimed *Rambo* series that begins with *First Blood* (1982) decisively demarcate an age of U.S. male heroism made possibly by unfeasibly large muscles. And in each case, the

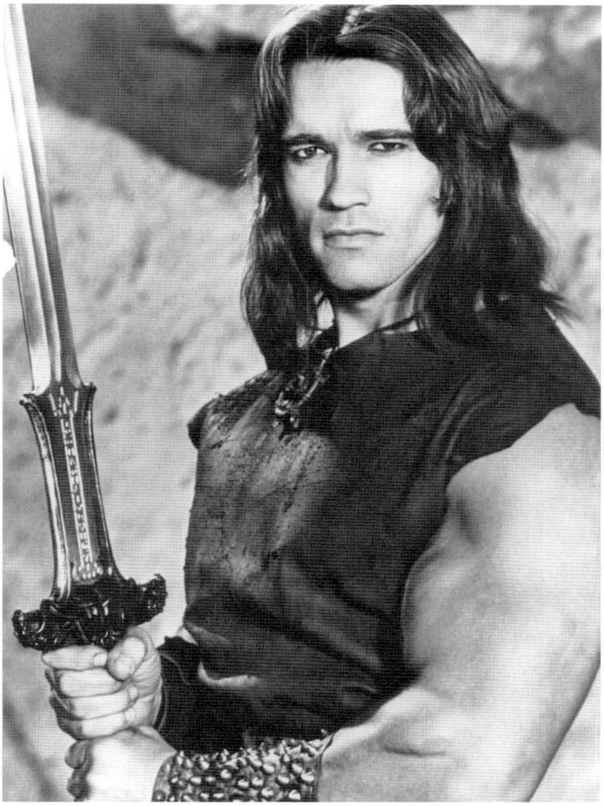

**Figure 6.5** Arnold Schwarzenegger as Conan the Barbarian, 1982. Photo by Mondadori Portfolio via Getty Images.

character has some degree of dehumanization, reduced to an object, an instrument, not only through military training, but also, one can add, by excessive muscle training. (Note also that there are dolls of all these characters, many of which are valuable collectors' items.)

Jeffords then observes a new relationship that she sees as epitomizing the Bush era just after Reagan (and which presages the new millennial cyborg doll-body to be discussed in the final chapter). As opposed to Rambo, who despite his forcefulness and implacability still shows signs of affect, and therefore, humanity, Batman offers us a new scenario:

> *Batman* shifts the focus on masculine identity away from hard-bodied heroism to a manhood divided and troubled. . . . . *Batman* exteriorizes that ambivalence by dividing the body and the emotions, depicting that body as something to be put on and off at will. . . . As in the Bush presidency, the hard body is being rejected and embraced, recognized as a burden and as a necessity, as something to hide at the interpersonal level and as something to display in the public arena, as a source of fear and of attraction, or goodness and destruction.[13]

What Jeffords describes is the ultimate ambivalence that occurs within the body-object, the body-as-sculpture, the body-as-doll in relation to "nature" and humanity. For if they exist together, as with Batman himself, it is always an agonistic union.

Among the more arresting, and amusing, accounts of the travails of bodybuilding are to be found in the memoir of the Oxford graduate-cum-competitive bodybuilder Samuel Fussell in his book *Muscle: Confessions of an Unlikely Bodybuilder*. He describes the staggering regimen of two workouts a day, the supplements, the steroids and the sleep, the manner in which people sculpt their own body, which becomes an obsession where they do not have much time for anything else. "'Bodybuilding. It's not just about size, it's about symmetry,' was a line as common in the gym as in the magazines, 'The Apollonian Ideal,' this symmetry was called, after classical Greek sculpture. The neck, the calves, the arms, should all be the same size.'"[14] Fussell, whose experience is embedded in the 1980s, was witness to a radicalization of the body that was not mere building, but sculpting—"body sculpting" is a now a stock phrase within the bodybuilding and wider gym repertoire—and the proponents would actively become sculptures, assuming classical poses such as the *contraposssto*, exemplified by Michelangelo's *David*.

In recalling his bodybuilding days in a more recent interview, Fussell confessed that he "had a girlfriend who simply stroked my arms and stared at them. I was reduced to a body part. But given I had reduced my own life to building a body part, how could I object that she was significantly more interested in my bicep than in me"?[15] Fussell mentions "The Walk," a gait proper to bodybuilders that is not only a result of their bulk, but a kind of somatic signature. In the lead-up to competitions, the body is subjected to a radical kind of diet intended to reduce the fat for the showing of muscle definition, a process that leads to vertigo and pain. He even deprived himself of toothpaste because of the sodium levels, which led to water retention.[16] Evidently, the price of the appearance of absolute "fitness" is extreme bodily disquiet. In preparation for his final competition, in order to "get ripped," shed fat, to be "shredded," "shrink-rapped," and "sliced and diced," Fussell recalls the way he was reduced to a vulnerable shadow, perceiving normal temperatures as cool, and with a fat content so low that the lack of padding on the soles of feet, given his body weight, made it painful to walk.[17] Unlike Kleist's marionette, in this pursuit of melon-like bulges, the professional bodybuilder, in becoming an objectivized ideal, becomes a paragon of self-consciousness.

## Hypermasculine queer

In the same way that Barbie's extreme feminization unmasks a contradiction, or paradox of gender identity and performance, the extreme masculinization in bodybuilding, in its overemphasis, is a kind of dragging. Indeed, Fussell recounts how his friends in Oxford, upon hearing of his abandonment of an academic career to pump iron, enter into a chorus of how he had turned gay ("Samuel *is* looking butch" progressed to the dismissive "obviously he's gone queer").[18] Since the social stamping of gay male identity in the late nineteenth century, and the climax in the scandal of the Wilde trial in 1895, gay men as individuals and as a once (and in some countries still) illegal social group struggled with the equation of being gay and femininity. The combat with this stereotype occurs at precisely the time when bodybuilding entered into the mainstream in the mid-to-late 1970s. One of the most familiar gay clones is the "Muscle Mary," or muscle-bound homosexual, more man than man. Understanding these tensions and contradictions in the exemplary and objectified forms of Barbie and the bodybuilder are essential in establishing the idea of the third identity of the queer, posthuman cyborg, the human introjected doll, or what Jean Baudrillard refers to as "transexuality,"[19] in the following chapter.

In keeping with one of the regular motifs of this book, the most masculine, or masculinizing—since not straight—model that men sought to emulate was a fabricated, unreal image. An outstanding model, and symptom, of the growing taste for manliness among gay men was the fictional creation of the Helsinki executive Touko Laaksonen, Tom of Finland. Tom of Finland was to the world of soft porn and comics what the Village People were to the disco set. Touko dressed in leather, "becoming" Tom, and dreaming up a whole menagerie of pumped, "ripped" guys, "a gay utopia" in the words of Guy Snaith, "full of horny lumberjacks, sailors, policemen and construction workers, all bursting out of their uniforms or their jeans and T-shirts. Tomland is a fantasy world in which masculinity is held up as the highest ideal."[20] Laaksonen invented a universe in which jutting chins and full, pursed lips gazed longingly at biceps and pectorals that bulged with exaggerated rotundity, or to use the correct gay expression: "big pecs, tight abs and bubble butt."[21] Snaith continues: "Through his fantasy of total maleness, Tom sought to eliminate gay guilt, to correct injustices, to validate gay men, their desires and their experience, to destroy the stereotype which equated homosexuality with effeminacy."[22] Laaksonen may have come from Europe, but his characters are definitely new world. Due to the American movie industry, American males, especially those of the working class were seen as more virile than their European counterparts, who bore the legacy of the aesthete, the effete, pruned and groomed dandy.[23] (Americans wear boots; Europeans wear suede loafers.)

Manliness and muscularity had already began to be popular with publications such as *Physique Pictorial* that had illustrations of groups of buff, scantily clad men; construction workers pausing for a drink was a favorite.[24] Laaksonen did his own cover illustration for this magazine in 1968, and this time, with penises straining within the tightest of pants, there was little left to the imagination. For Tom of Finland took masculinity to an absurd extreme that went so far as to parody heterosexual aspirations, transposing it into the gay-o-sphere. Heterosexual pornography had long relied on exaggeration—huge tits, long legs, small waist, big lips—which was best realized in the comic blonde in *Roger Rabbit*, and Tom did the same with manliness. But it was so tipped as to be a threat to heterosexual male desire, not the least because it confronted straight men with traits that they aspired to as well. The effect of Tom of Finland on the male gay community was immense, liberating many from inhibitions, and to assert that "maleness," such as it is, is an idea to be shared between gay and straight men. But what became certain is the uncertainty of the reducibility of maleness. With the gay male clone, over-pronounced maleness was a performance of a man in male drag, a man playing the part to an inanimate and artificial ideal.

## The anatomic shell and death: Bodybuilding and AIDS

If we are to imagine that a line could be drawn of the old former human and humanist age to the age of the cyborg, the human doll, the cyborg, it is not quite 1977, but rather 1981, the beginning of the Reagan era, and the date of the first diagnosis of the AIDS in the Western world. It is this date that marks the beginning of a definitive set of changes to the era of the cyborg and the technologized body. While Schwarzenegger, Stallone and others were defining the new age of muscled action hero that was very much a different breed from the "sensitive seventies,"[25] the body is henceforward a site of infinite modification and transformation that oscillates between paranoia and mania. The paranoid body is one that, thanks to the information revolution and media hype, is acutely conscious of agents that threaten the body, such as unwelcome chemicals in the air or chemical additives in food. The paranoid body is also terrified of ageing. This fear of ageing overlaps with the maniacal body that is obsessed with "body maintenance"—the connotations of body and machine ought not to go unnoticed—and bodily improvement. The maniacal body turns to any means available to push the bodies to the extremes of "perfection," a notion that *exceeds* the limits of a body without steroids or prosthetic enhancements. While anabolic steroids were available before this era, and instances of cosmetic breast augmentation are evident since the mid-twentieth century (in fact, the earliest recorded instances was as early as 1895 with the German surgeon Vincenz Czerny), it was only in 1980s that these means of radical body mediation became widespread.

Unlike the pumped body of bodybuilding, the AIDS body was a body degraded and broken down. Unlike other viruses, it is adaptable to the antibodies that seek to fight it. It is referred to as an "intelligent virus." But it is also at this time that aberrations in technical systems are universally called "viruses." Musing on the AIDS epidemic and its relation to the technologically encoded body, Baudrillard writes:

> It is logical that AIDS (and cancer) should have become the prototypes for our modern pathology and for all lethal virality. When the body is exposed to artificial prostheses and, at the same time, to genetic fantasies, its defense systems are disorganized, its biological logic is destroyed. This fractal body, fated to see its own external functions multiply, is at the same time doomed to unstoppable internal division among its own cells. It metastasizes: the internal, biological metastases are in a way symmetrical with those external metastases, the prostheses, the networks, the connections.[26]

Metaphorically at least, AIDS is the disease of the cyborg body, a catastrophic *Zeitgeist*. The bodybuilder and the AIDS body are historically and conceptually two sides of the same coin: One is a studied unity through the laboring of parts; the other is a body divided and reorganized, reduced to the scene of its own gradual demise bit by bit. The bodybuilder and the cyborg then conjoin with the figure of the Terminator (*Terminator*, 1984), perhaps Schwarzenegger's most famous role. Appropriately enough, in his analysis of Schwarzenegger's Terminator, Sean French draws a parallel with Boris Karloff's Frankenstein.[27]

# 7

# GENETICALLY BAROQUE BEINGS: CYBERGENDER, TRANSEXUALITY AND NATRIFICIALITY

*Faust: What am I then, when there is no possibility,*
*To win humanity's crown,*
*To which every sense compels?*
*Mephistopheles: In the end you are – who you are.*

—GOETHE[1]

*Take La Cicciolina. Is there any more wonderful embodiment of sex, of the pornographic innocence of sex? She has been contrasted with Madonna, the virgin product of aerobics and a glacial aesthetic, devoid of all charm and sensuality, a muscled android, ripe for precisely that reason for conversion into a computer-generated idol on account of the strange deterrence she generates. But, if we think about it, is not La Cicciolina also a transexual? Her long, platinum-blonde hair, her ample pneumatic breasts, her ideal blow-up-doll forms, her lypophilized-cartoon or science-fiction eroticism and, above all, the exaggeration of the sexual discourse (never perverse, never libertine), total transgression on a plate; the ideal telephone chat-line woman, plus a carnivorous erotic ideology which no woman today would sign up to—except, precisely, a transsexual, a transvestite: they alone, as we know, live by the exaggerated, carnivorous sign of sexuality. Here the fleshy ectoplasm La Cicciolina meets the artificial nitroglycerine of Madonna or the androgynous Frankenstein charm of Michael Jackson. They are all mutants, transvestites, genetically baroque beings, whose erotic "look" conceals their gender indeterminacy. They are all 'gender-benders' as they say in the USA.*

—JEAN BAUDRILLARD[2]

Baudrillard's statement, written in 1987, is more valid today than ever, which is why it warrants one important correction, namely, that women, and men, are "signing up" in droves. Coterminous with the dramatic transition of bodybuilders from fanatics and freaks to desirable and enviable, the perception of altering one's body has moved from vain and mildly insane to sheer good sense if you can afford it, and perhaps even better, sense if you cannot since the procedure might change the direction of your life for the better. But as we have begun to see throughout this book, what is better—aesthetically or morally—is open to conjecture and often leads to a Faustian wager.

The new standard of body—muscleman or Barbie doll—tends to isolate a fictive but still present antagonism in the philosophical definition and approach to the "natural" body. For it would seem then the concept of the natural body had a dual birth that would result in an oscillation between an ideal image, on one hand, and the laxity born from freedom, on the other—the latter being a legacy of the 1960s and 1970s. One needed to discipline the body to maintain its "natural" beauty, yet, as the opposing view would have it, we must also let the body follow its own natural course. This contradiction has stayed with us to this day, and underlies people's personal predilections for or against plastic surgery, for example. With growing sophistication in medicine and the intervention of technology, the aspiration for the perfect body, whatever that is, has transmuted from emulation of a particular "real" (and realizable) body type to one that is less real and more imaginary, and either impossible to attain or partly attainable through technological intervention, hence the rhetoric of the cyborg body. This change in approach contrasts the now historical classical body that would then be a fashionable body with clothes, with the body that is self-consciously worn. The body is altered by more than "natural" means such as sport and other exertions—and today it has now become "natural" for us to do so. We are now in an era in which there is free choice to look more or less like a doll, and also to have a relationship with one. This could either be with the person who looks like a doll or a doll that looks like a person.

We are also in the era when naturalness is more relative, literary and arbitrary than ever before. In a sense, we are all cyborgs to some degree or another, having been subject to myriad modifications, be they teeth straightening devices and bridges, eyebrow tattoos, Botoxed brows, ears pinned back, hair implants, hip replacements or temporary modifications such as face creams, waxing, manicuring, even simple things we take for granted such as shaving or having our hair cut and styled. If we think closely, we are subject to modifications every day, many of which are, by dint of habit, imperceptible to us. It is left to the reader's judgment and personal disposition as to what measures are appropriate and when they tip to extremes. But the reader might also give pause to too severe a judgment, simply for the fact that ideas about body modification are changing. For we are now already in an era when unnatural and off outcomes for plastic surgery are deemed, in some smaller circles, desirable, just as punks in the 1970s, in all their theatrical dereliction, may have found one another attractive.

## Plastic surgery

The sophistication of and advancement in cosmetic and restorative surgery in the last thirty years has led to the improvement and recuperation of hundreds of thousands of lives. Anyone skeptical about surgical intervention need only look at photographs of the horrors of, say, the First World War, of myriad gouged faces, imponderably disfigured and robbed of any prospect of eking out a normal existence. Or we could consider the developments in breast reconstruction such that women afflicted with cancer and facing a biopsy of one or both breasts need no longer look to a future of insecurity and unattractiveness, but if the cancer is not malignant, may walk out with better breasts than what they once had. Other forms of prosthetic enhancements were prompted by the spread of polio in the 1950s. But within this biological and emotive topos, there is no qualitative point of demarcation between salvaging dignity from tragedy to where cosmetic surgery is used for self-improvement. And from thereon, we have addiction, where the perennial patient becomes obsessively all-body much as bodybuilders play brinkmanship with their health in order to be the appearance of health's paragon.

But it is also this muddy transition from compassionate restoration, a salutary benefit of the technological age—on par with mending bunions, replacing teeth or removing moles—and the relative difference between necessity and the necessity impelled by desire, that is also the cause of some critical disquiet. As Suzanne Fraser adds, for

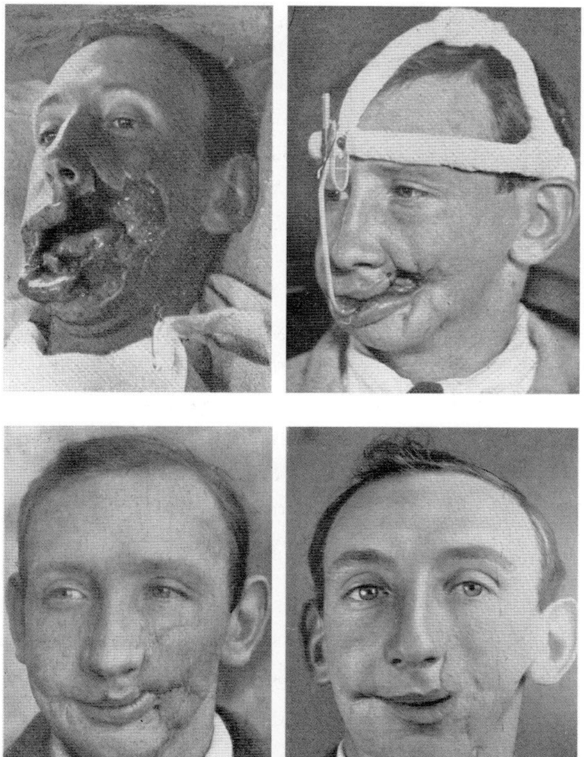

**Figure 7.1** Four photographs documenting the facial reconstruction of a soldier whose cheek was extensively wounded in the Battle of the Somme (July 1916). Taken from *Plastic Surgery of the Face: Based on Selected Cases of War Injuries of the Face Including Burns* by H. D. Gillies, 1920. Photo by SSPL/Getty Images.

feminists, a dramatic divide exists between reconstructing a syphilitic nose and "the reasons why appearance should be so important as to compel women to risk injury, disfigurement or death in a procedure on a healthy, and by all accounts, normal, body."[3] Her counterargument to this is that women who undergo such surgery seek a new level of social attainment, where appearance is an undeniably central component.[4] Katherine Hayles rues the "nightmare of a culture inhabited by posthumans who regard their bodies as fashion accessories rather than the ground of being."[5] Moreover, for those who seek a certain ideal type, there are concerns over race that are seldom voiced in discussions of body modification. Arnold, Barbie and Ken are, after all, white.[6]

As Elizabeth Haiken correctly observes in one of the earlier cultural studies on cosmetic surgery, "Cosmetic surgery lies at the nexus of medicine and consumer culture."[7] As opposed to the soft anarchy of the hippie culture of the protest era of the 1960s and 1970s, plastic surgery plays its part in bringing people to a common standard advanced through repeated media representations and stereotypes. In the quest for what is desirable and enviable, people find themselves locked into the oblivion of sameness. As Haiken remarks, "the widespread adoption of the surgical solution reveals a frightening vision of Americans as conformists, bent on achieving a commodified, advertising-driven standard of perfection."[8] She traces this trend back to the early twentieth century when restorative surgeons began to observe a growing market of people wanting to participate physically in a mass culture that was repeatedly doling out judgments as to what was desirable and was undesirable. A citable early case was when the Jewish actress Fanny Brice in 1923 decided to have a nose job, prompting Dorothy Parker's much-repeated quip that she has "cut off her nose to spite her race."[9] But the culture of mobility and capitalism also conspired to create a view that beauty could be acquired rather than an inherited trait.[10] Beauty to the highest bidder.

Fanny Brice's surgical improvement was one of what were to be many attempts to erase the signs of race and creed, real or perceived. Today, an entire industry is given over to lifting the fold over the eyes to what plastic surgeons call "optimalizing" "Asian eyes"[11]—something that occurs more prevalently in a Western and Caucasian cultural setting—or to sharpen rounded features of African Americans. The signal case in all of this is Michael Jackson, whose "Frankenstein charm" comes at the expense of countless procedures that altered his bone structure, including reducing his nose to an elfin sprig. He alleged to Oprah Winfrey in 1993 that the lightness of his skin owed itself to a skin condition, but even if this were true, this does not mitigate the fact that he had been on a campaign to make himself less black. Despite his grotesquerie, Jackson's example caused more Afro-Americans to seek out surgery, the ones, that is, that could afford it.[12] In thrall with their brother (who had been in thrall of Diana Ross), Jackson's sisters Janet and La Toya followed suit, primping their noses and sharpening their check bones. Comparing pictures of them in the early 1990s reveals the siblings to resemble one another. Surgically, they had become clones. Barbie, in a sense, lies waiting in the shadows. M. G. Lord rightly argues that Barbie has become something of a fixed standard by which Americans measure themselves, and thereby, a standard by which "aliens" are compared. She has become a certainty principle in an age of purported pluralism.[13]

It is important to stress that more often than not, Barbie lurks as a covert, not an overt, standard. With more than 90 percent of girls in the United States having one, she is still, in the words of Urla and Swedlund, "an incredibly resilient visual and tactile model of femininity for pre-pubescent girls headed straight for the twenty-first century."[14] With this compelling thought, in what is a paradox that has eluded most surgery-seeking individuals, Rhian Parker explains that in opting for plastic surgery, most women want to be normal, while they remain obscure as to what exactly "normal" is. "Achieving a natural look was seen as important so that they did not stand out. But again, 'natural' was not clearly defined. The repertoires of 'natural' and 'normal' were also part of the doctor's narratives about cosmetic surgery."[15] Moreover, the motivations remain equally obscure: While many women, according to Parker, claimed to want surgery for themselves, it was inevitably to achieve a greater degree of social approbation.[16] But the strongest argument is that "normal" is a fictional center, that is, at best, of a foreign, artificial, shape.

Again, we veer back to the highly porous, shifting, and ultimately, amorphous concept of nature. In this vague questing after the natural, Suzanne Fraser stipulates that first we must not forget the gendering of nature as female as against the maleness of science and culture. Constructions of nature have, she argues, opened up the field of cosmetic

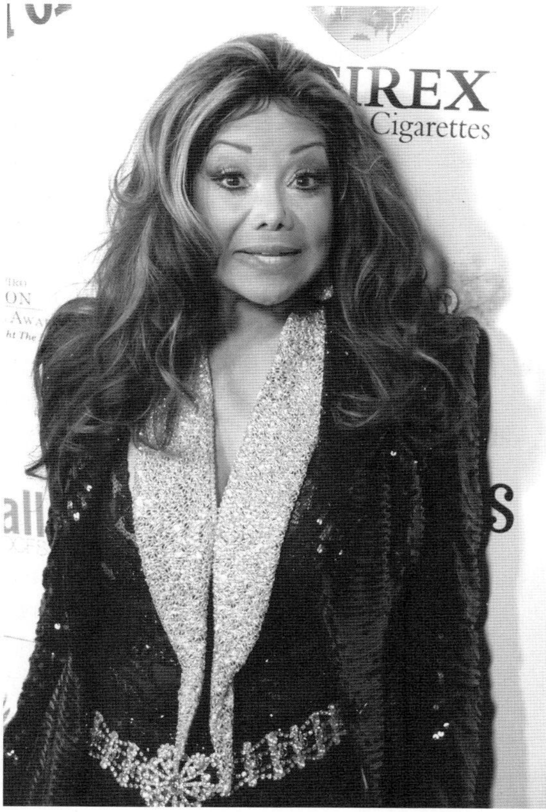


**Figure 7.2** La Toya Jackson attends the annual Summer Spectacular Under the Stars for the Brent Shapiro for Alcohol and Drug Awareness, September 13, 2014, Beverly Hills, California. © Getty Images.

surgery, since it created the possibility of, as it were, attaining a greater or better state of nature. One version of nature is as "the inert raw materials that culture sets to work," while the Enlightenment view that has held sway to this day is an elevated view that brings it "to the status of Ideal model for culture."[17] Drawing on the work of Haraway, Fraser rejects both positions—"nature as origin and resource"— to reframe nature as "a set of objects, practices and places," a position that has strong ramifications for ecology and for "human nature."[18] At the root of Haraway's (and subsequently, Fraser's) reorientation is the attempt to unmask, and finally, disrupt a philosophically Christian model of technoscience whose teleology is Edenic bliss, a redeemed and sanitized space whose Janus face, for Haraway, is genocide and ecological catastrophe.[19] The "mutant" that she invokes sidesteps this narrative and opens up a new set of myths whose negative ramifications are less horrifying.

To extrapolate, for Haraway, Frankenstein's monster and Barbie, that is, the disabled and ideal, the monstrous and the angelic, are effectively one. Haraway used the term *prosthetics* to this end as it has the double meaning of substitute for a lost limb and a supplement as an enabler beyond "natural" limits. Although she doesn't mention them, the bionic man ("Gentlemen, we can rebuild him") and woman enter into this territory. Such types marry human flesh with the machine, thus perturbing the kinds of ethics and assumptions built on humanist precepts, to "force a rethinking of kin."[20] Allied to the ethos of queer, the cyborg is thus a "mixed breed," who is, in the words of Sharon Betcher, "a fugitive, from Christian salvation history."[21] But Betcher refutes Haraway's position as impracticable in practice as people with prostheses remain deeply other, a gender subclass.[22] Her suspicion is that Haraway's exhortation that "we are all cyborgs" is simply the same humanist holism in a different shell.[23] Timothy Lender, in his essay "Techno-Humanism," echoes similar concerns, stating that the human and the digital must cease to be two separate entities, and that we must dispense with the cyborg as a "a human-machine hybrid, where the machine is a (possibly dangerous) supplement, tool, and extension of the human."[24] Such a view vouches for the additive ethical model of cosmetic surgery that Fraser advances. But it is a position that also courts its likely set of detractors, from accusations of vanity (which particularly crop up in the *Schadenfreude* accompanying publication of "plastic surgery disasters")[25] to technological excess and a kind of techno-bodily greed. But to return to the main point, this desire, which does lapse into greed, continually converges on the same imaginary points, of a body whose facets exist outside the realm of nature, but which nevertheless epitomize nature. Hence, in the words of Fraser, "'Natural' is a word that always replaces a complex of (often) less convincing, powerful or controllable ideas and issues. It is a rhetorical device, where its power to persuade is frequently taken for granted, indeed, relied upon."[26] Similarly, as prototypes, the Arnie, the Barbie and the Ken, are bodily equivalents of "rhetorical devices" that are "taken for granted, indeed, relied upon."[27]

## Performing monstrosities: Orlan

Mireille Suzanne Francette Porte (b. 1947), better known as Orlan, is the artist best known for undergoing a series of surgical procedures under the banner of performance art. In the words of Haiken, "The infamous Henry Schireson, in 1938, asserted that a plastic surgeon could reproduce, in thirty minutes, the eyes of the Mona Lisa, on which Da Vinci labored for four years. Today, the Parisian artist lives out Schireson's claim."[28] She renamed herself Orlan in 1971; in 1990, under the general rubric of "The Reincarnation of St. Orlan," her project was to remake herself into a fantastic composite based on paragons of beauty by male artists. (Note also that *reincarnation* is a term used by many transsexual conversions.)[29] In a series of heavily publicized events under the title *Omnipresence*, her surgeries were broadcast in preeminent venues such as the Centre Georges Pompidou, Paris; the Sandra Gehring Gallery, New York; and the McLuhan Centre, Toronto. Orlan slowly transformed herself into a feminine ideal, or rather, a hybrid ideal. Where, since the 1980s, feminist artists had appropriated from historical examples of male representations of women for the sake of feminist redress, Orlan appropriated various attributes onto herself. In the process, she made herself into a flamboyant somatic anthology derived from the Western canon of painting, with the chin from Botticelli's Venus, the forehead of Mona Lisa, lips from Gustave Moreau's Europa, nose from Gérard's Psyche and eyes of Diana as painted by an anonymous member of the sixteenth-century school of Fontainebleau. These were apparently chosen not simply as examples of beauty, but because of their associated narratives and histories.[30] (Orlan later remarked that it was ironic that the program *Extreme Makeover* came out six months after the operation, not to do with her, but rather as a sign of the times.)[31] Further, the recombination of parts, was not quite the quest for ultimate beauty, but a refashioning of parts to emphasize the fractured nature of all our bodies. The recombining, or anthologizing of parts of paintings prompts Parveen Adams to state that Orlan "is effectively disfiguring the image, the image comes apart from itself in the surgery." The result is that "Nothing 'fits' any longer. Her operation destroys the distinction between the inside and the outside."[32] This is because the body is treated as raw material: Orlan repudiates the original self as normal, or indeed, authentic; authenticity exists in the serial acts of alteration. As she herself states of her "reincarnation," it "is not the story of a martyr, but of a character that dissolves through added multiplicity."[33]

In her review of Orlan's exhibition at Espacio AV in Murcia, Spain, in 2008, Rhonda Garelick states that Orlan's work raises key questions that have dogged humans since modernism and have since become even more exigent: "How is identity performed? What renders us recognizable? Where, or how, beneath our many layers of tailored roles, do we exist?"[34] She is an artist who challenges "our most basic assumptions about beauty, religion, art history, sexuality and, ultimately, about the stability of the self,"[35] who wishes to violate its wholeness as a sanctified human.[36] Disposed to modification from the start and calling her body her "software,"[37] Orlan states that "one must always mistrust the person one was,"[38] and refers to her work as "rhizomatic," a root genus (e.g., ginger) that is used by philosophers Gilles Deleuze and Félix Guattari to characterize arbitrarily proliferating, nonbinary systems.[39] "In future times," Orlan proclaims, "we'll change our bodies as easily as our hair colour,"[40] a comment that is as implausible as it is outlandish, although it is unequivocal about the attitude to the morphous self. Orlan conforms to a logic, in the words of Michela Marzano, of "and-and," where "everything is always possible, each decision reversible, each choice not definitive."[41] We need only think of reversal

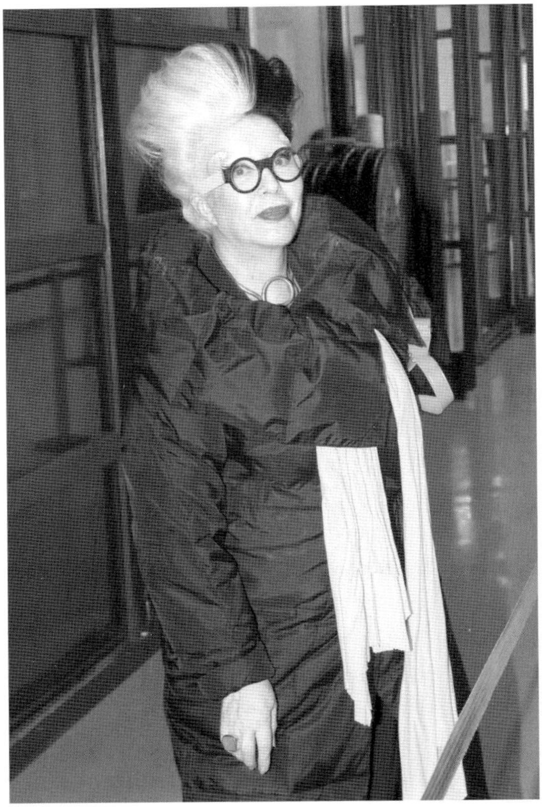

**Figure 7.3** Orlan attends the Jeff Koons retrospective opening evening at the Beaubourg in Paris, November 24, 2014. © Getty Images.

surgery, and also the rise of tattoo removal clinics. Everything is impermanent and no commitment is absolute.

Yet, her highly ritualized alterations do destabilize the habitual and too glib notions of naturalness, as Jill O'Bryan evocatively observes:

> if there is a conflict between what is *natural* in the mind and what is biologically inherited (*natural*) in the body, then how can one judge which *natural* image should or should not be portrayed? Considering the contemporary emphasis on body as image, the fact that the process of surgical alteration leaves one's body in a state of flux, and the fact that she is injecting into her body images of *ideal* beauty, is Orlan's new (future) form stable? Is the possible instability of her image undermining her attempts to stabilize an altered one? Is Orlan authoring a failure or a success? And finally, specifically addressing the art/medicine binary, exactly *who* is authoring this work, the surgeons or Orlan?[42]

Orlan's work lends provocative ironic force to those addicted to plastic surgery who call their bodies a work of art, as the work is both commentary and complicity.

In remembering the earlier discussion in this book of dolls and the commedia dell'arte, Orlan's last procedure in 1993 was with a large Harlequin hat on her head, while the medical team wore motley commedia-inspired clothing designed by Issey Miyake. During the surgery, Orlan read from a philosophical prose poem by Michel Serres where he places Harlequin as "an avatar of human freedom and radical otherness, as a figure of profound epistemological daring."[43] Reminiscent of Haraway's cyborg, Serres's Harlequin is, to quote Garelick again, "a grave yet fanciful figure, a performer whose being conjures the possibility of infinite identities coexisting." Further, in Orlan's photographs in various guises, her "recognizability, like the Harlequin's, resides in her theatrical persona, and not within any kind of 'authentic' flesh-and-blood self lying beneath it."[44] Garelick's final words are also worth quoting. In the 2008 exhibition:

> We enter the Harlequin's permeable character and he enters us, and we are haunted by the void or lack that underlies all attempts to define one's self. We're faced with the impossibility of fixed identities. While disturbing, however, this impossibility comes to us in a playful, mischievous way, via the spirit of the Harlequin, the mysterious clown that roams among us.[45]

It is against this framework, which is not confined to femininity, that Orlan's work must be seen. She embodies the open terrain of the new body, the queer, the "third gender"—it is no surprise then that Orlan refers to her work as "blasphemous,"[46] but also at the threshold of camp.[47] In celebration of the body's mutability by natural and artificial means, she had herself photographed just after her surgery, and would parcel out bodily remnants—scalp with hair on it or clumps of fat, even bloodied gauze—as relics for sale in the name of her art.

The irrepressible aspect of Orlan's work, and something the artist returns to again and again, is the pain of the process. As she herself reinforces, her art is not meant to discomfort in order for her audience to make more pertinent realizations about themselves. "Orlan's performances" states Alyda Faber, "command attention because she puts her own body at risk in order to create awareness of the extent to which we all discipline our own bodies, in more or less painful ways, to conform to current social norms."[48] Certainly, Orlan's campaign of surgery was an ambiguous one as it drew attention to the rigors that women have to endure for an imaginary picture-book image of beauty, while also reaping the benefits. She herself identifies her transformation as a "woman-woman transsexualism."[49] Predating Baudrillard's coinage, this transsexualism is homologous to the concept, drawn out in the previous chapter on bodybuilders, that they are men in male drag. What Orlan locates is that the women who seek out plastic surgery to be more "natural" compensate for a perceived lack that they need technology to address; to feel natural is therefore on condition that you are a woman playing woman, or maybe just *a* woman playing *a* woman, often a fictitious one.

But in this way, Orlan also highlights a contradiction in such efforts: To become ourselves (again?), we have to resort to the objectification of the body. In her own words:

> [Orlan's] carnal art is a work of *self-portraiture* in the classical sense, but with technological means that are of their time. It oscillates between *disfigurement* and *refiguring*. It is inscribed in the flesh because our era offers this possibility. The body becomes a *modified readymade* because it is no longer that *ideal readymade* which carries a signature [*qu'il suffit de signer*].[50]

This said, there is an epistemic instability of which the artist, surely, is only too aware. That is, that she reduces herself to an object but it is she, the subject, who performs this reduction. It is a contradiction already pregnant in her pseudonym, which is not only a synecdoche of "Orlando," Virginia Woolf's gender bender, but where the *O* implies zero: zero subject, zero gender.[51] This opens up a very contemporary ethical and psychological issue as to whether a person who has surgery performed is a subject with things attached or a new subject altogether. She may feel new and revitalized (or misshapen), but then there is the new concept of epigenetics to consider, the way in which external factors shape our genes; the way in which our genetic make-up is altered by environmental conditions, which also means refashioning bodily tissue. We are not the hermetically sealed genetic package we once thought we were.[52]

By the seventh surgery in 1993, when she had lumps put in above the side of each eyebrow, Orlan does begin to tip into the realm of odd, much as many others addicted to cosmetic surgery. Sarah Wilson calls the performance procedure as "a Passion Play of our times . . . followed by the triumphal resurrection of unscarred flesh."[53] Other procedures followed that certified her as tipping the boundary of the benign. Two operations later, Orlan had liposuction performed on her for the fabrication of neon and plexiglass reliquaries. Yet, if her work is blasphemous, her work also risks resacralizing itself, with herself as the martyr, the filmed procedures an ersatz ritual.[54] It also speaks to the hubris of technological society to have it all. Or, to echo Mephistopheles to Faust, you always are who you are. Body alteration just makes the statement more enigmatic.

## Porn, sex, dolls and the natrificial

Barbara Rose makes a useful and unusual observation about Orlan:

> Orlan's medium, finally, is media, if that sounds redundant, she means it to be. Her critical method is based on a sophisticated feedback system, a vicious circle of echoing and self-generating images, spawning a progeny of hybrid media production. This continuous feedback loop is difficult to escape long enough to gain sufficient distance to decode the meaning of her performances and their afterlife as documents, relics and replicated image banks.[55]

Although not intended to be read this way, her words can insightfully applied to contemporary pornography, pornography in the age of the Internet. And in this light, we can also safely say that Orlan's work is highly pornographic. Here "pornography" has to be taken in its less literal sense, to mean a feckless playing-up to salacious voyeurism, where there is no shame or inhibition. It is also a cheapening of things, their reduction as absurdum, a displacement of intimacy by parading it in the public realm. In doing so, Orlan, in effect, confronted pornography with the pornographic, achieved through the spectacle of "monstrous femininity." As Kate Ince argues, this is precisely what is not permitted in "the male imaginary" because it is not a viable prospect of the male gaze. But in broadcasting the belly-churning ugliness leading to the pursuit of greater beauty she was confronting "the male imaginary with its own abjected content."[56] The gaze of anticipation and desire was also confronted with all the repressed conditions of the object of desire.

Contemporary with Orlan's performances was the growth of the Internet pornography industry, an industry that is now immeasurably large, although conservative lobby groups may have had a hand in the public hysteria caused by overinflated estimates.[57] This explosion (most figures of speech become infelicitous when discussing matters such as these) had numerous effects, one of which was to make a certain default narrative sequence discernible, and the other was to perpetuate certain expectations about the body. There are many alternative kinds of pornography, but as alternatives, these only serve to enforce the rule. Through dint of sheer quantity, what becomes evident is that the convention for the porn body is that woman follow a roughly Barbie-like model and the man somewhere between Ken and bodybuilder. But as the body culture accelerated in the 1980s, so did the pornography industry, and the two worlds were never too far away from one another. If one way for bodybuilders to earn a living was personal training, another was pornography.[58] Note, too, the interrelationship between a bodybuilder's work and that of the pornographer: one labors without any palpable result except that the commodity become himself, while the other performs an act whose biological trajectory is to reproduce the species, but where no reproduction takes place, and instead, the corporeal, carnal act becomes commodified.

The sexual permissiveness of the 1960s, and the birth of pornographic brands such as *Hustler* (1974) and *Playboy* (1953) signaled a significant break with the pornography of the previous era. This was a new theatricality in which quasi-celebrities like John Holmes, and later, Anna Nicole Smith played a part. As pornography became increasingly stylized and the body types more fixed, the travesty and sham within the pornographic representation is there for all to see. So the "natrificial" enshrines two factors within straight porn over the Internet: The first is its rejection of naturalness—as opposed to, say, the verisimilitude of the filmic love scene—and the second is the looks and body types it prefers. There is a discernible "porn body" that is as much *worn* as possessed. This is the paradox of natrificiality: It announces its contrivance as a given; the pornographic image recognizes itself always already as surrogate. Dress fetishes persist, but these exist *together* with a "porn body." In contradistinction to the "actress" who may or may not have had the attributes the gazer is looking for, the porn body imposes itself onto the viewer to achieve what the viewer cannot without the experience, assistance, of the pornographic representation. It is also one of the ironies within historical symmetries that the first saline breast implant was introduced in France in 1964, while the silicone prosthetic breast was invented in America in 1961, which is only just before the beginning of the new genre of porn star. Another significant stage in the manipulated body image is at the end of the 1980s, which witnessed a highly sexualized and busty feminine ideal, around the time of the bra's centenary, 1989.[59] A little after arrives the fashion for washboard stomachs ("six packs") and bulging pectorals, disseminated by the likes of Calvin Klein and the brand's highly successful black-and-white underwear advertisements.

Another key aspect of natrificiality is it is not just played out on the surface, but in the way in which the body moves. The body is therefore not only the site of technology (work), but performs technologically. Note the ungainly poses in straight porn so as to reveal all for the camera. For example, the position when the man is lying down but behind and the woman, also lying down raises her leg to reveal the act of penetration— this is the body as marionette. Further, the woman is more often than not wearing a garment that has been lowered at the top and hiked at the bottom. Thus, to dress up as the porn actor is to anticipate the state of semi-undress. The intimate is made specular and the body mimics, or becomes, the clown of technology, delimiting coupling and love to a genital act.

The natrificiality of straight porn is a condition that in "natural," nonpornographic sexual relations is always repressed, namely, that we clothe the other with our needs, desires and expectations. Natrificiality is the space of fantasy, desire and lack grafted on the body in an exaggerated way, where tattoos, body modification, cosmetic surgery, athletic work, make-up, shoes and other fetishes become one. The paradox of the "worn body" of porn is that it is at an extreme pole to classical nude, but much in the manner of the political horseshoe. The classical nude is uninhibited, and in its beauty, suggests harmony between culture/humanity and nature, while pornographic nakedness is presents a kind of orchestrated violence that is not natural, but rather all about artificiality and exaggeration, celebrated through the ritualized repetition of the conventionalized professional straight porn sequence. This repetition engenders a rhetorical naturalness that rivals, and undermines, the "natural" sexual act.[60]

The overwhelming quantity, together with the repetitive presence of certain conventions in bodies and activities has percolated down into fashion culture, with the now mainstream currency of terms like "pornification,"[61] "pornochic,"[62] and "pornostyle."[63] These designations are to the interrelation of body and dress, but more recently, similar categorizations have devolved to the body alone. In March 2015, the German national newspaper *Die Welt* announced a new type of man, categorized by his resemblance to the pornographic model, thus confirming the latter as a somewhat autonomous and universally recognizable type. He is the "spornosexual," a hybrid of the athlete and the porn star.[64] He is the successor of the metrosexual, or rather the "updated" model.[65] The spornosexual is like an athlete like David Beckham, but with more pronounced bulges—one of the poster boy pundits of this new genus is the Munich-based designer Philipp Plein who uses models with minimal fat, a narrow waist, pronounced pectorals and shoulders, with shortly cropped hair and an expressionless face, reminiscent of G.I. Joe, but more angular (Plein sports a similar build, although he himself does smile from time to time). It is also not uncommon for such models, like Plein himself, to have tattoos. Unsurprisingly this look has little to do with real, outdoor, participatory sport, but "the combination of sport and porn is rather obvious, since in both cases it is about function and aesthetics."[66]

## No need for life: RealDolls are here

Sexual substitutes and onanistic aides are about as old as the oldest profession. The invention of plastics and polymers made it all the easier to create sexual dolls, of which Hoffmann's Olimpia is no doubt a darkly allegoric fantasy. Inflatable sex dolls have come with the consolation that they are tawdry and ridiculous, in their caricatural approximation of the human. But the sex dolls of more recent time are a completely different breed, something analogous to the leap from the original Terminator to the quicksilver model.

A careful construction of silicone flesh around a PVC skeleton supported by a steel frame, RealDolls first entered the market in 1996, the brainchild of Matt McCullen. Although based in San Marcos, California, the company has offices throughout Europe, where the dolls also enjoy a healthy popularity. They are posable dolls, designed for participatory sex, with a body weight approximated to an actual human body of the same size (Figure 61). A visit to the site reveals a host of different permutations of the same (post-Barbie/Ken) for both men and women. The female dolls are mostly with D or DD breasts, a hairless pubis and long legs. There is a list of bodily accessories, from merkins (pubic wigs) to longer nails, which are also sold to ensure a custom type. (In parallel to this, children's toys have also evolved from the idea of a core type—G.I. Joe and Barbie—to an eminently manipulable body, with removable parts, down to the eye color, for the ultimate tailor-made body—assuming, that is, that children know what they want.)

In 2003, the company introduced a face-replacement system, or "Face-X," presumably if a person became tired of his or her partner or wanted to pretend to be a Lothario. Despite the fluency that Face-X provides, each "edition" is marketed pre-Christened with a name, but with a Terminator-type name addition: "'Michelle' Body A, Face A"; "'Renee' Body C, Head L"; "'Olivia' Configuration 2, Body A." Or, if so inclined, customers may try "Nick" who is "Male Body Type B, Face Type B." One of the more astonishing of the male dolls is the punk who is advertised with vinyl pants and gloves holding drumsticks.[67] Make-up can be applied to the faces, and the company sells an assortment of clothing and fetish-accoutrements. Thanks to the scruples of hygiene, the mouth and vagina contain removable inserts for cleaning, and at one point in production, customers could get robot hip actuators for the ultimate illusion of sexual gyration. The cost of the dolls exceeds the U.S. $5,000-mark, which makes the dolls serious business. As a maker of the most sophisticated sexual fetishes yet available, the company is aptly called Abyss, because that is, after all, what a fetish is expected to fill. With the innumerable options available, and the countless permutations it can undergo, the RealDolls is truly an apogee of Pygmalionism. For a fee, any man (or woman) can produce the ideal other, which includes transgender types.[68]

Before RealDolls, the market where highly contrived sex dolls flourished was Japan. In his detailed account of sex dolls and fetishes, Marquard Smith explains how the Japanese doll can be linked to the ancient doll culture, *ningyõ* "with its own historically and culturally locatable fantasies of animism and anthropomorphism."[69] It is also connected with the crisis of masculinity that befell Japanese men after the defeat of the Second World War which among other things was expressed through sexual violence. From the onset of its

Westernization in the nineteenth century, Japanese taste and talent for popular culture grew frenetically, and with it kitsch, erotic and pornographic culture. While Japan has strict social mores and decency laws,

> At the same time, it is a culture with a fanatical interest in toys, models and model figures, trinkets, robots and AI's [sic] "intelligent agents." It also has a long tradition of recreational participation with inanimate objects that have human form, including dolls, figurines, puppets, mechanized wind-up dolls (*karakuri*), realistic life-sized "living dolls" (*iki-ningyõ)* and automata. So, perhaps, accusations of a broader obsession with the ludic potential of all things miniature (and animistic, animatable and enlivenable) are closer to the mark.[70]

The aesthetic that has predominated for such specimens has been that of *kawaii*, or cuteness, which subsequently took the form of the Manga form of the exceptionally large heads that supported massive doe eyes, that can be taken for psychological depth or the opposite. The infantilizing nature of this aesthetic is duplicated across the spectrum: from dolls to anime to young women themselves in cosplay or as their own version of cuteness clone, such as the Lolita good-bad-girl school uniform look. The Japanese sex dolls are strongly uniform. The body is that of a teenage girl with bulbous silicone enhanced-style breasts, enormous doe eyes above a sharply tapered pointing chin. As Smith points out, Japan's traditions of making dolls predate that of ancient Greece. While serving the pan-cultural function of components in both birth and funerary rituals, they were also thought to bring good luck. Shinto traditions of animism dictated that dolls were vessels for spirits.[71]

Which brings us back to the RealDoll, which in more isolated cases, now serves not only sexual functions but as life partners. Vessels for spirits they may not fully be, RealDolls are now functioning members of our global society, if a universally taciturn. The RealDoll, largely she, has made her imprint on popular culture, from television series ranging from *Nip/Tuck* to *Sons of Anarchy*. But its strongest presence is in the home. The men drawn to such fetishes are largely introverted or come from specialist "geek" professions such as IT, and who confess to having had disturbing experiences with the opposite sex.[72] Sometimes calling themselves agalmatophiles or iDollators, these men use these dolls as active surrogates. As Smith states, "they manage their loneliness and their sentimental attachment to inanimate human form" with otherwise "normal" acts of canoodling, by changing clothes daily, giving them massages and anything else that may win them approval.[73] These relations can be so ongoing and intense that the male hosts even confer on their inanimate mates the emotional dynamics of mood swings and dispositional intricacies.[74] The ease with which they pick up such play can, in many cases, be accounted for in their childhood interaction with dolls such as G.I. Joe and Barbie.[75] While there is growing culture of RealDoll lovers, there is also a subgroup that uses them for unspeakable acts. Smith cites examples of crude dismemberment and evidence of savage sodomizing that rendered her anal cavity a "ragged crevasse."[76] It is evidence again of the sliding scale of morality when it comes to artificial bodies, dolls and plastic surgery recipients. On one hand, we have the salutary results of restorative surgery, men and women given a boost of confidence through a bit of surgical maintenance; on the other, there are those addicted to surgery, who have altered themselves beyond recognition. Here, the extremes of beauty meet with those who willingly transform themselves into beasts. They are the living embodiments of technology gone amuck.

## Living dolls

In the depths of California lives one of the serial types that have undergone radical transformation to look like Barbie. What is special, if not remarkable, about Blondie Bennett is that her metamorphosis to become a living doll is more than skin deep. She has weekly hypnotherapy sessions in order to make her more stupid, to which she proudly testifies is successful. A newspaper report from 2014 states that she had taken three hours to arrive to her mother's house because she had lost her way. On another occasion, when picking up a friend from the airport, she did not know whether to go to departures or arrivals.[77] Now around forty years old, she confesses that her obsession with Barbie began as a young girl. As a teenager, she dressed like Barbie and drove a Corvette (Barbie's favorite car), and got odd jobs in toy stores impersonating Barbie. At age thirty-eight, she had her fifth breast enlargement augmenting her H implants to a whopping JJ, "assets" that require her to walk in a careful semi-mechanical way. This was followed by chin liposuction, while regularly using Botox and lip fillers. As she boasts, "Some other women pretend they are human Barbie dolls but I take it to the next level. I want people to see me as a plastic sex doll and being brainless is a big part of that. People criticize me but this is who I am: I want my transformation to be head to toe, inside and out." An admirable ambition, no doubt. A television interview with her includes excerpts of her taking the hypnotherapy, and footage of her in public, where people's reactions to her can only be described as amusing.[78] She earns her living through male "sponsors" and "patrons" to whom she shows her breasts, and she confesses also to having one special patron, making her a kind of cyber-courtesan.

Blondie's contemporary rival is the Moldovan-Ukrainian model Valeria Valeryevna Lukyanova. Born in 1985, she gained her fame began in 2007 when she won the "Miss Diamond Crown of the World" contest over 300 contestants, a competition with no stipulations against body alteration. While she cannot boast the virtue of not knowing that picking up someone from the airport means going to arrivals, her resemblance to Barbie is truly uncanny, and haunting, assisted not only by an inherited body type, but also by eye surgery (unconfirmed) and distinctive make-up, making her eyes more prominent, a procedure not unique to her as there is now another cult of women who want to turn themselves out as Manga dolls. But it is these gaping eyes that have earned her the occasional appellation of "Space Barbie."[79] Patrick Sandberg, writing in *VMagazine*, comments that "her pretended look is so calculated as seemingly artificial that it borders on CGI."[80] When the Gawker Media Site *Jezebel* posted her image in April 2012, things went viral, "chatter reached soprano pitch."[81] But while Blondie Bennett attempts to make herself vacuous, Lukyanova explores a different form of evacuation, in the form of "astral projection," or out-of-body travel, claiming that her spiritual name is "Amatue." In the interview with her in the same magazine, she promises that through the School of Out-of-Body, we may leave

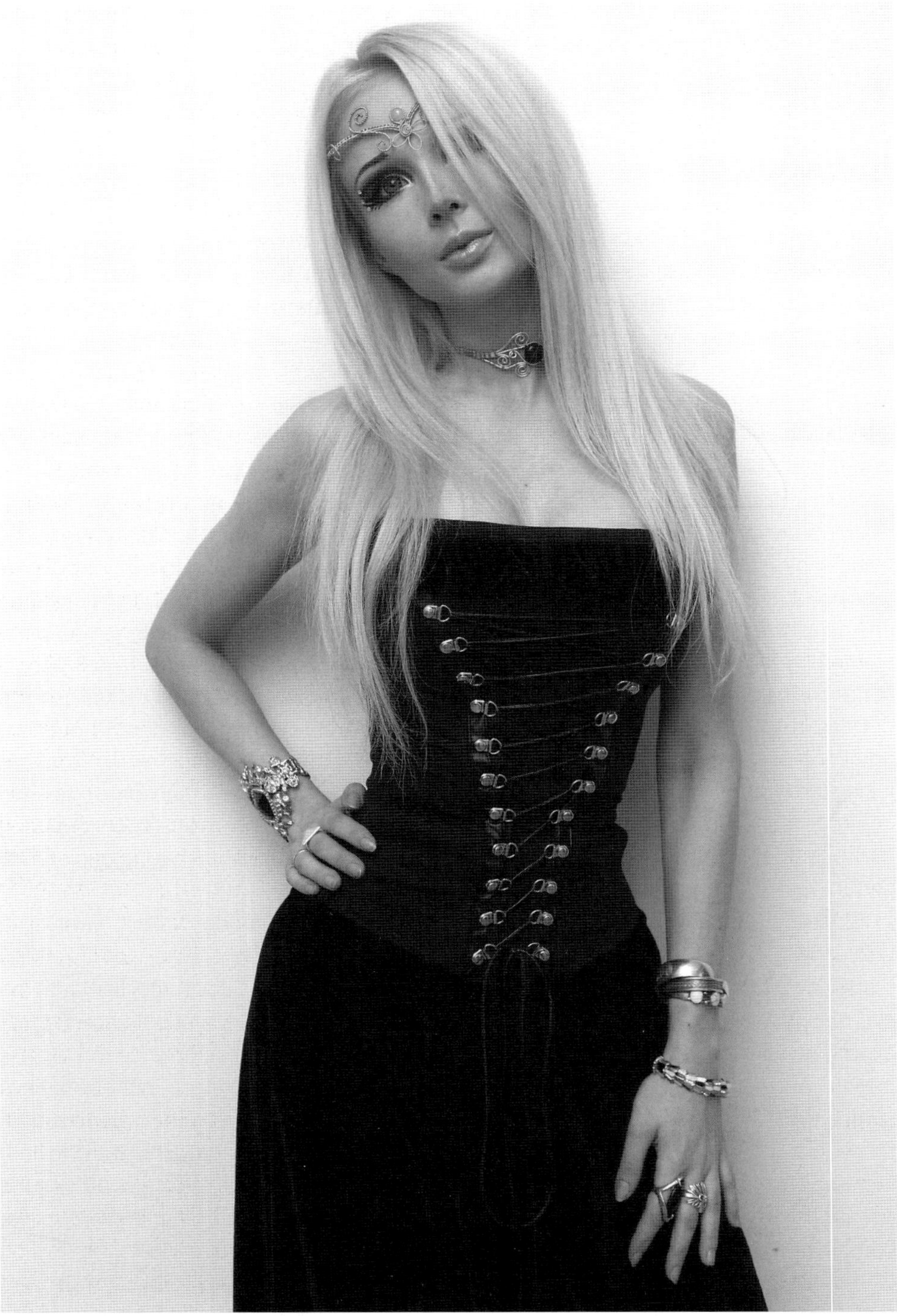

**Figure 7.4** Valeria Lukyanova attends the *Quelli Che Il Calcio*: TV show, 1 February, 2015, in Milan. © Getty Images.

our physical body to "visit any place on the planet and in the universe. I know that this is the future of mankind." When asked about plastic surgery, she is notoriously reticent and obtuse, but in commenting about the many speculations circulating about her on the Internet, she admits that "I am happy I seem unreal to them, it means I'm doing a good job."[82] With Lukyanova, the reality and illusion of the cyborg find their cryptic and hallucinogenic union. In her words, "The aim of my life is to come to this planet to help people realize that it is necessary to move from the role of the 'human consumer' to the role of 'human demigod.'" She also confesses to wanting "to be powered by solar energy."[83] With this her major aim, she says that she never sought to look like a doll. "I just like everything beautiful, feminine and refined. It just happens that dolls are based on the image of refined girls."[84] She forgot to add, "that are white."

In what could have been a marriage made in heaven (or outer space), Lukyanova was paired with her male equivalent, Justin Jedlica, who has sculpted himself into a human Ken doll, having spent more than $150,000 and over a 125 procedures doing so (Plate 19). Not only has he had his face modified into saturnine plasticity, including five rhinoplasties (nose jobs), but he is also riddled with implants all over his body, including pectorals, triceps and shoulders. His allegiances are unequivocal. In one video, he introduces himself as "Justin Jedlica, and I'm a living doll!"[85] The same promotional documentary, which can also be found on his website,[86] has him sculpting a torso in preparation for creating abdominal implants and then visiting a plastic surgeon for such an operation. The skeptical surgeon declares, "Beauty is strategic perfection; I think you really want super perfection." "Correct," replies Jedlica. Surgeon: "With all due respect, you are not conforming to common dictates of taste, but a cartoon version of it." Jedlica nods in assent. In another interview, he admits to "like looking a little overdone."[87] Jedlica, a lover of Japanese anime, refers to his body and his processes as his form of expression and himself as a living work of art. Later in the film, he and his friends are seen preparing for a "Plastics Ball," which Jedlica explains "is the celebration of anything plastic, superficial and dollish, so it's only fitting I make an appearance."[88] He regularly makes appearances wearing a singlet bearing the words, "Proud to be Plastic." Jedlica is the pop artist to Orlan's conceptual artist, he is the plasti-Koons to her plasti-Duchamp, and looks to supersede arguably the first human Barbie, Cindy Jackson, a record holder for the greatest number of plastic surgery procedures. Adding to the connection between body modification and art, Jackson's tertiary education was at the Royal College of Art, London. In all cases, these figures seek to elide their birth and become their own creation, a complex self-fetishization that recalls the detail about Barbie that she has no parents. In the words of Rogers, "Barbie has no doll parents nor has she ever married or given birth. Barbie is the center of Barbie's world."[89] Thus, autonomy and immaculate conception also mask a particular aggressiveness. Note that Cindy Jackson stated that her transformation into Barbie was the best way of exacting revenge on men.[90] There is a certain prestige attributed to the heavily altered human. Labor and capital are made to be, or appear, permanent and tactile, as it is literally worn on the body. The extremities of beauty express advantage and seek to elicit envy. What Jackson may not have been aware of is the symbol of her unattainability which was her power over men was also the very unattainability of the ideal itself that she was following.

The example of Jedlica, who is representative of a growing cohort of convergent clones, is to emphasize the persistently, and obsessively, queer nature of extreme body modification. This does not only hinge on Jedlica being a gay man, but more philosophically the close relationship between queerness, artificiality and excess. In one publicity stunt, Jedlica even wages war with his human Barbie counterpart, Valeria. In what can only be the most twisted semantics, Jedlica assured Veleria of being "a fake" and to prove that anything could be achieved with make-up dressed up in drag as her "busted twin sister."[91] As Baudrillard remarks apropos of transexuality, that unlike sexuality, which is based in pleasure,

> Transexuality is underpinned by artifice—be it the artifice of actually changing sex or the artifice of the transvestite who plays with the sartorial, morphological, or gestural signs of sex. But whether the matter in question is surgical or semi-surgical, whether it involves organs or signs, we are in any case concerned with replacement parts, and since today the body is fated to become a prosthesis, it is logical enough that our model of sexuality should have become transsexuality, and that transsexuality should have everywhere become the locus of seduction.[92]

The site of pleasure is eternally displaced through its highly mediated and ambiguous other. It is angel and a homunculus that have melded into one. Further, "The sexual revolution, by liberating all the potentialities of desire, raises another fundamental question, 'Am I a man or a woman?'"[93]

## The incorporated doll and the internalized fetish

The examples of Cindy Jackson, Lukyanova or Jedlica are but a few among what is a world-wide trend in which people seek to consume happiness through wholesale body modification. The need to undergo an excessive number of plastic surgeries is typically understood as an extreme form of body dysmorphia, a dissatisfaction with one's body coupled by a need to change it, a need that can range from a hankering to a violent urge. Considering the body rendered doll by surgical intervention from another psychological standpoint is in terms of introjection such that we might come to speculate on a new condition of the "incorporated doll." In psychoanalysis "incorporation" is the failed or corrupted form of introjection. Coined by Sandor Ferenczi in 1912, *introjection* is defined as "an extension to the external world of original autoerotic interests, by including its objects in the ego." Thus, "man can love only himself; if he loves an object he takes it into his ego."[94] In her famous analysis of this essay, "The Illness of Mourning and the Fantasy of the Exquisite Corpse," Maria Torok observes that introjection is not about the loss of the love-object, which would in fact bring the process to an end. Rather, introjection "does not tend toward compensation, but growth . . . enriching the ego."[95] Incorporation resembles introjection but is instigated by loss as opposed to love, and it is this loss that prevents introjection from taking place. As Torok puts it:

> Incorporation may operate by means of representations, affects, or bodily states, or use two or three of these means simultaneously. But, whatever the instrument, incorporation is invariably distinct from introjection (a gradual process) because it is instantaneous and magical. The object of pleasure being absent, incorporation obeys the pleasure principle and functions by way of processes similar to hallucinatory fulfillments.[96]

Moreover, as Torok explains it is this "magic'" that surmounts the possibility of revealing its inner nature or cause. In the case of the incorporated doll, the human as "normally," consensually, conceived is disavowed and used only as a canvas or working material. Torok continues: "Refusing both the object's and reality's verdict, incorporation is an eminently illegal act; it must hide from view along with the introjection it masks; it must hide even from the ego. Secrecy is imperative for its survival."[97] In this regard, it is a highly mournful act that not only disavows the self, but also disavows the mutability of the self in the immanence of aging. "While introjection of desires puts an end to objectal dependency, incorporation of the object creates or reinforces imaginary ties and hence dependency."[98] The incorporated doll is entirely dependent on the fabricated image it mimics. Thus, the body inhabits its own other, as Carole Spitzack suggests, women's bodies "are replaced by replicas or 'fictions' of women."[99] To become plastic, as Rogers terms it,[100] is a transformation as tragic as it is liberating, occurring on several levels of the imaginary. It also relies on a continuous physically coercive act of persuasion ("can you see what I resemble?"), for unlike something natural, we are tied to our facsimile and to people who can make the connection, without which, we are criminals, monsters or mad. By being something fictional, a comic book, we are eminently bound to failure because we are, for all intents and purposes, living and real. It is a Faustian pact with technology—until inexorable old age sets in, then death.

To extend this line of thinking, the incorporated doll is also the attempt to internalize the fetish, to conjoin the subject and object, real and imaginary, into one. Where once the doll was a role model, the incorporated doll becomes that model and assumes that role. Here, surgical procedures are that of a continual line of partial fulfillments, which are effectively consumed on the surface of the body. As opposed to "maintenance" as a result of minor dysmorphic disorder, or the need to render ourselves more "natural," with the incorporated doll flight from nature is key, and maintenance becomes displaced in the act of new creation. Its celebratory face hides what is truly a highly mournful act, for unlike the disgruntled housewife who seeks improvements in the attainment of a "lifelike" model, the incorporated doll wants to be something that does, and cannot, exist.

# 8
# FUTURE POSTSCRIPT: SHELLS AND GHOSTS, BODIES AND SOULS

*Most of the little ones want above all to see the soul, some after a little recreation, others straight away. It is the greater or lesser invasion of desire that determines the greater or smaller longevity of the toy. I feel I don't have the gumption to reproach this childhood mania: it's the first metaphysical tendency. When the desire is stuck in the marrow of the child's brain it fills his fingers and nails with a singular agility and force. The child twists his toy and twists it again, scratches it, shakes it, beating it on walls, throwing it on the ground. From time to time, he makes it do its mechanical movements again, sometimes in an inverse direction. The life of marvels ends. The child, like the people sitting in the Tuileries, makes a supreme effort: finally he opens it up with all his strength. But where is the soul? This is where the confusion and sadness begins.*

—CHARLES BAUDELAIRE[1]

The eternal problem of the doll and the soul, of life and the perception of life, of feeling and the illusion of feeling are at the epicenter of Mamoru Oshii's anime film *Ghost in the Shell* (1995) and the later sequel *Ghost in the Shell 2: Innocence* (2004). Both are about the plight of automata policemen, who at turns find themselves in dilemmas considered germane to humans and not machines. Their confusion must be carried out in secret as there is no prevailing way to account for the nature of affect in something that is not bona fide human. While all animated and fictional, the films elide the anxiety that surfaces from the Enlightenment onward over whether machines will surpass humans by insisting that this relationship is far more manifold and confused, with cyborg and the robot now a central component to society and sociability. Writing at around the same time as when the first manga series from Masamune Shirow, *The Ghost in the Shell*, was aired (1989), Baudrillard presciently points out that "The cybernetic revolution, in view of the equivalence of brain and computer, places humanity before the crucial question, 'Am I a man or a machine?' The genetic revolution that is taking place at the moment raises the question, 'Am I a man or just a clone?'"[2]

*Ghost in the Shell* tells of a world that is a vast electronically connected network to which humanity has access through "shells," which are artificial, cybernetic bodies. The main protagonist is Major Motoko Kusanagi, who has been charged to lead an assault team to hunt down a hacker called the Puppet Master. It shortly becomes clear that the lines between human, part-human and cyborg have all but been destroyed; everything is filtered with technology one or another degree; there are robots, there are cyborgs and there are "ghost hacked humans." Kusanagi is a cyborg imbued with affect, she sleeps and her life is one of lonely melancholy. As a technological enhanced being, Kasanagi is capable of superhuman actions. One suspect is a garbage man who was brainwashed to make him believe he has a wife and child when in "reality" he had been living alone all along. Human memories are just so much information, which in the scheme of things is just a "drop in the bucket." Somewhere near the middle of the film, Kusanagi asks her off-sider Batou, "How much of your body is original?"—after which she gives him a small lecture about her superiority to humans, including her ability to process alcohol, enabling her to knock back liquor endlessly without negative effects. "I suppose an occasional tune-up is a small price to pay for all this." But this technological bliss is at the price of being at the behest of the state; to retire is to forego "augmented brains and cyborg bodies. There wouldn't be much left after that!"[3] This suggests that humans and machines have found their integrated complement.

Dialogues such as these raise the suspicion, which rise as the film unfolds, that the inventive, lush animated tableaux and the plot itself, is itself a visual and narrative apparatus that is a meditation on what this integration of human and machine actually constitutes, and how this cybernetic ontology is systematically defined. In another bout of soul searching, Kusanagi asks Batou if he thinks that he saw a similarity between her and a robot, admitting that "cyborgs like myself have a tendency to be paranoid about our origins. Sometimes I suspect I'm not who I think I am: like maybe I died a long time ago and someone took my brain and stuck it in this body. Maybe there never was a real me in the first place I'm completely synthetic like that thing." Batou replies that she is treated like other humans, "so stop with the angst," a curious word to use, even if in translation, since it is so often applied to describe quintessential existential conflict. But it is only the way she is treated, she replies, that is the only things that makes her feel human. The robot, suspected to be inhabited by the Puppet Master challenges a human over the proof of his existence, "how can you? When neither modern science nor philosophy can explain what life is." He explains that he "is a living thinking entity that was created in the sea of information," and not artificial intelligence. The film's denouement occurs with the Puppet Master merging with Kusanagi who, at the end, exits the film like a melancholy lone gun, but one uncertain as to whom she is.

The ambiguity that she faces between her and a robot mirrors, or displaces, the relationship between her and a human. For the issue of contention is not only one of affect, it is one of control. The word *robot* was coined by the Czech writer Karel Capek for his 1920 play *R.U.R.* about a group of mechanical bodies used as labouers who rise up against their makers. In Capek's Czech, the word was *robotoi*, which he related to the Latin word *servitude*, the word *rab*, meaning "slave."[4] At least humans bask in the myth of the bedrock of nature, the irrational but material source of life. With their own mythic logic, robots and cyborgs have some rational element immanent to them: They have been made with someone or something with the technology to do so, and with some intent. At least, humans do not know whence they sprang. For a cyborg or robot not to know is a lapse in data, a misprision or the presence of some clandestine secret. Or then, there could still be some ambiguity analogous to what humans feel. But the question is whether it is truly analogous or arising from a wholly different order.

In the sequel, the song to the opening credits is a choral piece by Kawai Kenji—reprised throughout the film in three different variants—entitled *Song of Puppets* (*Kugutsu uta*) in which a *nue*, a chimera-like creature with the head of a monkey, raccoon dog's body, tiger's legs and the tail of a snake, bemoans the spirits of flowers "their dreams having faded away" and awaits a time when the "gods will descend." From the outset, the song indicates from the extinction of the real or organic human and a dark Miltonian Fall from innocence and beauty, yet also anticipating a new framework of being.[5]

We are returned to Batou, still an operative for Section 9, who is called on to investigate some deaths caused by malfunctions in gynoids, female robots, specifically "sexoids," sex robots. As it transpires, the gynoids have been inserted with an inappropriate "ghost." When Batou and his partner Togusa visit the robot maintenance lab, they are told that among the many reasons for dangerous malfunctions in robots is degeneration through lack of maintenance, for "no robot wants to be treated like a disposable item." The particular quality about the androids and gynoids is that they had no utilitarian purpose; they were more like pets. "I wonder why" asks the lab worker, "humans are obsessed with creating robots that resemble them." This then leads to a philosophical conversation completely unbefitting a conventional discussion among policemen. The lab worker discusses the child's use of dolls, and adults' commensurate relation to children, concluding that children are the best solution to the ancient dream of creating animate life. Batou then opens into a monologue about Descartes, supporting the probably apocryphal story his "doll" used to replace his daughter Francine after her death. When they turn to leave, a portion of the outer membrane of the lab worker's eye and brow raise, showing herself to be a cyborg or robot, even though she had been smoking.[6]

Amid many moody, sinister and some violent moments, the most intriguing scene is when Batou and Togusa visit the residence of former soldier now hacker, Kim, who subsists within the shell of a humanoid marionette. His opulent mansion is filled with haunting curiosities, such as a tableau vivant of mannequins at table, to a glassed-in room with holographic birds. The rogue company that had manufactured the faulty gynoids is called Locus Solus ("solitary place"), which is also the title of a novel from 1914 by Raymond Roussel about the sumptuous property containing all manner of wonders, including tableaux vivants and cadavers in preservative liquid.[7] The offending company and the eyrie of Kim's solitude are somehow enfolded.

When they meet Kim, he, or his mechanical shell, is feigning death. Accompanying him in the sham is a hologram that reads, "Life and death come and go like marionettes dancing on a table. Once their strings are cut, they easily crumble." These already manifested on the wall of a crumbling mausoleum, and will again appear painted on a wall of Locus Solus.[8] Kim, who has an obsession with dolls and life-forms that bestride life and death, embarks on another remarkable philosophical monologue:

> I don't understand those who want to replicate humans by breathing souls into dolls. The definition of a truly beautiful doll is a living breathing body devoid of a soul. It's nothing but an unyielding corpse, tiptoeing on the brink of collapse.
>
> Humans are no match for a doll, in form or elegance. You see my dear Batou, the inadequacies of human cognitive ability are the cause for the imperfection of reality. Perfection is possible only for those without consciousness, or with infinite consciousness, in other words, dolls, or gods.[9]

Such sentiments were already presaged in the quotation that opens the film, taken from Villiers's *Future Eve*: "If our gods and hopes are nothing but scientific phenomena, then it must be said that our love is scientific as well."

The policemen are transported into a parallel realm where they revisit the entry into Kim's mansion, but now Togusa faces not the marionette effigy of Kim but his own mechanical doppelgänger, who begins to taunt him.

> You doubt whether a creature that certainly appears to be alive, is really alive. Conversely, you doubt that a lifeless object might actually be alive. The eeriness of dolls come solely from the fact that they are completely modelled on human beings. In fact, they are nothing but human, really. They make us face the fear of being reduced to simple mechanisms and matter. In other words, they make us face the fear that, fundamentally, all humans belong to the void.
>
> Science, seeking to unlock the secret of life, also brought about this fear. The notion that nature can be calculated inevitably leads to the conclusion that humans too can be reduced to basic mechanical parts.[10]

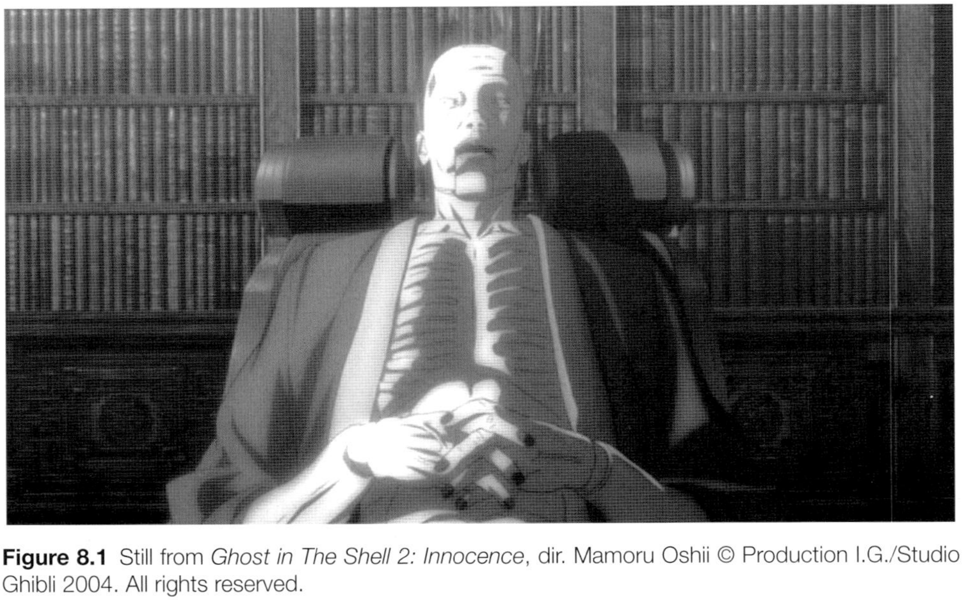

**Figure 8.1** Still from *Ghost in The Shell 2: Innocence*, dir. Mamoru Oshii © Production I.G./Studio Ghibli 2004. 

Whereupon the phlegmatic Batou, extraordinarily, adds, "La Mettrie said that the human is a machine which winds its own springs. It is the living example of perpetual motion." Kim continues:

> The modern technologies of robotics and electronic neurology resurrected the eighteenth century theory of man as machine. From the time computers have made eternal memory possible, humans have pursued self-mechanization aggressively in order to expand the limits of their own function. Determined to leave Darwinian natural selection behind, this human determination to beat evolutionary odds also reveals the desire to transcend nature, the very things that gave birth to humankind. The mirage of life, equipped with perfect hardware, is the very source of this nightmare.[11]

Togusa's confrontation with his mechanically activated double recalls what Freud observes of the uncanny, that is, can be precipitated when "what is human is perceived as merely mechanical" as when the body convulses from epilepsy or illness or the movements of somnambulism. The obverse is just true for automata since "what is perceived as human is in fact mechanical."[12] The film ensures that these relationships remain tightly woven, and therefore, completely confounded.

When Batou infiltrates the Locus Solus ship, he is confronted with an army of gynoids that bear a startling resemblance to Hans Bellmer's ball-jointed dolls, and the way in which they break up and distort when fired only confirms this. Then he encounters a portion of Kusanagi's ghost inhabiting one of the generics. She assists him in confronting another battery of dolls that continue to writhe and disarticulate as if in homage to Bellmer. Bellmer's presence throughout the movie is strong to the point of allegorical, with references that begin with the doll in the opening sequence that commits suicide by pulling out her own innards, a direct allusion to a drawing by Bellmer of a girl opening up her torso and staring at her innards.[13] In the course of his investigation, Batou chances on a copy of the Bellmer book, *The Doll*, which Steven Brown sees as an encounter that reveals the film's very conceptual fulcrum:

> By situating the holographic image of the missing girl inside the book of *The Doll* by Bellmer, Oshii provides us with a visual metaphor that anticipates Batou's eventual discovery of the kidnapped girls held by Locus Solus for the purpose of ghost-dubbing. In effect, just as Bellmer's book on artificial dolls [sic] contains the simulacrum of the captive girl inside it, so too, the Locus Solus gynoids have been instilled with the simulacrum of the adolescent girls held captive. In this way, the reversibility of inside and outside that so deeply interested Bellmer is reenvisionsed by Oshii as a critique of the anthropomorphization of gynoids and other robots. Why is it necessary to make robots in our own image? Is it possible to coexist with forms of artificial intelligence without forcing them into the human mould?[14]

For her part, Kusanagi only imperfectly inhabits the gynoid as the machine's capacity for data storage is commensurate to its designed intention. Yet, it is through this fractured habitation that Kusanagi finds some contentment.

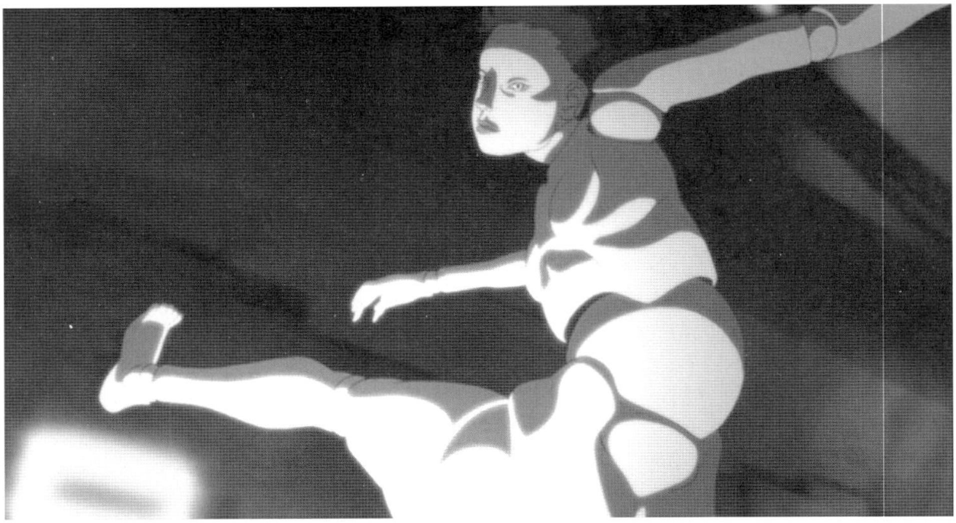

**Figure 8.2** Still from *Ghost in The Shell 2: Innocence*, dir. Mamoru Oshii © Production I.G./Studio Ghibli 2004. All rights reserved.

Toward the end, they both stand in the manufacturing plant and Kusanagi falls into a reverie: "If the dolls could speak no doubt they'd scream, 'I don't want to become human!'" Batou: "Can I ask yourself a question? Do you consider yourself finally happy now?" Kusanagi: "A nostalgic value I suppose; to be happy. At least I am free of dilemma now, and that's nice." In the film's conclusion, Batou and Togusa say their goodbyes in

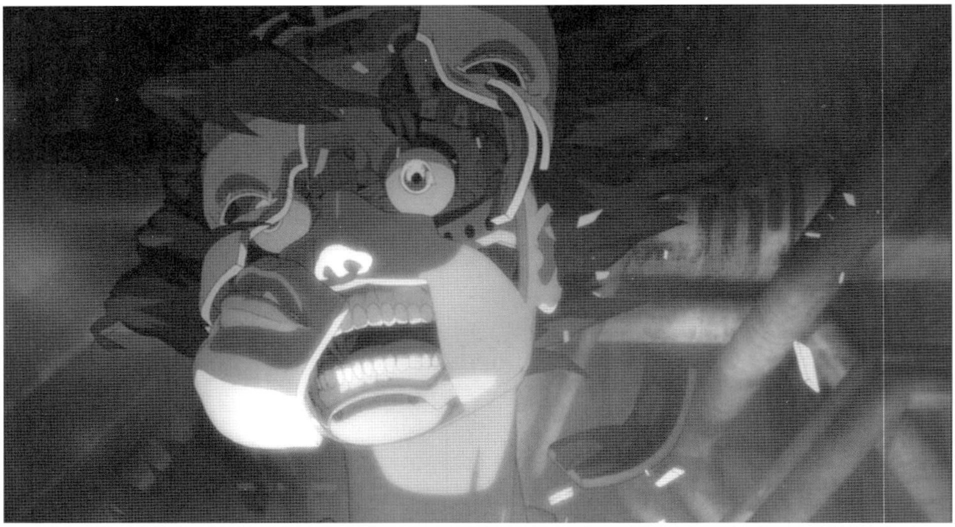

**Figure 8.3** Still from *Ghost in The Shell 2: Innocence*, dir. Mamoru Oshii © Production I.G./Studio Ghibli 2004. All rights reserved.

front of the latter's house. When Togusa's daughter sees her father, she runs to him as he hands her his gift, a doll. A close-up of the doll's face is with a mixture of innocence and menace. Batou, holding his dog, his own ersatz doll, but with more visible affect than he, stares impassively on. Fade out.[15]

While Oshii's two films allow us to embrace in myriad ways the nature of the posthuman future, when the boundary between natural and artificial has eroded to the point of providing a new horizon for consciousness and of ontology itself, it does so using a welter of references that, among those not already mentioned, range from Confucius to Plato to Jacob Grimm. It also contains many allusions to the venerable history of Japan's mechanical dolls, or *mizukumi ningyo*.[16] Whether or not the present cannot do without the past is one matter, but another is whether human versus human doll binary cannot be successfully united or resolved because it is tied in a fundamental agonism, that has to do with humanity's irresolute reaction to death, and the permeability of character, human nature and being. As Kenneth Gross poetically and enigmatically puts it:

> The story of puppets becomes the story of embodied souls and ensouled objects; it insists that our souls are never perfectly our own, as our bodies are never our own. Puppets are entities smaller and larger than any selves we think we know, selves capable of gaining life by giving themselves away. The blackness of the puppet is a blackness of the spirit that is also the blackness of matter, dead preserving moulded, unlighted earth, the blackness of our interior selves, the black hole that is inside our skulls yet made part of the outside world.[17]

This is the allure and the terror of the doll. And perhaps, the desire to become the doll is also the temptation to be able to view the existential drama from the outside, and to grasp Nietzsche's "thought of thoughts" about the finite minuteness of life, with the same mute equanimity as the puppet. For it is the puppet that manages to maintain lifeliness and deathliness all at once. To become the doll is to want to become both the exception and the rule, and thereby, to defy the rules of biological origin or of fate.

# CONCLUSION: BETWEEN BEAUTY AND TERROR

*Would the puppet theater be big? Big and wide? How would the curtain look? A small hole has to cut into it as soon as possible because there was also a peephole in the State Theatre's curtain. . . . Had Grandma or Miss Severin—because Grandma can't do everything—found the decorations needed for Fidelio? As soon as it was morning he would decide on a site and do a show all on his own . . . And already the figures in his heart began singing, because music had immediately bound him close to the theatre.*

—THOMAS MANN, *BUDDENBROOKS*[1]

This vignette out of the life of the young Hanno is indicative of the innocent open experience of children. In the age when puppet theater was an active part of children's lives, it was normal for plots of plays, operas and legends to be transcribed as a foretaste of the more complex adult experience to come. They were pared, accessibly diminutive narrative models, much as dolls since antiquity had been a way of instilling in girls qualities of womanly virtue. The irony of her awaiting with such delight at the adaptation of Beethoven's opera about conjugal love and human dignity is not lost on readers, given that Hanno's mother had endured shame from not one, but two marriages. Temporarily insulated from the grimness of life, her sentiments are of the welcoming variety, and perhaps, just before the Baudelairean rage kicks in, the first metaphysical conflict that reveals the inadequacy and opacity of the world. The next reference to puppets is startling more chilling and frank: When Thomas contemplates the body of his deceased mother, he is overwhelmed by the inert materiality of the corpse, such that she reminds him of being a mere puppet, a lifeless human shell.[2]

This is the evolution, the osmosis of the doll that this book has traced: first from benign ventriloquism, then to trepidation and fear, and finally, to the odd synthesis between doll and human. This can take many forms. It may be as an idea in which the doll is the corrective the arbitrariness and nonspecificity of what we deem to be our soul. It may be an expedient in which we are compelled to combine with prosthetics for survival. Or it can be aesthetic in the disavowal of one's physical humanity, a flight from the "warts and all" to a new plastic transcendence.

There are still more conditions, such as when adults adapt their lives to dolls. But without childishness, without the simple wonder at the world, adult play, and finally, adult over-identification with their objects of play, ends grotesquely. This is because the confusion of adult life and play ritualizes a contradiction that highlights a need to reimagine, rerender the world according to a regressive formula, resulting in circumstances that are comic and tragic. One of the more memorable instances of this in literature is the scene in the second part of Cervantes's *Don Quixote* when Don Quixote believes a puppet theater to be real and attacks the set. The story he witnesses is a knight who goes to rescue his wife from the hands of the Moors. At the peak of the drama, embroiled in the story to a hallucinatory pitch:

> Don Quixote, seeing such a number of Moors, and hearing such alarm, thought it high time to assist the flying lovers; and starting up, "It shall never be said while I live," cried he aloud, "That I suffered such a wrong to be done to so famous a knight and so daring a lover as Don Gayferos. Forbear then your unjust pursuit, ye base rascals: stop, or prepare to meet my furious resentment." Then drawing out his sword, to make good his threats, at one spring he gets to the show, and with violent fury lays at the Moorish puppets, cutting and slashing in a most terrible manner; some he overthrows, and beheads others; maims this, and cleaves that in pieces.[3]

Don Quixote makes good on his destruction by refunding the puppet-master, Master Peter, for his misdeeds. Other tales do not end so neatly, and when applied to the present day, those who have relationships with dolls, do so less out of gormless, hotheaded reaction, and more as a conscious choice, a suspension of belief in certain ways of the world.

But we cannot necessarily decry these kinds of human affect as they have evolved, or transmogrified, into the present. It is a reaction to having felt unscrupulously played, manipulated and controlled by the wiles of the adult world. This suspicion is not confined to an exceptional and lonely few, it is that of many who feel suffocated by their powerlessness. This experience has its greatest dramatic expression in Ibsen's *Doll's House* about a woman who feels oppressed by her world and her lack of agency within it. In the third act she confesses to her husband, that she has never been happy, despite or because of, the pantomime that her life has been:

> . . . you have always been so kind to me. But our house has been nothing but a playroom. I have been your doll-wife, just as at home I was papa's doll-child; and here the children have been my dolls. I thought it great fun when you played with me, just as they thought it great fun when I played with them. That is what our marriage has been, Torvald.[4]

Her penultimate line to her husband is, "Oh Torvald, I don't believe any longer in wonderful things happening."[5] It is the antithesis of the innocent, playful dolls of childhood that introduce the potentialities of life. But at the same time, a child pins his or her hopes on something far different from an adult.

When this is tipped to the extreme, the doll is the rattling carapace for what is well beyond our grasp. It is not only the extension of a physical limit, but a moral limit as well. In André Gide's novella *Isabelle*, the mysterious eponymous figure appears to the narrator in dream, the only figure dressed in white amid a somber crowd:

> She at first appeared to as charming, quite similar to what that locket had depicted, but in an instant I was struck by the immobility of her features, the fixity of her gaze, and suddenly I understand what someone had whispered into her ear: this was not the real Isabella here but a puppet resembling her that had been put in her place in absence of the real one. For me now this puppet appeared horrible; I was disturbed, to the point of anguish, at its air of pretentious stupidity. . . .[6]

This is a common theme that is exploited in any number of modern doll tales and movies: the charming face turned horrible in an instant, the symbolic sudden transition from childhood ingenuousness to the realization of the true gruesomeness of the world, human cruelty, the impassability of fate, the implacability of death.

Anyone with a taste for the horror genre will know the doll subgenre. It begins perhaps with Ernst Lubitsch's *The Doll* (1919) and Paul Leni's *Waxworks* (1924), although neither are strictly ranked as horror. Tod Browning, five years after the classic *Dracula* (1931), directed *The Devil-Doll* (1936) about a scientist who is working on a formula to reduce people to a sixth of their size in order to conserve the world's resources. Films about possessed dolls include *Dolly Dearest* (1991) and *Annabelle* (2014)—a prequel to *The Conjuring*, which contains the line "we are all dolls!"—one of the highest grossing horror films of all time.

The living dolls, such as models and celebrities, began once as dolls, but take on a new persona in the very same age as the growth of bodybuilding and the mass-corporatization of celebrity in the 1980s. Perhaps the first supermodel was the Swedish born Lisa Fonssagrives, whose fame reached her height in the 1940s and 1950s, especially with the photographic eye of Horst. In the 1960s and 1970s, celebrities such as Brigitte Bardot and Talitha Getty were also models. Notwithstanding, it was only a decade later that the phenomenon of the supermodel came into her own, a figure endowed with the embodied symbolic power of celebrity itself. She was defined by a special paradox, namely, that she was uniquely herself—a woman with a personality and a history—who was ably able to inhabit myriad forms, roles and looks. She was therefore both particular and generic. The original supermodels of this age (Linda Evangelista, Naomi Campbell, Iman, Cindy Crawford) were distinct from the actor since the role play, and the in-habiting, was simultaneously inscribed by the sine qua non of personality, albeit suspended. They are simultaneously mannequins and themselves.

This wavering between self and nonself, and the intriguing oscillation between life and nonlife constitutes our relationship with the doll. In light of technology, it is a relationship from which it is harder for us to distance. For whether it be extreme cases of living dolls, digital photographic retouching or the virtual spectacles of CGI, this is an era when the doll is present both physically and psychologically. With all the contradictions that this will allow, it is the mute and inanimate conscience of human modified from its birthed image as well as the avatar, or the decoy, that hints at a new way of understanding the self, especially in innumerable ways in which the illusion of self coalesces as a result of illusions we exert on our world and the alterations, innocuously miniscule or crushingly violent, wrought on our body. In the doll, and its multiple incarnations, we face, with joy or with apprehension, our dissolution. And it is the continual presentiment, and reminder, of this dissolution that confers the ability for us to think ourselves whole, and to delude ourselves that we are autonomous and independent of them.

# NOTES

## Introduction

1 Plutarch, *Makers of Rome*, trans. and ed. Ian Scott-Kilvert (Harmondsworth: Penguin, 1965), 50.

2 Slavoj Zizek, *The Most Sublime Hysteric: Hegel with Lacan*, trans. Thomas Scott-Railton (London: Polity, 2014), 27.

3 Kate Elderkin, "Jointed Dolls of Antiquity," *American Journal of Archaeology* 34, no. 4 (October–December 1930).

4 Rudolf Degen, "Kinderspielzeug ist seit den ältesten Epochen der Menschheit bekannt und findet sich zu allen Zeiten und allen Kulturen. 'Römischen Puppenhaus Octodorus/Martigny'," *Helvetia archaeologica* 28 (1997): 18.

5 See, for example, Richard Carter and Perry Mason, "Selection and Use of Puppets in Counseling," *Professional School Counseling* 1, no. 5 (June 1998): 50–53, or Florence Brady, "The Use of Marionettes in Theatre," *English Elementary Review* 22, no. 5 (May 1945): 182–185. Brady's essay is an early but still instructive example of such pedagogical literature in which she vouches for the benefits of community activity as well as auditory and visual development.

6 See, for example, Katharina Sommer, *Maskenspiel in Therapie und Pädagogik* (Bielefeld and Basel: Edition Sirius, 2009).

7 John Styles, "The Appeal of Mr. Punch," Laurence Kominz and Mark Levenson eds, *The Language of the Puppet* (Vancouver and Washington: Pacific Puppetry Center Press, 1990), 82.

8 Kenneth Gross, *The Dream of Moving Stone* (Ithaca and London: Cornell U.P., 1992), 33.

9 See, for example, Talia Welsh, "Child's Play: Anatomically Correct Dolls and Embodiment," *Human Studies* 30, no. 3 (September 2007): 255–267; and Gail Goodman and Christine Aman, "Children's Use of Anatomically Detailed Dolls to Describe an Event," *Child Development* 61, no. 6 (December 1990): 1859–1871.

10 For an excellent examination of the Real Doll phenomenon, see Marquard Smith, "RealDoll: Intimacy, Domesticity and Brutality," *The Erotic Doll: A Modern Fetish* (New Haven and London: Yale U.P., 2013).

11 Slavoj Zizek, *Tarrying With the Negative* (Durham: Duke U.P., 1993), 12.

12 Ibid., 15.

13 Ibid., 84.

14 Plato, *Laws* (360 B.C.E.), Book VII, trans. Benjamin Jowett, MIT classics, available at http://classics.mit.edu/Plato/laws.7.vii.html.

15 "May we not conceive each of us living beings to be a puppet of the Gods, either their plaything only, or created with a purpose—which of the two we cannot know?" Plato, *Laws*, Book I, available at http://classics.mit.edu/Plato/laws.1.i.html.

**16** Immanuel Kant, *Critique of Practical Reason*, trans. L. W. Beck (New York and London: Palgrave Macmillan, 1956), 152–153.

**17** Slavoj Zizek, "Fichte's Laughter," in Markus Gabriel and Slavoj Zizek, *Mythology, Madness and Laughter: Subjectivity in German Idealism* (London and New York: Continuum, 2009), 140–141.

**18** See Kate Berridge, *Waxing Mythical: The Life and Legend of Madame Tussaud* (London: John Murray, 2006), 41.

**19** In his argument for the formalistic model of acting in Shakespeare, Marvin Rosenberg concludes "The drama of Shakespeare's time was an explosion of art in which the artists—playwrights—shaped their conceptions of human nature and human dreams into acting materials much too rich and diverse to fit into fixed categories." Marvin Rosenberg, "Elizabethan Actors: Men or Marionettes?" *PML A* 69, no. 4 (September 1954): 925.

**20** See Harold Segel, *Pinocchio's Progeny: Puppets, Marionettes, Automatons and Robots in Modernist and Avant-Garde Drama* (Baltimore and London: Johns Hopkins U.P., 1995), 49.

**21** Ibid., 51.

**22** Note that we (Vicki Karaminas and I) use this essay to open our book *Queer Style* as a way of introducing the relationship of queer identity to artificiality. Adam Geczy and Vicki Karaminas, *Queer Style* (New York and London: Bloomsbury, 2013).

**23** Heinrich von Kleist (1810), "Über das Marionettentheater," *Sämtliche Werke* (Leipzig: Im Insel Verlag, n.d.).

**24** For a good study on Pygmalion and the attendant myths and compulsions, see Kenneth Gross, *The Dream of the Moving Statue* (Ithaca and London: Cornell U.P., 1992).

**25** Ibid., 42.

**26** Charles Dickens, *The Old Curiosity Shop* (1841) (Harmondsworth: Penguin, 1972), 288.

**27** Ibid., 289.

**28** Judith Halberstam and Ira Livingston, eds, *Posthuman Bodies* (Bloomington: Indiana U.P., 1995), 3ff.

**29** Available at http://www.i-am-bored.com/bored_link.cfm?link_id=98068 (Last accessed February 15, 2015).

**30** See, for example, Meredith Jones, *Skintight: An Anatomy of Cosmetic Surgery* (London and New York: Berg, 2008); and Anne Balsamo, "Plastic Surgery and the Technological Production of the Gendered Body," in Nicholas Mirzoeff ed., *The Visual Culture Reader*, 2nd edn. (London and New York: Routledge, 2002). On the cultural phenomenon of the body builder phenomenon in film and the 1980s, see Susan Jeffords, *Hard Bodies: Hollywood Masculinity in the Reagan Era* (New Brunswick: Rutgers U.P., 1994).

**31** Writing as "early" as 2000, Zizek observes that "although sociopolitical life and its structure were always-already the outcome of hegemonic struggle, it is none the less only today, in our specific historical constellation—in the 'postmodern' universe of globalized contingency—that the radically contingent-hegemonic nature of political processes is finally allowed to 'come/return to itself', to free itself of 'essentialist' baggage. . . ." There is no need to get bogged down in the details of this passage, but rather to emphasize that this book proposes the same radical break *mutatis mutandis* with regard to our bodies. Zizek, "Holding the Place," in Judith Butler, Ernesto Laclau and Slavoj Zizek, *Contingency, Hegemony, Universality* (London and New York: Verso, 2000), 319.

**32** Paul Hazard, *La Crise de la conscience européenne 1680–1715* (Paris: Fayard, 1961).

**33** Stefan Herbrechter, "The Posthuman Subject in *The Matrix*," in Myriam Diocaretz and Stefan Herbrecher, eds, *The* Matrix *in Theory* (Amsterdam and New York: Rodopi, 2006), 286.

**34** Theodor W. Adorno, *Zur Metcritique der Erkentnisstheorie; Drei Studien zu Hegel* (Frankfurt am Main: Suhrkamp, 1970), 35.

**35** Zizek, *Tarrying*, 40.

**36** Donna Harraway, "Manifesto for cyborgs: science, technology, and socialist feminism in the 1980s," *Socialist Review* 80, 1985, 65–108, reprinted as "A Cyborg Manifesto: Science, Technology and Socialist-Feminism in the Late Twentieth Century," in Donna Harraway, *Simians, Cyborgs and Women: The Reinvention of Nature* (London and New York: Routledge, 1991).

**37** Elaine Graham, "Cyborgs or Goddesses? Becoming Divine in a Postfeminist Age," in Eileen Green and Alison Adam, eds, *Virtual gender: Technology, Consumption and Identity* (London and New York: Routledge, 2001), 307.

**38** Ibid., 308.

**39** Available at https://www.youtube.com/watch?v=wow2utprEoM (Last accessed February 15, 2015).

**40** Sigmund Freud, *Civilization and its Discontents*, trans. James Strachey, in Peter Gay, ed., *The Freud Reader* (New York: Norton, 1995), 738.

**41** As Katherine Hayles writes, in the posthuman paradigm, "human functionality expands because the parameters of the cognitive system it inhabits expand. In this model, it is not a question of leaving the body behind, but rather of extending embodied awareness in highly specific, local, and material ways that would be impossible without electronic prosthesis." *How We Became Posthuman* (Chicago and London: Chicago U.P., 1999), 290–291.

**42** A few disclaimers, as the still modest filmography at the back of this book will show, dolls, automata and artificial intelligence are an important and very rich subject in film dating from its beginning in films such as Fritz Lang's *Metropolis*. This book uses film but purposely avoids the temptation to go too far into that direction, simply because the area is vast, worth the subject of its own discrete study, and therefore, beyond the reach of this book. Similarly, dolls from Asia and Southeast Asia, for instance, such as Baraku in Japan or the shadow theater of Wayang of Java in Indonesia, are not featured here, again not out of artful neglect, but because the examples explored within the book help to formulate the various issues regarding the aesthetic, moral and practical relationships we have with artificial bodies. The elisions are for the sake of economy and balance.

## 1 Clothes of Carnival: Personal Puppeteering and Role Play

**1** Molière, *Le Malade imaginaire*, *Œuvres complètes 4* (Paris: Flammarion, 1979), 409. "Ah! ah! ah! ah! comme je leur ai donné l'épouvante! Volià less sottes gens d'avoir peur de moi, qui ai peur des autres. Ma foi! il n'est que de jouer d'adresse en ce monde. Si je n'avais tranché du grande seigneur, et n'avais fait le brave, ils n'auraient pas manqué de me happer. Ah! ah! ah! ah!"

**2** Commentators vary on this point. For instance, Robert Henke, asserts that "The term 'commedia dell'arte' can be traced to the eighteenth century but may well have been in circulation before then." *Performance and Literature in the Commedia Dell'Arte* (Cambridge and New York: Cambridge U.P., 2002), 5.

**3** Constant Mic, *La Commedia dell'arte, ou le théatre des comediens italiens des XVIe, XVIIe et XVIIIe siècles* (Paris: Librairie Théatrale, 1980), 25; and Henke, *Performance and Literature in the Commedia Dell'Arte*, 5.

**4** Natalie Crohn Schmitt, "Improvisation in the Commedia dell'Arte in its Golden Age: Why, What, How," *Renaissance Drama* 38 (2010): 225–249. This essay reflects this and cites a sizeable amount of literature in this regard.

**5** Franco Tonelli, "Molière's *Don Juan* and the Space of the Commedia dell'Arte," *Theatre Journal* 37, no. 4, December (1985): 443.

**6** Gustave Attinger, *L'Esprit de la Commedia dell'arte dans le théâtre français* (Paris and Neuchâtel: Librairie Théâtral, 1950) 433.

**7** Max Wolff, "Zur Commedia dell'arte," *Zeitschrift für Französische Sprache und Literatur* 58, no. 7/8 (1934): 422.

**8** Ibid., 227.

**9** Kathleen McGill, "Women and Performance: The Development of Improvisation by the Sixteenth-Century," *Theatre Journal* 43, no. 1 (March 1991): 59–69; Jane Tylus, "'Women at the Windows: 'Commedia dell'arte' and Theatrical Practice in Early Modern Italy," *Theatre Journal* 49, no. 3 (October 1997): 323–342.

**10** For an extended examination of the influence of the commedia dell'arte on Elizabethan theater, see Winifred Smith, "Italian and Elizabethan Comedy," *Modern Philology* 5, no. 4 (April 1908): 555–567.

**11** David George, "Joan Brossa and the 'Commedia dell'arte," *Anales de la literatura española contemporánea* 20, no. 3, Drama/Theater (1995): 343.

**12** In the words of Jindrich Honzl, "the greatest historical exception to our current understanding of dramatic character is the *commedia dell'arte*, where conventional stage figures like Harlequin and Pantalone were transformed from one scenario to another." Cit. Michael Quinn, "Svek's Stage Figure: Illustration, Design, and the Representation of Character," *Comparative Drama* 31, no. 3 (September 1988): 330.

**13** Anne McNeil, *Music and Women of the Commedia dell'Arte in the late Sixteenth Century* (Oxford and New York: Oxford U.P., 2003), 1.

**14** See Allerdyce Nicoll, *Masks, Mimes and Miracles* (New York: Cooper Square, 1963); and Kathleen Lea, *Italian Popular Comedy: A Study in the Commedia Dell'Arte 1560–1620* (New York: Russell and Russell, 1962).

**15** Paul Castagno, *The Early Commedia Dell' Arte, 1550–1621: The Mannerist Context* (New York: Peter Lang, 1994), 85.

**16** Ibid.

**17** Arnold Hauser, *Mannerism* (Belknap Press of Harvard U.P., 1965), 329.

**18** See also the interesting but now largely outdated book by Efrat Tseëlon, *Masquerade and Identities: Essays in Gender, Sexuality and Marginality* (London: Routledge, 2001). As Tseëlon comments: "Masks, says Eliade (1990) are a means of dealing with otherness. Indeed, they represent the quintessential Other, its inversion, and the impossibility of transcending it." 3.

**19** Mic, *La Commedia dell'arte*, 162–163.

**20** Charles Sterling, "Early Paintings of the Commedia Dell'Arte un France," *The Metropolitan Museum of Art Bulletin*, New series, 2, no. 1 (Summer 1943): 16.

**21** There are numerous and conflicting sources for these types. This list refers principally to that supplied by Bernard Joubert, in *La Commedia dell'arte et son influence en France du XVIe au XVIIIe siècle* (Paris: L'Harmattan, 1999), 45.

**22** R. Reynolds, "Criticism of Individuals in Roman Popular Tragedy," *Classical Quarterly* 37, no. 1/2 (January–April 1943): 41.

**23** Ibid.

**24** Antonis Petrides, "Plautus Between Greek Comedy and Atellan Farce: Assessments and Reassessments," in Michael Fontaine and Adele Scafuro eds, *The Oxford Handbook of Greek and Roman Comedy* (Oxford and New York: Oxford U.P., 2014), 425.

25 Judith Hallett, "Plautine Ingredients in the Performance of 'Pseudolis'," *The Classical World* 87, no. 1 (September–October 1993): 26.

26 See documentation in ibid., 25–28.

27 B. Joubert, *La Commedia dell'arte*, 45.

28 Jane Cody, "The 'Senex Amator' in Plautus' Casina," *Hermes*, 104, no. 4 (1976): 467, 474–475.

29 Pierre-Louis Duchartre, *The Italian Comedy*, trans. Randolph Weaver (New York: Dover [1929], 1966), 18.

30 Petrides, "Plautus Between Greek Comedy and Atellan Farce," in Fontaine and Scafuro eds, *The Oxford Handbook of Greek and Roman Comedy*, 425, 434–437.

31 Ibid., 437–438.

32 See Herschel Gerfein, Mel Gordon and Gennaro Tuci, "The Adriani Lazzi of the Commedia Dell'Arte," *The Drama Review: TDR* 22, no. 1, Italian Theatre Issue (March 1978): 3–12.

33 John McDowell, "Some Pictorial Aspects of Early 'Commedia dell'arte' Acting," *Studies in Philology* 39, no. 1 (January 1942): 56.

34 Tseëlon, *Masquerade and Identities*, 3.

35 George Speaight, "Punch and Judy" in Brunela Ernuli ed., *Policinelle* (Chareleville-Mézières: Cahiers Robinson, 1999), 49.

36 Michael Byrom, *Punch in the Italian Puppet Theatre* (Sussex and London: Centaur Press, 1983), 8.

37 Duchartre, *The Italian Comedy*, 209.

38 Ibid., 9.

39 Catherine Velay-Vallantin, "Polichinelle dans le colportage au XIXème siècle," in B. Ernuli ed., *Policinelle*, 92.

40 Purschke, *Die Entwicklung des Puppenspiels*, 18.

41 Charles Mazouer, "Polchinelle en France jusqu'aux théâtres de la Foire," in B. Ernuli ed., *Policinelle*, 19–25.

42 Paul Valéry, "Descartes," *Œuvres I* (Paris: Gallimard Pléiade 1957), 804.

43 The extended passage reads: "Je désire, dis-je, que vous considériez que ces fonctions suivent tous naturellement, en cette machine, de la seule disposition de ses organs, ne plus ne moins que font les mouvements d'une horloge, ou autre automate, de celle de ses contrepoids et de ses roués; en sorte qu'il ne faut point à leur occasion concevoir en elle aucune autre âme vegetative, ni sensitive, ni aucun autre principe de movement et de vie, que son sang et ses esprits, agités par la chaleur du feu qui brûle continuellement dans son cœur, et qui n'est point d'autre nature que tous les feux qui sont dans les corps inanimés." René Descartes, *Le Monde, l'homme* (1630–3), ed. Annie Bitbol-Hespériès and Jean-Pierre Verdet (Paris: Seuil, 1996), 168.

44 Cit. and trans. Desmond Clarke, *Descartes: A Biography* (Cambridge and London: Cambridge U.P., [2006] 2012), 93.

45 Ibid., 92.

46 Ibid.

47 Ibid., 93.

48 Antoine Furetière, *Dictionnaire universel contenant généralement tous les mots François, tant vieux que modernes, & les termes de toutes les sciences et des arts* (The Hague and Rotterdam: Arnout & Reiner Leers, 1690), 3 vols., repr. Paris: Le Robert, 1978, 1984, v. 2, n.p.

**49** Michel Manson, "Policinelle, un jouet pas comme les autres. Quelques pistes de recherché, XVII$^{e}$-XIX$^{e}$ siècles," in B. Ernuli ed., *Policinelle*, 133.

**50** Descartes, *Discours de la méthode* (1637) (Paris: Flammarion, 2000), 67.

**51** Domenico Scafoglio, "Pulcinella/Policinelle: Meéthodologique et perspectives de recherche," in B. Ernuli ed., *Policinelle*, 14. See also Gerald Sandy: "Habinnas" slave takes up some of the slack, giving samples of his virtuoso abilities as a "Vergilianist" and as a performer of Atellan farces (68, no. 4–5), with his master reporting additional details of his talent as a mimus (68, no. 6-7; cf. 69, no. 4–5). It is of some interest that the slave's mingling of different verse forms is reminiscent of Livy's famous description of the introduction of drama, that is, Atellan farce, to Rome (7.2.II). "Scaenica Petronia," *Transactions of the American Philological Association (1974–)* 104 (1974): 336.

**52** Ferdinando Taviani and Mirella Schino, *The Secret de la commedia dell'arte*, trans. Fr. Yves Liebert (Florence: La Casa Usher, 1984), 129–162.

**53** Available at http://en.wikipedia.org/wiki/Zanni.

**54** Michel Foucault, *Madness and Civilization: A History of Insanity in the Age of Reason* (1960), trans. Richard Howard (New York: Random House, 1965).

**55** Duchartre, *The Italian Comedy*, 22.

**56** Ibid., 49. See also Mic: "Tout d'abord, l'acteur qui pose un masque sur son visage, fonde don jeu non plus sur la mobilité de sa physiognomie, mais sur les mouvements de son corps." *La Commedia dell'arte*, 117.

**57** "Ce faquin Harlequin combine/L'enlèvement de Columbine/Et pirouette quatre fois." Paul Verlaine, *Fêtes galantes*, *Poèmes saturniens suivi par Fêtes galantes* (Paris: Livre de Poche, 1972), 135.

**58** Mic, *La Commedia dell'arte*, 118.

**59** Ibid., 119–120.

**60** Joubert, *La Commedia dell'arte*, 20.

**61** See also Segel, *Pinocchio's Progeny*, 40–41.

**62** Sterling, "Early Paintings of the Commedia Dell'Arte un France," 18–20. For a more comprehensive account of early examples of iconography of the commedia, see Paul Castagno, "The International Style of Mannerism and Early Commedia Dell'Arte Iconography," *The Early Commedia Dell'Arte*, 125–143.

**63** See also John McDowell, "Some Pictorial Aspects of Early 'Commedia dell'arte' Acting."

**64** Günther Hansen, *Formern der Commedia dell'Arte in Deitschland* (Emsdetten: Verlag Lechte, 1984), 155.

# 2 A Soul in Control: The Art of the Automaton

**1** Dénis Diderot, *Paradoxe sur le comedien; Entretiens sur le fils natural* (Paris: Flammarion, 1981), 186–187, 151.

**2** Marquard Smith, *The Erotic Doll: A Modern Fetish* (New Haven and London: Yale U.P., 2013).

**3** Joseph Needham, *Science and Civilization in China* (Cambridge and London: Cambridge U.P., 1986), 2:53.

**4** Linda Safran, *Heaven on Earth: Art and the Church in Byzantium* (Pittsburgh: Penn State Press, 1998), 30.

**5** Helmut Swoboda, *Der künstliche Mensch* (Munich: Heimeran, 1967), 64, 72.

**6** Geneviève Rodis-Lewis, "Limitations of the Mechanical Model in the Cartesian Cocneption of the Organism," in Michael Hooker ed., *Descartes: Critical and Interpretative Essays* (Baltimore and London: Johns Hopkins U.P., 1978), 157.

**7** Anthony Grafton, "The Devil as Automaton," in Jessica Riskin ed., *Genesis Redux: Essays in the History and Philosophy of Artificial Life* (Chicago and London: Chicago U.P., 2007), 48.

**8** Ibid., 54.

**9** Ibid., 59.

**10** See the title of Marquard Smith's first chapter: "Visions of Pygmalion: 'I know very well but all the same . . .'," in *The Erotic Doll*, 31ff.

**11** Ovid, *Metamorphoses*, Book 10, trans. Samuel Garth, John Dryden et al., available at http://classics.mit.edu/Ovid/metam.10.tenth.html (Last accessed February 15, 2015).

**12** Jean-Jacques Rousseau, *Œuvres Completes*, ed. Bernard Gagnebin and Marcel Raymond, 4 vols (Paris: Gallimard, 1964), 2:1230–1231. See also Smith, *The Erotic Doll*, 41; and J. L. Carr, "Pygmalion and the *Philosophes*: Animated Statues in Eighteenth-Century France," *Journal of the Warburg and Courtauld Institutes* 23 (1960): 239–255.

**13** Ibid., 46.

**14** Paul de Man, *Allegories of Reading: Figural Language in Rousseau, Nietzsche, Rilke and Proust* (New Haven and London: Yale U.P., 1979), 187.

**15** Descartes, Letter to Plempius Fromondus, January 3, 1637, cit. Rodis-Lewis, "Limitations of the Mechanical Model," in Hooker ed., *Descartes*, 157–158.

**16** Michael Hooker, ed. *Descartes: Critical and Interpretative Essays* (Baltimore and London: Johns Hopkins U.P., 1978), 157.

**17** Descartes, Letter to More, February 5, 1649, cit. ibid., 159.

**18** See Hayles, *How We Became Posthuman*, 194ff; and Elizabeth Grosz, *Volatile Bodies: Toward a Corporeal Feminism* (Bloomington: Indiana U.P., 1994). Grosz's main contenders for study include, Freud, Merleau-Ponty, Nietzsche, Lacan, Foucault, and Deleuze and Guattari.

**19** Gilles Deleuze, *Spinoza: Philosophie pratique* (Paris: Minuit, 1981), 28.

**20** Jessica Riskin, "The Defacating Duck, Or, The Ambiguous Origins of Artificial Life," *Critical Inquiry*, 29, no. 4 (Summer 2003): 602–604.

**21** Cit. Joan Landes, "The Anatomy of Artificial Life: An Eighteenth Century Perspective," in Riskin ed., *Genesis Redux*, 97.

**22** Ibid., 96ff.

**23** Jean-Claude Heudin, *Les Créateures artificielles: des automates aux mondes virtuels* (Paris: Odile Jacob, 2008), 56.

**24** ". . . automate ayant figure humaine & qui, par le moyen de certains resorts, &c. bien disposes, agit & fait finctions extérieurement semblables à celles de l'homme." Jean d'Alembert, "Androïde" (1751), in Dénis Diderot and d'Alenbert eds, *Encyclopédie, ou dictionnaire raisonné des sciences, des arts, et des métiers*, 17 vols (Paris, 1751–1772), I: 448.

**25** Ibid., 57.

**26** JacquesVaucanson, "Letter to the Abbé Desfontaines" (1742 [1738]), *Le Mécanisme du fluteur automate*, trans. J. T. Desaguliers (The Netherlands: Buren, 1979), 21.

**27** Riskin, "The Defacating Duck," 602.

**28** Heudin, *Les Créateures artificielles*, 59.

**29** "Vaucanson's automata were philosophical experiments, attempts to discern which aspects of living creatures could be reproduced in machinery, and to what degree, and what such reproductions might reveal about their natural subjects." Riskin, "The Defacating Duck," 601.

**30** Heudin, *Les Créateures artificielles*, 60.

**31** Sylvia Berryman, "The Imitation of Life in Ancient Greek Philosophy," in Riskin ed., *Genesis Redux*, 36–37.

**32** See Jeanne Abrams, *Revolutionary Medicine: The Founding Fathers and Mothers in Sickness and in Health* (New York: New York U.P., 2014).

**33** See Riskin, "The Defacating Duck," 609.

**34** Cit. Ibid.

**35** Francine du Plessix Gray, *At Home with the Marquis de Sade* (1998) (London: Pimlico, 2000), 46.

**36** Ibid., 61.

**37** Swoboda, *Der künstliche Mensch*, 113–115.

**38** In 1770, the *Vossische Zeitung* reported that a Herr Mowsstyn sold a mobile wooden horse for 100 ducats. Ibid., 120.

**39** Zizek *Tarrying with the Negative*, 126.

**40** Adelheid Voskuhl, "Motions and Passions: Music-Playing Women Automata and the Culture of Affect in Late Eighteenth-Century Germany," in Riskin ed., *Genesis Redux*, 309.

**41** Ibid., 310.

**42** See also M. Smith, *The Erotic Doll*, 72ff.

**43** Mladen Dolar, "At First Sight," in Renata Salecl and Slavoj Zizek eds., *Gaze and Voice as Love Objects* (Durham and London: Duke University Press, 1996), 143.

**44** Ibid.

**45** See also Jeffrey Cox, "The Parasite and the Puppet: Diderot's Neveu and Kleist's 'Marionettentheater'," *Comparative Literature*, 38, no. 3 (Summer 1986): 258–263.

**46** Swoboda, *Der künstliche Mensch*, 127, 135.

**47** Cit. Heudin, *Les Créatures artificiels*, 65–66.

**48** John Johnston, *The Allure of Machanic Life: Cybernetics, Artificial Life, and the New AI* (Cambridge, MA: MIT Press, 2008), 99ff.

**49** Charles Gottlieb de Windisch, *Inanimate Reason, or A Circumstantial Account of that Astonishing Piece of Mechanism, M. De Kempelin's Chess-Player* (London: S. Bladon 1784), vii.

**50** Ibid., 12–13.

**51** Ibid., 31.

**52** Ibid., 32.

**53** Ibid., 26.

**54** Jean Paul, *Werke*, ed. Norbert Miller and Wilhelm Schmidt-Biggermann (Munich: Carl Hanser, 1976), pt 2, 1:1029.

**55** Ibid.

**56** Ibid.

**57** Ibid., 1030, See also Voskuhl, "Motions and Passions" in Riskin ed., *Genesis Redux*, 299–303.

**58** Mark Sussman, "Performing the Intelligent Machine: Deception and Enchantment in the Life of the Automaton Chess Player," in John Bell ed., *Puppets, Masks and Performing Objects* (Cambridge, MA: MIT Press, 2001), 82.

**59** Charles Carroll, *The Great Chess Automaton* (New York: Dover, 1975), 1–2.

**60** Ibid., 39.

**61** Alex Wetmore, "Sympathy Machines: Men of Feeling and the Automaton," *Eighteenth-Century Studies*, 43.1, (Fall 2009), available at http://search.proquest.com.ezproxy1.library.usyd.edu.au/docview/198664826?accountid=14757; my emphasis. Wetmore refers to Adam Freguson and his *An Essay on the History of Civil Society*, 1767.

**62** Ibid.

# 3 Dark Doubles: Dolls as a Solution to the Fallible Body

**1** Edward Gordon Craig, *On the Art of Theatre* (London: Heinemann, 1914), 94.

**2** Maurice Maeterlinck, "The Old Man in *Intérieur*" (1894), in *Théâtre* I-III (Paris and Geneva: Slatkine, 1979), 2:181.

**3** Smith, *The Erotic Doll*, 81.

**4** Augé, *Le Dieu objet* (Paris: Flammarion, 1988), 69–70.

**5** Jean Paul, "Der Machinen-Man nebst seinen Eigenschaften," *Werke* (Munich: Carl Hanser Verlag, 1959–1963), 2: 446–447.

**6** Ibid., 449.

**7** Ibid., 451.

**8** Ibid., 452.

**9** Ibid., 453.

**10** Ibid.

**11** Ibid., 452.

**12** This is expressed gnomically in the famous line by Dostoyevsky, "If God is dead, then everything is possible."

**13** Heinrich von Kleist, "Über das Marionettentheater" (1810), *Sämtliche Werke* (Leipzig: Im Insel Verlag, n.d.), 1142.

**14** Kleist, 1138.

**15** "Etwas über die erste Menschengesellschaft nach dem Leitfaden der mosaischen Urkunde." See also James A. Rushing, "The Limitations of the Fencing Bear: Kleist's 'Über das Marionettentheater' as Ironic Fiction," *The German Quarterly* 61, no. 4 (Autumn 1988): 530.

**16** Ibid., 530.

**17** Peter Michalzik, *Kleist: Dichter, Krieger, Seelensucher* (Berlin: Propyläen, 2011), 428.

**18** Ibid., 428–429.

**19** J. C. F. von Schiller, *Über Anmut und Würde* (1793), available at http://gutenberg.spiegel.de/buch/ueber-anmuth-und-wurde-3320/2.

**20** Ibid.

**21** Ibid.

**22** Maria Glotzbach,*"Strahlend und herrschend"—Kleist's Anspruche an de Graze und ihre Verköerperung im mechanischen Wesen* (Norderstedt: Grin, 2004), 6.

**23** Ibid., 8.

**24** Giorgio Agamben, "The Last Chapter in the History of the World," *Nudities* (2009), trans. David Kishik and Stefan Pedatella (Stanford: Stanford U.P., 2011), 114.

**25** Frank Kermode, "The Dancer," *Romantic Image* (London: Routledge, 1957), 49–91.

**26** Cit. Kermode, 85–86.

**27** "'O du herrliches, du tiefes Gemüt', reif Nathaniel auf seiner Stube: 'nur von dir, von dir allein werd' ich ganz verstanden." E. T. A. Hoffmann, *Der Sandman* (Stuttgart: Philipp Reclam, 1991), 34.

**28** M. Dolar, in Salecl and Zizek eds, *Gaze and Voice as Love Objects*, 144.

**29** Ibid.

**30** Hoffmann, 35.

**31** Rushing, 537.

**32** Theodor W. Adorno, *Aesthetische Theorie* (Frankfurt am Main: Suhrkamp Verlag, 1970), 180–181.

**33** Adorno, 182–183.

**34** Lucia Ruprecht, *Dances of Self in Heinrich von Kleist, E. T. A. Hoffmann and Heinrich Heine* (Hampshire: Ashgate, 2006), 13.

**35** Ibid., 13–14.

**36** Annie Gilles, *Images de la marionette dans la littérature* (Charleville-Mézières and Nancy: Éditions Institut Internationale de la Marionnette and Presses Universitaires de Nancy, 1993), 91–97.

**37** Maurice Maeterlinck, "Menus Propos—Le théâtre' (1890), in Didier Plassard ed., *Les Mains de la lumière: Anthologie des écrits sur l'art de la marionnette* (Charleville-Mézières: Institut International de la Marionnette, 1996), 200.

**38** See Katherine Hayles, *How We Became Posthuman: Virtual Bodies in Cybernetics, Literature and Infomatics* (Chicago and London: Chicago U.P., 1999), 288; and Stefan Herbrecheter, *Posthumanism: A Critical Analysis* (London and New York: Bloomsbury, 2013), 95–101.

**39** See also Segel, *Pinocchio's Progeny*, 49–54.

**40** See James Fisher, "Harlequinade: Commedia dell'Arte on the Early Twentieth-Century British Stage," *Theatre Journal* 41, no.1 (March 1989): 30–44.

**41** Marjorie Garber, "Out of Joint," in David Hillman and Carla Mazzio eds, *The Body in Parts: Fantasies of Corporeality in Early Modern Europe* (New York and London: Routledge, 1997), 39.

**42** Craig, *On the Art of Theatre*, 80.

**43** Ibid., 81.

**44** Ibid., 82.

**45** Ibid., 83. In a related essay, "The Artists of the Theatre of the Future," Craig expresses his abhorrence of theatrical naturalism, and although artificiality is prone to insipidity, he advises "not to forget that there is such a thing as *noble* artificiality," 35.

**46** Ibid., 84.

**47** Craig, "Gentlemen, The Marionette," in Michael Walton ed., *Craig on Theatre* (London: Methuen, 1983), 26.

**48** C. Moody, "Vsevolod Meyerhold and the 'Commedia dell'arte'," *The Modern Language Review* 73, no. 4 (October 1978): 859–860.

**49** Ibid., 860–861.

**50** Ibid., 865.

**51** Ibid., 868.

**52** Rainer Maria Rilke, "Das Theater des Maeterlink" (1901), *Sämtliche Werke* vol. 5 (Frankfurt: Insel Verlag, 1965), 482.

**53** Cristina Grazioli, "*Mensch (Tod) und Kunstfigur*: Figures of Death and Otherness in the Reflections of Rainer Maria Rilke and Oskar Schlemmer," in Carole Guidicelli ed., *Surmarionettes et mannequins: Craig, Kantor et leurs heritages contemporains* (Lavérune and Charleville-Mézières: L'Entretemps Édtions and Institut International des Marionettes, 2013), 167.

**54** Rilke, "Brief an eine Shauspielerin," *Sämtliche Werke* 6 (1966): 1178–1191.

**55** Ibid., 1189.

**56** Rilke, *Die Gedichte* (Frankfurt am Main: Insel Verlag, 1986), 41.

**57** Grazioli, "*Mensch (Tod) und Kunstfigur*," 168.

**58** Rilke, "Puppen: Zu den Wachs-Puppen Lotte Prizel," *Sämtliche Werke* 6, 1063.

**59** Ibid., 1066.

**60** See the epigraph to the final chapter of this book.

**61** Rilke, "Puppen," *Sämtliche Werke* 6, 1072.

**62** Ibid., 1068.

**63** Ibid., 1072.

**64** Rilke, *Die Gedichte*, 641–642.

**65** ". . . wenn mir zumut ist,
zu warten vor der Puppenbühne, nein,
so vollig hinzuschauen, um mein Shauen
am Ende aufzuweigen, dort as Spieler
ein Engel hinmuss, der die Balge hochreisst.
Engel und Puppe: dann ist endlich Shauspiel.
Dann kommt zusammen, was wir immerfort
entzwein, indem wir da sind. Dann entsteht
aus unseren Jahreszeiten erst der Umkreis
des ganzen Wandelns. Über uns hinüber
spielt dann der Engel. Sieh, die Sterbenden.
Sollten sie nicht vermuten, wie voll Vorwand
das alles is ist, was wir lesiten. Alles
ist nicht es selbst. O Stunden in der Kindheit,
da hinter den Figuren mehr als nur
Vergangenes war und vor uns nicht die Zukunft."
Ibid., 643.

**66** Gross, *The Dream of Moving Stone*, 156.

**67** Cit. Marquard Smith, *The Erotic Doll*, 124.

**68** For the best account of Kokoschka's obsession, see ibid., 108–135.

# 4 Between Torture and Transcendence: The Doll in Art

**1** Friedrich Schlegel, *Lucinde* (Frankfurt am Main: Insel Verlag, 1985), 26.

**2** Edith Wharton, *The House of Mirth* (London: Dent, 1993), 33.

**3** George Gordon, Lord Byron, "Prometheus," *Byron*, ed. Jerome McGann (Oxford and New York: Oxford U.P., 1986), 266.

**4** Available at http://www.galleryhistoricalfigures.com/index.html (Last accessed February 15, 2015).

**5** Juliette Koss, "Bauhaus Theater of Human Dolls," *The Art Bulletin* 85, no. 4 (December 2003): 724. See also Susanne Lahusen, "Oskar Schlemmer: Mechanical Ballets?" *Dance Research: The Journal of the Society for Dance Research* 4, no. 2 (Autumn, 1986): 65–77.

**6** Céline Masson, *La Fabrique de la pouppée chez Hans Bellmer* (Paris: Harmatton, 2000); Therese Lichtenstein, *Behind Closed Doors: The Art of Hans Bellmer* (Berkeley and London: California U.P., 2001); Sue Taylor, *Hans Bellmer: The Anatomy of Anxiety* (Cambridge, MA: MIT Press, 2002); Marquard Smith, *The Erotic Doll.*

**7** Lichtenstein, *Behind Closed Doors*, 13.

**8** Hans Bellmer, 1902–1975; Michel de Ghelderode, 1898–1962.

**9** Paul Levitt, "Ghelderode and Puppet Theatre," *The French Review* 48, no. 6 (May 1975): 975–976. See also Michel de Ghelderode, *Théâtre*, 5 vols. (Paris: Gallimard, 1950–1957).

**10** Segel, *Pinocchio's Progeny*, 119–120.

**11** Cit. Jacqueline Blancart-Cassou, "Du grotesque hugolien au grotesque de Ghelderode: l'influence, rencontres, divergences," *Revue d'Histoire littéraire de la France* 100, no. 5 (September–October 2000): 1348–1349.

**12** Cit. Helen Hellman, "Hallucination and Cruelty in Artaud and Ghelderode," *The French Review* 41, no. 1 (October, 1967): 3.

**13** Cit. ibid., 6.

**14** Lichtenstein, *Behind Closed Doors*, 1–6.

**15** Cit. ibid., 6.

**16** Ibid., 7.

**17** Ibid., 35.

**18** Cit. Peter Webb, *The Erotic Arts*, rev. ed. (New York: Farrar, Strauss & Giroux: 1983), 370.

**19** Hans Bellmer, Postscript to Unica Zürn, *Hexentexte*, 1954, reproduced in ibid., 175.

**20** Luce Irigaray, *Parler n'est jamais neutre* (Paris: Minuit, 1985), 172.

**21** Bellmer, *Die Puppe* (Karlsruhe: Th. Eckstein, 1934); I have used the French translation *La Poupée*, trans. Robert Valancay (Paris: Guy Lévis-Mano, 1936), n.p.

**22** Hal Foster, *Compulsive Beauty* (Cambridge, MA: MIT Press, 1993), 115.

**23** Hal Foster, "Armour Fou," *October* 56 (Spring 1991): 90.

**24** Cit. Lichtenstein, *Behind Closed Doors*, 143. For another lengthy, if more jumbled, recent account of Bellmer, see Jessica Burstein, *Cold Modernism: Nature, fashion, Art* (University Park: PA: Penn State Press, 2012).

**25** Amada Cruz, "Movies, Monstrosities and Masks: Twenty Years of Cindy Sherman," in *Cindy Sherman: A Retrospective*, exn. cat. (London, Chicago, Los Angeles: Thames and Hudson, Museum of Contemporary Art Chicago and The Museum of Contemporary Art, Los Angeles, 1997), 10ff.

26 Glenn Collins, "A Portraitist's Romp Through Art History," *New York Times*, February 1, 1990, available at http://www.nytimes.com/1990/02/01/arts/a-portraitist-s-romp-through-art-history.html (Last accessed February 15, 2015).

27 Hal Foster, "Obscene, Abject, Traumatic," *October* 78 (Autumn 1996): 110.

28 Ibid., 111.

29 Ibid., 113.

30 The main watershed comes with the exhibition curated by Yve-Alain Bois and Rosalind Krauss, and the subsequent publication *L'informe: mode d'emploi* (Paris: Centre Georges Pompidou, 1996). See also Adam Geczy and Jacqueline Millner, "Less is Less: Formlessness, *Fashionable Art*" (New York and London: Bloomsbury, 2015), 75–90.

31 Rudolphe Gasché, *Georges Bataille: Phenomenology and Phantasmatology*, trans. Roland Végsö (Stanford, CA: Stanford University Press, 2012), 81.

32 Cindy Sherman, cit. *Cindy Sherman: A Retrospective*, exn. cat. (London, Chicago, Los Angeles: Thames and Hudson, Museum of Contemporary Art Chicago and The Museum of Contemporary Art, Los Angeles, 1997), 164.

33 Kelly Grovier, "*Dead Dad* (1996–97): Ron Mueck," *100 Works of Art that Will Define Our Age* (London: Thames and Hudson, 2013), 194.

34 Craig Raine, "From *Dead Dad* to *A Girl," Ron Mueck*, exn. cat. (Tokyo: Foil, 2008), 67.

35 Robert Nelson, "Sam Jinks: Distortions," *The Age* 31 (August 2005), repr., available at http://www.samjinks.com/essay.html.

36 Available at http://www.patriciapiccinini.net/104/61 (Last accessed February 15, 2015).

37 Kim Toffoletti, *Cyborgs and Barbie Dolls: Feminism and the Posthuman Body* (London: I.B. Tauris, 2007), 156.

38 Robert Rosenblum, "Bodies and Souls," *Ron Mueck*, exn. cat. (Paris: Fondation Cartier pour l'art contemporain, 2006), 52–53.

39 Herbrechter, *Posthumanism*, 132.

40 Gilles Deleuze, *Spinoza et le problème de l'expression* (Paris: Minuit, 1968), 225–226; emphasis in original.

# 5 A Model Subject: The Window Dummy, the Fashion Doll and the Double

1 See Adam Geczy and Vicki Karaminas, *Fashion's Double: Representations of Fashion in Painting, Photography and Film* (London and New York: Bloomsbury, 2015).

2 Giacomo Leopardi, "Dialogue Between Fashion and Death," *Dialogues*, available at http://www.bartleby.com/380/prose/840.html (Last accessed February 15, 2015).

3 *Sosie* was, in fact, taken from a character in Molière's rendition of Plautus's *Amphytrion*. Sosie is confronted with an imposter who pretends to be him, Sosie, leading to the original Sosie doubting himself. See also Alenka Zupancic, *The Odd One In: On Comedy* (Cambridge, MA: MIT Press, 2008), 77–78. Note also that Sosie is male.

4 Adam Geczy, "Straight Internet Porn and the Natrificial: Body and Dress," *Fashion Theory* 18, no. 2 (Special Issue: Pornography): 169–188.

5 Nancy Troy, *Couture Culture: A Study in Modern Art and Fashion* (Cambridge, MA: MIT Press, 2003), passim.

**6** Daniel Harris, "Some Reflections on the Facial Expressions of Fashion Models: 100 Years of Vogue," *Salmagundi* 98/99 (Spring-Summer 1993): 133: "Such thoughtlessness is of crucial importance to glamor because it suggests that the relation between the woman and the dress is one of the utmost carelessness and haste, that the dress is in fact an after-thought, something she just threw on that morning, an outfit that involved a minimum of premeditation (an effect that also explains the strangely agitated poses of many models, the way they are now represented jumping or kicking, acts meant not only to break the staid decorum of traditionally immobile poses but to express indifference to the apparel itself)."

**7** Caroline Evans, "The Ontology of the Fashion Model," *AA Files* 63 (2011): 58–59.

**8** Juliette Peers, *The Fashion Doll: From Bébé Jumeau to Barbie* (Oxford and New York: Berg, 2004), 16–17.

**9** Cit. Yassana Croizat, "'Living Dolls': François Ier Dresses His Women," *Renaissance Quarterly* 60, no. 1 (Spring 2007): 98.

**10** Ibid., 94.

**11** Cit. ibid., 97.

**12** Ibid., 101.

**13** Ibid., 105.

**14** Ibid., 119.

**15** Leslie Reinhardt, "Daughters, Dress, and Female Virtue in the Eighteenth Century," *American Art* 20, no. 2 (Summer 2006): 38.

**16** Ibid.

**17** Ibid., 39. Reinhardt echoes and confirms much of what has already been stated with respect to girls and their ascent into adolescence and womanhood: "Girls could see in these dolls, which were dressed in adult styles, pictures of womanhood and imagine the women they would become. Conversely, grown women could look to the dolls' apparel for hints on fashionable attire. Even with dolls clearly intended as toys for little girls of this period, there were constant references to adult interest and involvement in both production and reception. For example, Thomas Shippen was aware of the wider implications when he sent the English doll to his niece Peggy Livingston, a contemporary of Elizabeth Gilmor, in America. This doll had been dressed entirely by workshop adult professionals, and he knew that women as well as his niece would study it."

**18** Ibid.

**19** Karen de Perthuis, *Dying to Be Born Again: Mortality, Immortality and the Fashion Model*, Ph.D. dissertation, The University of Sydney, 2003, 72–73.

**20** Ibid., 73.

**21** Croizat, "Living Dolls," 119.

**22** Ibid., 9.

**23** See, for example, Georg Simmel, "Psychologie der Mode," *Aufsätze und Abhandlungen 1894–1900* (Frankfurt am Main: Suhrkamp, 1992), 110–111.

**24** Peers, *The Fashion Doll*, 9.

**25** See also Marianne Thesander, *The Feminine Ideal* (London: Reaktion, 1997), 81ff.

**26** Peers, *The Fashion Doll*, 43.

**27** Ibid., 45–46.

**28** Meryle Secrest, *Elsa Schiaparelli: A Biography* (New York: Knopf, 2014), 293.

**29** Ibid., 293–295.

**30** Ibid., 296.

**31** Peers, *The Fashion Doll*, 170–171.

**32** Viktor Horsting and Rolf Snoeren, "Interview with Susannah Frankel," in Caroline Evans and Susannah Frankel, ed. Jane Alison and Ariella Yedgar, *The House of Viktor & Rolf*, exn. cat. (London and New York: Merrell and the Barbican Centre, 2008), 23.

**33** Alison Matthews David, *Cutting a Figure: Tailoring, Technology and Social Identity in Nineteenth-Century Paris*, Ph.D. dissertation, Department of Art and Art History, Stanford University, August 2002, 80–82.

**34** Étienne-François Bazot, *The Nouvelles Parisiennes*, cit. Evans, "The Ontology of the Fashion Model," 63.

**35** David, *Cutting a Figure*, 81; see also Evans, "The Ontology of the Fashion Model," 60.

**36** Ibid.

**37** Auguste Villiers de l'Isle-Adam, *L'Eve Future* (1886), available at http://www.gutenberg.org/files/26681/26681-h/26681-h.htm.

**38** Ibid.

**39** Evans, "The Ontology of the Fashion Model," 64.

**40** Rhonda Garelick, *Mademoiselle: Coco Chanel and the Pulse of History* (New York: Random House, 2014), 85.

**41** Evans, *The Mechanical Smile*, 187.

**42** Meredith Etherington-Smith, and Jeremy Rilcher, *The It Girls: Lucy, Lady Duff Gordon the Couturiere "Lucile" and Elinor Glyn, Romantic Novelist* (London: H. Hamilton, 1986), 76. See also de Perhuis, *Dying to Be Born Again*, 99–100.

**43** C. Evans, "The Enchanted Spectacle," *Fashion Theory* 5, no. 2 (2001): n. 2, 307.

**44** Etherington-Smith, and Rilcher, *The It Girls*, 162ff.

**45** Evans, *The Mechanical Smile*, 185.

**46** See also Evans, "The Enchanted Spectacle," 271–310, and Evans, ibid.

**47** Garelick, *Mademoiselle*, 151.

**48** See also Peter Wollen, *Raiding the Icebox: Reflections on Twentieth-Century Culture* (London and New York: Verso, 1993), 20–21, 44.

**49** Caroline Evans, *The Mechanical Smile: Modernism and the First Fashion Shows in France and America, 1900–1929* (New Haven and London: Yale U.P., 2013), 3.

**50** Ibid., 4.

**51** Ibid., 4–6, 29ff.

**52** Cit. Evans, *The Mechanical Smile*, 192.

**53** Evans, *The Mechanical Smile*, 192.

**54** Ibid., 376.

**55** Cit. Garelick, ibid.

**56** M. G. Lord, *Forever Barbie* (New York: William Morrow and Co., 1994), 7–8.

**57** Mary Rogers, *Barbie Culture* (London: Sage, 1999), 1.

**58** Ibid., 3.

**59** David Groves, "A Doll's Life," *Los Angeles Times*, December 15, 1994, cit. Kristin Weissman, *Barbie: The Icon, the Image, the Ideal* (United States: Universal Publishers, 1999), 11.

**60** Weissman, ibid., 12.

**61** Laura Jacobs, *Barbie™: What a Doll!* (New York and London: Artabras of Abbeville, 1994), 42.

**62** Catherine Driscoll, "Girl-Doll: Barbie as Puberty Manual," *Counterpoints*, 245: Seven Going on Seventeen: Tween Studies in the Culture of Girlhood, 2005, 224–241.

**63** Erica Rand, *Barbie's Queer Accessories* (Durham, NC: Duke U.P., 1995), 9.

**64** Peers, *The Fashion Doll*, 174–175.

**65** Ibid., 176.

**66** Rogers, *Barbie Culture*, 4.

**67** Judith Butler, *Gender Trouble: Feminism and the Subversion of Identity* (London and New York: Routledge, 1990), 137; emphasis in the original.

**68** Rand, *Barbie's Queer Accessories*, chapter two, "Younger Heads on Older Bodies," 93–148.

**69** For a detailed discussion of queer identity and artificiality, see Adam Geczy and Vicki Karaminas, *Queer Style* (London and New York: Bloomsbury, 2013), "Introduction" and passim.

**70** Rand, *Barbie's Queer Accessories*, 109–111.

**71** Ibid., 115.

**72** Ibid., 150.

**73** Rogers, *Barbie Culture*, 90ff.

**74** "Interview with Nancie Martin (Mattel)," in Justine Cassell and Henry Jenkins eds, *From Barbie to Mortal Kombat: Gender and Computer Games* (Cambridge, MA: MIT Press, 2000), 145–146.

## 6 Extreme Hellene: Sport, Superheroes and the Modern *Übermensch*

**1** Cit. Garelick, *Mademoiselle*, 426.

**2** Bodo Kirschoff, *Body-Building: Erzählung; Schauspiel: Essay* (Frankfurt am Main: Suhrkamp, 1980), 154.

**3** Available at http://bodybuilding.about.com/od/bodybuildingcompetition/ss/The-Eight-Mandatory-Poses-In-Bodybuilding_8.htm§ep-heading.

**4** Ruprecht, *Dances of the Self*, 13.

**5** Kenneth Clark, *The Nude: A Study in Ideal Form* (Princeton, NJ: Princeton U.P. 1956), passim.

**6** Thucydides, *History of the Peloponnesian War*, trans. Rex Warner (Harmondsworth: Penguin, 1954), 38. See also R. Sennett, *Flesh and Stone: The Body and the City in Western Civilization* (London: Faber and Faber 1994), 33.

**7** Ibid.

**8** Thomas Holland, *Girls' Toys from the Fifties and Sixties: Memorable Catalog Pages from the Legendary Sears Christmas Wishbooks 1950–1969* (Sherman Oaks, CA: Windmill Press, 1997), 210.

**9** See also T. Attfield, "Barbie and Action Man: Adult Toys for Girls and Boys," in *The Gendered Object*, Pat Kirkham (ed.) (Manchester: Manchester U.P., 1996), 58; and Anna Wagner-Ott, "Analysis of Gender Identity Through Doll and Action Figure Politics in Art Education," *Studies in Art Education*, 43, no. 3 (Spring 2002): 251–252.

**10** Teresa Winge, "Costuming the Imagination: Origins of Anime and Manga," *Mechademia*, 1, *Emerging Worlds of Anime and Manga* (2006): 66–67.

**11** David McVeigh and Scott McVeigh, *Iron and Beyond*, 2002. Available at https://www.youtube.com/watch?v=wiXxifU5ilQ (Last accessed February 15, 2015).

**12** Ibid.

**13** Susan Jeffords, *Hard Bodies: Hollywood Masculinity in the Reagan Era* (New Brunswick, NJ: Rutgers U.P., 1994), 97.

**14** Samuel Fussell, *Muscle: Confessions of an Unlikely Bodybuilder* (New York: Avon Books, 1991), 185.

**15** Michael Joyner, "Sam Fussell: An Interview with the Author of Muscle," *Human* Limits, June 10, 2014, available at http://www.drmichaeljoyner.com/sam-fussell-an-interview-with-the-author-of-muscle/ (Last accessed February 15, 2015).

**16** Fussell, *Muscle*, 223.

**17** Ibid., 216.

**18** Ibid., 146.

**19** "Transsexuality," in Jean Baudrillard, *The Transparency of Evil: Essays on Extreme Phenomena* (1990), trans. James Benedict (London and New York: Verso, 1993).

**20** Guy Snaith, "Tom's Men: The Masculinization of Homosexuality and the Homosexualization of Masculinity at the End of the Twentieth Century," *Paragraph* 26 (2003): 77.

**21** Ibid., 78.

**22** Ibid., 77.

**23** Vito Russo, *The Celluloid Closet*, rev. ed. (New York: Harper and Row, 1987), 32ff.

**24** See Reed, *Art and Homosexuality* (Oxford and New York: Oxford U.P., 2011), 167–169.

**25** *Iron and Beyond.*

**26** Jean Baudrillard, "AIDS: Virulence or Prophylaxis?" (1987), in *Screened Out*, trans. Chris Turner (London and New York: Verso, 2002), 3.

**27** Sean French, *The Terminator* (London: British Film Institute, 1996), 34.

# 7 Genetically Baroque Beings: Cybergender, Transexuality and Natrificiality

**1** Johann Wolfgang Goethe, *Faust* (Munich: Deutsche Taschenbuch Verlag, 2010), 54.

**2** Jean Baudrillard, "We Are All Transsexuals Now" (1987), in *Screened Out*, 10.

**3** Suzanne Fraser, *Cosmetic Surgery, Gender and Culture* (Hampshire and New York: Palgrave Macmillan, 2003), 5.

**4** Ibid., 5–6.

**5** K. Hayles, *How We Became Posthuman*, 5.

**6** Ibid., 6.

**7** Elizabeth Haiken, *Venus Envy* (Baltimore and London: Johns Hopkins U.P., 1997), 12.

**8** Ibid., 15.

**9** Ibid., 96.

**10** Ibid., 97.

**11** I am grateful to Dr. Darryl Hodgkinson for this correction of an earlier version.

**12** Ibid., 209.

**13** Lord, *Forever Barbie*, 177.

**14** J. Urla and A. Swedlund, "The Anthropometry of Barbie: Unsettling Ideals of the Feminine Body in Popular Culture," in *Feminism and the Body*, Londa Schiebinger ed. (Oxford and New York: Oxford U.P., 2000), 389.

**15** Rhian Parker, *Women, Doctors and Cosmetic Surgery: Noegotiating the "Normal" Body* (Hampshire and New York: Palgrave Macmillan, 2010), 175. See also Fraser, 70ff.

**16** Ibid.

**17** Fraser, *Cosmetic Surgery*, 65.

**18** Ibid., 66.

**19** Haraway, *Simeans*, 149–153.

**20** D. Haraway, *Modest_Witness@Second_Millennium.FemaleMan _Meets_OncoMouse(tm): Feminism and Technoscience* (New York: Routledge, 1997), 119.

**21** Sharon Betcher, "Putting My Foot (Prosthesis, Crutches, Phantom) Down: Considering Technology as Transcendence in the Writings of Donna Harraway," *Women's Studies Quarterly* 29(3/4): 39.

**22** Ibid., 42.

**23** Ibid., 43.

**24** Timothy Lender, "Techno-Humanism," in *Genesis Redux*, Riskin (ed.), 216.

**25** See also Parker, *Women, Doctors and Cosmetic Surgery*, 193–194.

**26** Fraser, *Cosmetic Surgery*, 67.

**27** Ibid.

**28** Haiken, *Venus Envy,* 297.

**29** Kate Ince, *Orlan: Millenial Female* (Oxford and New York: Berg, 2000), 120.

**30** "I constructed my self-portrait by mixing representations of goddesses from Greek mythology: chosen not for the canons of beauty they are supposed to represent, but for their histories. . . . These representations of feminine personages have served as an inspiration to me and are there deep beneath my work in a symbolic manner. In this way, their images can resurface in works that I produce, with regard to their histories." Orlan, "Carnal Art," trans. Tanya Augsburg and Michel Moos, in Duncan McCorquodale ed., *Orlan: Ceci est mon corps . . . ceci est logiciel/This is my body . . . this is my software* (London: Black Dog, 1996), 84.

**31** Orlan and Paul Virilio, "Transgression/Transfiguration: A Conversation," in *Fabulous Harlequin: Orlan and the Patchwork Self*, Jorge Veneciano and Rhonda Garelick eds (Lincoln and London: Nebraska U.P., 2010), 57.

**32** Parveen Adams, "Operation Orlan," in ibid., 67.

**33** Orlan, "In Retrospect," trans. Simon Donger, in Simon Donger, Simon Shepherd and Orlan eds, *Orlan: A Hybrid Body of Artworks* (London and New York: Routledge, 2010), 111.

**34** Rhonda Garelick, "Fashioning Hybridity," *TDR* 53, no. 2 (Summer 2009): 150. See also Veneciano and Garelick eds, *Fabulous Harlequin*, 9–17.

**35** Ibid., 150–151.

**36** Carey Lovelace, "Orlan: Offensive Acts," *Performing Arts Journal* 17, no. 1 (January 1995): 25.

**37** Duncan McCorquodale ed., *Orlan: Ceci est mon corps . . . ceci est logiciel/This is my body . . . this is my software*.

**38** Cit. ibid., 151.

**39** Gilles Deleuze and Félix Guattari, *Milles plateaux* (Paris: Minuit, 1981).

**40** Lovelace, "Orlan: Offensive Acts," 13–14.

**41** Michela Marzano, "Ceci mon corps: Orlan ou l'identité incertain," *Cités* 21 (Refaire son corps: Corps sexué et identities, 2005), 98.

**42** Jill O'Bryan, "Saint Orlan Faces Reincarnation," *Art Journal* 56, no. 4, Performance Art: (Some) Theory and (Selected) Practice at the End of This Century (Winter 1997): 52, emphasis in the original.

**43** Garelick, "Fashioning Hybridity," 151.

**44** Ibid., 154.

**45** Ibid., 157.

**46** Alyda Faber, "Saint Orlan: Ritual as Violent Spectacle and Cultural Criticism," *TDR* 46.1 (Spring 2002): 86.

**47** Lovelace, "Orlan: Offensive Acts," 23.

**48** Ibid., 90.

**49** Orlan, "Carnal Art," 88.

**50** Orlan, "Conférence," *De l'art charnel au baiser de l'artiste* (Paris: Jean-Michel Place & Fils., 1997), 1. See also Marzano, "Ceci mon corps," 90.

**51** Marzano, ibid., 92, n. 2.

**52** See, for example, Richard Francis, *Epigenetics: How Environment Shapes Our Genes* (London and New York: Norton, 2011).

**53** Sarah Wilson, "L'histoire d'O, Sacred and Profane," in Duncan McCorquodale ed., *Orlan: This is my body . . . this is my software*, 15.

**54** See also Faber, 91 and passim.

**55** Barbara Rose, "Is it Art? Orlan and the Transgressive Act," *Art in America* 81, no. 2 (February 1993): 125.

**56** Ince, *Orlan*, 71.

**57** Estimates vary as the number is shrinking and expanding on a daily basis. Susanna Paasonen contends that the number has been diminishing since the 1990s, and "of the approximately 100 million sites currently available, an estimated 1.5 to 5 percent are pornographic—although some sources, including ones associated with filtering software and conservative Christian groups in the US, offer numbers as high as 12 percent or 260 million pages. Since such inflated figures, are enthusiastically circulated and presented as statistical facts, they are also referenced as objective findings in overviews of online pornography." "Porn Futures" in Susanna Paasonen et al. eds, *Pornification: Sex and Sexuality in Media Culture* (Oxford and New York: Berg, 2007), 167.

**58** See also Fussell, *Muscle*, 140.

**59** Marianne Thesander, *The Feminine Ideal* (1994), trans. Nicholas Hills (London: Reaktion, 1997), 218.

**60** See also my "Straight Internet Porn and the Natrificial: Body and Dress," 169–188.

**61** See Susanna Paasonen et al. eds, *Pornification*.

**62** Annette Lynch, *Porn Chic. Exploring the Contours of Raunch Eroticism* (Oxford and New York: Berg, 2012). See also Adam Geczy and Vicki Karamainas, Chapter 5: "Music Video, Pornochic and Retro-Elegance" in *Fashion's Double: Representations of Fashion in Painting, Photography and Film* (New York and London: Bloomsbury, 2015).

**63** Pamela Church Gibson, "Pornostyle: Sexualized Dress and the Fracturing of Feminism," in *Fashion Theory, The Journal of Dress, Body and Culture, Special Issue, Fashion and Porn*, Pamela Church Gibson and Vicki Karaminas eds, 18(2): 189–202.

**64** Adriano Sack, "Was Will der spornosexualle Mann?" *Die Welt*, 2 March, 2015, available at http://www.welt.de/icon/article129588106/Was-will-der-spornosexuelle-Mann.html (Last accessed February 15, 2015).

**65** Ibid.

**66** Ibid.

**67** Available at https://secure.realdoll.com/male-realdoll2-custom-build/ (Last accessed February 15, 2015).

**68** Available at https://secure.realdoll.com/ (Last accessed February 15, 2015).

**69** Marquard Smith, *The Erotic Doll*, 205.

**70** Ibid., 206.

**71** Ibid., 210–211.

**72** Ibid., 227ff.

**73** Ibid., 231.

**74** Ibid., 231–232.

**75** Ibid., 233.

**76** Ibid., 242.

**77** Deni Kirkova, "'I want people to treat me like a plastic sex doll': Woman has hypnotherapy to make her 'brainless like Barbie' after spending £25,000 on breast enhancements," available at http://www.dailymail.co.uk/femail/article-2562870/I-want-people-treat-like-plastic-sex-doll-Woman-hypnotherapy-make-brainless-like-Barbie-spending-25-000-breast-enhancements.html (Last accessed February 15, 2015).

**78** Available at https://www.youtube.com/watch?v=VO4M2VT4F-o (Last accessed February 15, 2015).

**79** Dominique Mosbergen, "Real-Life Barbie Documentary: Valeria Lukyanova, 'Living Barbie,' Featured by Vice (VIDEO)," *The Huffington Post*, July 29, 2013, available at http://www.huffingtonpost.com/2013/07/29/valeria-lukyanova-vice_n_3672260.html (Last accessed February 15, 2015).

**80** Patrick Sandberg, "Living Doll," available at http://www.vmagazine.com/site/content/261/living-doll (Last accessed February 15, 2015).

**81** Ibid.

**82** Ibid.

**83** Kate Jackson, "Bizarre Confessions of real-life Barbie," *The Sun*, available at http://www.thesun.co.uk/sol/homepage/features/4771200/real-life-barbie-valeria-lukyanova-on-her-obsession-to-be-like-iconic-toy.html (Last accessed February 15, 2015).

**84** Sandberg, "Living Doll."

**85** Available at https://www.youtube.com/watch?v=oLK0myrbSzQ (Last accessed February 15, 2015).

**86** Available at http://www.justinjedlica.com/press.html#prettyPhoto[rv]/11/ (Last accessed February 15, 2015).

**87** Available at https://www.youtube.com/watch?v=MGVrLuMIbdc (Last accessed February 15, 2015).

**88** Available at https://www.youtube.com/watch?v=oLK0myrbSzQ (Last accessed February 15, 2015).

**89** Rogers, *Barbie Culture*, 15.

**90** Weissman, *Barbie*, 35.

**91** Available at https://www.youtube.com/watch?v=XQYF6HcnKdk (Last accessed February 15, 2015).

**92** J. Baudrillard, "Transsexuality," in *The Transparency of Evil: Essays on Extreme Phenomena* (1990), trans. James Benedict (London and New York: Verso, 1993), 20.

**93** Ibid., 24.

**94** Sandor Ferenczi, *Final Contributions to the Problems and Methods of Psycho-Analysis* (New York: Brunner/Mazel, 1980), 316–317.

**95** Maria Torok, "The Illness of Mourning and the Fantasy of the Exquisite Corpse" (1968), in Nicholas Abraham and Maria Torok, *The Shell and the Kernel: Renewals of Psychoanalysis*, trans and ed. Nicholas Rand (Chicago and London: Chicago U.P., 1994), 113.

**96** Ibid.

**97** Ibid., 114.

**98** Ibid.

**99** Carole Spitzack, *Confessing Excess: Women and the Politics of Body Reduction* (Albany NY: SUNY Press, 1990), cit. Rogers, *Barbie Culture*, 115.

**100** "Plastic Bodies," ibid., 112–135.

# 8 Future Postscript: Shells and Ghosts, Bodies and Souls

**1** Charles Baudelaire, "Moral du Joujou," in *Œuvres complètes* (Paris: Gallinard Pléiade, 1954), 687.

**2** Baudrillard, "Transsexuality," 24.

**3** *Ghost in the Shell*, dir. Mamoru Oshii, Production I.G., 1995.

**4** For this etymology as well as an eloquent gloss of the mechanical bodies of Greek mythology, such as the forge of Hephaestus, see Daniel Mendelsohn, "The Robots Are Winning," *The New York Review of Books* June 4 (2015): 51.

**5** See also Steven Brown, "Mechanic Desires: Hans Bellmer's Dolls and the Technological 'Ghosts in the Shell 2: Innocence,'" *Mechademia* 8, Limits of the Human (2008): 224.

**6** *Ghost in the Shell II*, dir. Mamoru Oshii, Production I.G./Studio Ghibli, 2004.

**7** Raymond Roussel, *Locus Solus* (1914) (Paris: Gallimard, 1979).

**8** S. Brown, "Mechanic Desires," 227.

**9** *Ghost in the Shell II*.

**10** Ibid.

**11** Ibid.

**12** Sigmund Freud, "The Uncanny," *The Standard Edition of the Complete Psychological Works of Sigmund Freud*, ed. and trans. James Strachey et al. (London: Hogarth, 1955), 17:226–-227.

**13** S. Brown, "Mechanic Desires," 239. For another analysis of *Ghost in the Shell: 2 Innocence* in light of Bellmer, see also Livia Monnet, "Anatomy of Permutational Desire: Perversion in Hans Bellmer and Oshii Mamoru," *Mechademia* 5, Fanthropologies (2010): 285–309.

**14** Ibid., 242.

**15** Ibid.

**16** S. Brown, "Mechanic Desires," 230–231.

**17** Kenneth Gross, *Puppet: An Essay in Uncanny Life* (Chicago and London: Chicago U.P., 2011), 118–119.

# Conclusion: Between Beauty and Terror

**1** Thomas Mann, *Buddenbrooks* (1901) (Frankfurt am Main: Fischer, 1993), 534.

**2** Ibid., 588.

**3** Miguel de Cervantes Saavedra, *Don Quixote* (no trans. noted) (Hertfordshire: Wordsworth Editions, 1993), 2:169.

**4** Henrik Ibsen, *A Doll's House* (1879), (no trans.), available at http://www.gutenberg.org/files/2542/2542-h/2542-h.htm#act3 (Last accessed February 15, 2015).

**5** Ibid.

**6** André Gide, *Isabelle* (Paris: Gallimard, 1921), 98–99.

# BIBLIOGRAPHY


Abrams, Jeanne. *Revolutionary Medicine: The Founding Fathers and Mothers in Sickness and in Health*. New York: New York U.P., 2014.

Adorno, Theodor W. *Aesthetische Theorie*. Frankfurt am Main: Suhrkamp Verlag, 1970a.

Adorno, Theodor W. *Zur Metcritique der Erkentnisstheorie; Drei Studien zu Hegel*. Frankfurt am Main: Suhrkamp Verlag, 1970b.

Agamben, Giorgio. *Nudities* (2009), trans. David Kishik and Stefan Pedatella. Stanford, CA: Stanford U.P., 2011.

Andrews, Richard. "Molière, commedia dell'arte, and the Question of Influence on Early Modern European Theatre." *Modern Language Review* 100, no. 2 (April 2005): 444–463.

Attinger, Gustave. *L'Esprit de la Commedia dell'arte dans le théâtre français*. Paris and Neuchâtel: Librairie Théâtral, 1950.

Augé, Marc. *Le Dieu objet*. Paris: Flammarion, 1988.

Aurelius, Marcus. *The Meditations*, 167 C.E., trans. George Long. Available at http://classics.mit.edu/Antoninus/meditations.html (Last accessed February 15, 2015).

Baird, Bill. *The Art of the Puppet*. New York: Macmillan, 1965.

Barkan, Leonard. *The Gods Made Flesh: Metamorphosis and the Pursuit of Paganism*. New Haven and London: Yale U.P., 1986.

Bataille, Georges. *La Part maudit (précédé de La Notion de dépense)*. Paris: Minuit, 1967.

Bataille, Georges. *Lascaux où la naissance de l'art* (1955) in *Œuvres complètes*, v. 9. Paris: Gallimard, 1979.

Bataille, Georges. *Erotism: Death and Sensuality*, trans. M. Dalwood. San Francisco: City Lights, 1986.

Baudelaire, Charles. "Moral du Joujou." In *Œuvres completes*. Paris: Gallinard Pléiade, 1954: 681–687.

Baudrillard, Jean. *The Transparency of Evil: Essays on Extreme Phenomena* (1990), trans. James Benedict. London and New York: Verso, 1993.

Baudrillard, Jean. *Screened Out*, trans. Chris Turner. London and New York: Verso, 2002.

Baum, Paul. "The Young Man Betrothed to a Statue." *PMLA* 34 (1919): 523–579.

Bauzano, Gianluca. *Mannequins Bonaveri: A History of Creativity, Fashion and Art*. Skira 2013.

Beaton, Mabel and Les. *The Complete Book of Marionettes*. New York: Dover, 2011.

Bell, John. *Strings, Hands, Shadows: A Modern Puppet History*, exn. cat. Detroit: Detroit Institute of Arts, 2000.

Bell, John, ed. *Puppets, Masks and Performing Objects*. Cambridge, MA: MIT Press, 2001.

Bell, John. *American Puppet Modernism: Essays on the Material World in Performance*. Hampshire and New York: Palgrave Macmillan, 2008.

Bellmer, Hans. *Die Puppe*. Karlsruhe: Th. Eckstein, 1934.

Bellmer, Hans. *La Poupée*, trans. Robert Valancay. Paris: Guy Lévis-Mano, 1936.

Betcher, Sharon. "Putting My Foot (Prosthesis, Crutches, Phantom) Down: Considering Technology as Transcendence in the Writings of Donna Haraway." *Women's Studies Quarterly* 29 (3/4): 39–53.

Bettini, Maurizio. *The Portrait of the Lover*, trans. Laura Gibbs. Berkeley and London: California U.P., 1999.

Blair, Lorrie, and Maya Shalmon. "Cosmetic Surgery and the Cultural Construction of Beauty." *Art Education* 58, no. 3 (May 2005): 14–18.

Blancart-Cassou, Jacqueline. "Du grotesque hugolien au grotesque de Ghelderode: l'influence, rencontres, divergences." *Revue d'Histoire littéraire de la France* 100, no. 5 (September–October 2000): 1337–1350.

Blumenthal, Eileen. *Puppetry: A World History*. New York: Harry Abrams, 2005.

Bois, Yve-Alain, and Rosalind Krauss, and the subsequent publication *L'informe: mode d'emploi*. Paris: Centre Georges Pompidou, 1996.

Brady, Florence. "The Use of Marionettes in Theatre." *English Elementary Review* 22 no. 5 (May 1945): 182–185.

Breward, Christopher, and Caroline Evans, eds. *Fashion and Modernity*. Oxford and New York: Berg, 2005.

Broadhurst, Susan, and Josephine Machon, eds. *Performance and Technology: Practices of Virtual Embodiment and Interactivity*. Hampshire and New York: Palgrave Macmillan, 2006.

Brown, Steven. "Mechanic Desires: Hans Bellmer's Dolls and the Technological 'Ghosts in the Shell 2: Innocence'." *Mechademia* 8, Limits of the Human (2008): 222–253.

Burstein, Jessica. *Cold Modernism: Nature, Fashion, Art*. University Park, PA: Penn State Press, 2012.

Butler, Judith. *Gender Trouble: Feminism and the Subversion of Identity*. London and New York: Routledge, 1990.

Butler, Judith. *Bodies That Matter*. New York and London: Routledge, 1993.

Butler, Judith, Ernesto Laclau and Slavoj Zizek. *Contingency, Hegemony, Universality*. London and New York, 2000.

Byrom, Michael. *Punch in the Italian Puppet Theatre*. Sussex and London: Centaur Press, 1983.

Byron, George Gordon, Lord, *Byron*, ed. Jerome McGann. Oxford and New York: Oxford U.P., 1986.

Cadullo, Bert, ed. *Theories of the Avant-Garde Theatre: A Casebook from Kleist to Camus*. Lanham and Toronto: The Scarecrow Press, 2013.

Carr, J. L. "Pygmalion and the *Philosophes*: Animated Statues in Eighteenth-Century France." *Journal of the Warburg and Courtauld Institutes* 23 (1960): 239–255.

Carter, Richard, and Perry Mason. "Selection and Use of Puppets in Counseling." *Professional School Counseling* 1, no. 5 (June 1998): 50–53.

Cassell, Justine, and Henry Jenkins, eds. *From Barbie to Mortal Kombat: Gender and Computer Games*. Cambridge, MA: MIT Press, 2000.

Castagno, Paul. *The Early Commedia Dell'Arte, 1550–1621: The Mannerist Context*. New York: Peter Lang, 1994.

Cervantes Saavedra, Miguel de. *Don Quixote* (no trans. noted). Hertfordshire: Wordsworth Editions, 1993.

Church Gibson, Pamela. "Pornostyle: Sexualized Dress and the Fracturing of Feminism." In *Fashion Theory, The Journal of Dress, Body and Culture, Special Issue, Fashion and Porn*. Pamela Church Gibson and Vicki Karaminas, eds. 18(2): 189–202.

*Cindy Sherman: A Retrospective*, exn. cat. London, Chicago, Los Angeles: Thames and Hudson, Museum of Contemporary Art Chicago and The Museum of Contemporary Art, Los Angeles, 1997.

Clark, Kenneth. *The Nude: A Study in Ideal Form*. Princeton, NJ: Princeton U.P., 1956.

Clarke, Desmond. *Descartes: A Biography*. Cambridge and London: Cambridge U.P., (2006) 2012.

Cody, Jane. "The 'Senex Amator' in Plautus' Casina." *Hermes* 104, no. 4 (1976): 453–476.

Cohen, Matthew. "Puppetry and the Destruction of the Object." *Performance Research* 12, no. 4 (2008): 123–131.

Collins, Glenn. "A Portraitist's Romp Through Art History." *New York Times*, February 1, 1990. Available at http://www.nytimes.com/1990/02/01/arts/a-portraitist-s-romp-through-art-history.html (Last accessed February 15, 2015).
Collodi, Carlo (Carlo Lorenzini). *The Adventures of Pinocchio: Story of a Puppet*, trans. Nicolas Parella. Berkeley and Los Angeles: California U.P., 1986.
Cox, Jeffrey. "The Parasite and the Puppet: Diderot's *Neveu* and Kleist's 'Marionettentheater'." *Comparative Literature* 38, no. 3 (Summer 1986): 256–269.
Craig, Edward Gordon. *On the Art of Theatre*. London: Heinemann, 1914.
Crohn Schmitt, Natalie. "Improvisation in the Commedia dell'Arte in its Golden Age: Why, What, How." *Renaissance Drama* 38 (2010): 225–249.
Croizat, Yassana. "'Living Dolls': François Ier Dresses His Women." *Renaissance Quarterly* 60.1 (Spring 2007): 94–130.
Currell, David. *Puppets and Puppet Theatre*. London: Crowood Press, 1999.
Curtis, H. S. *Education Through Play*. New York: Macmillan, 1915.
D'Ambra, E. *Roman Women*. Cambridge: Cambridge U.P., 2007.
Davis, Emily. "Doll Family Traced to Stone Age and 'Adam'." *Science News-Letter* 11, no. 305 (February 12, 1927): 93–94, 97–98.
de Man, Paul. *Allegories of Reading: Figural Language in Rousseau, Nietzsche, Rilke and Proust*. New Haven and London: Yale U.P., 1979.
Degen, Rudolf. "Römischen Puppenhaus Octodorus/Martigny." *Helvetia archaeologica*, 28 (1997): 15–38.
Deleuze, Gilles. *Spinoza et le problème de l'expression*. Paris: Minuit, 1968.
Deleuze, Gilles. *Spinoza: Philosophie practique*. Paris: Minuit, 1981.
Deleuze, Gilles, and Félix Guattari. *Milles plateaux*. Paris: Minuit, 1981.
Descartes, René. *Le Monde, l'homme* (1630), ed. Annie Bitbol-Hespériès and Jean-Pierre Verdet. Paris: Seuil, 1996.
Descartes, René. *Discours de la méthode* (1637). Paris: Flammarion, 2000.
Dickens, Charles. *The Old Curiosity Shop* (1841). Harmondsworth: Penguin, 1972.
Dickinson, Janice. *Everything About Me is Fake . . . and I'm Perfect*. New York: Harper Collins, 2004.
Diderot, Dénis, and d'Alenbert, eds. *Encyclopédie, ou dictionnaire raisonné des sciences, des arts, et des métiers*. 17 vols, vol. 1. Paris. 1751–1772.
Diderot, Dénis. *Paradoxe sur le comedien; Entretiens sur le fils natural*. Paris: Flammarion, 1981.
Diocaretz, Myriam, and Stefan Herbrecher, eds. *The* Matrix *in Theory*. Amsterdam and New York: Rodopi, 2006.
Dolansky, Fanny. "'Playing with Gender: Girls, Dolls, and Adult Ideals in the Roman World." *Classical Antiquity* 31, no. 2 (October 2012): 256–292.
Donger, Simon, and Simon Shepherd and Orlan, eds. *Orlan: A Hybrid Body of Artworks*. London and New York: Routledge, 2010.
Dörig, José. "Von Griechischen Puppen." *Antike Kunst* 1, no. 2 (1958): 41–52.
Decharme, P. *Note sur un fragment des Daedala de Plutarque*. Paris: Mélanges Henri Weil, 1898.
Driscoll, Catherine. "Girl-Doll: Barbie as Puberty Manual." *Counterpoints*, 245; Seven Going on Seventeen: Tween Studies in the Culture of Girlhood, 2005, 224–241.
Duchartre, Pierre Louis. *The Italian Comedy*, trans. Randolph Weaver. New York: Dover, (1929) 1966.
Elderkin. "Jointed Dolls of Antiquity." *American Journal of Archaeology* 34, no. 4 (October–December 1930): 455–479.
Ernuli, Brunela, ed. *Polcinelle*. Chareleville-Mézières: Cahiers Robinson, 1999.
Etherington-Smith, Meredith, and Jeremy Rilcher. *The It Girls: Lucy, Lady Duff Gordon the Couturiere "Lucile" & Elinor Glyn, Romantic Novelist*. London: H. Hamilton, 1986.
Evans, Caroline. "The Enchanted Spectacle." *Fashion Theory*, 5, no. 2 (2001): 271–310.
Evans, Caroline. "The Ontology of the Fashion Model." *AA Files* 63 (2011): 56–69.

Evans, Caroline. *The Mechanical Smile: Modernism and the First Fashion Shows in France and America, 1900–1929*. New Haven and London: Yale U.P., 2013.

Evans, Caroline, and Susannah Frankel, ed. Jane Alison and Ariella Yedgar. *The House of Viktor & Rolf*, exn. cat. London and New York: Merrell and the Barbican Centre, 2008.

Faber, Alyda. "Saint Orlan: Ritual As Violent Spectacle and Cultural Criticism." *TDR* 46, no. 1 (Spring 2002): 85–92.

Faraone, Christopher. "Binding and Burying the Forces of Evil: The Defensive Use of 'Voodoo' Dolls in Ancient Greece." *Classical Antiquity* 10, no. 2 (October 1991): 165–205, 207–220.

Ferenczi, Sandor. *Final Contributions to the Problems and Methods of Psycho-Analysis*. New York: Brunner/Mazel, 1980.

Fisher, James. "Harlequinade: Commedia dell'Arte on the Early Twentieth-Century British Stage." *Theatre Journal* 41, no. 1 (March 1989): 30–44.

Fontaine, Montaine, and Adele Scafuro. *The Oxford Handbook of Greek and Roman Comedy*. Oxford and New York: Oxford U.P., 2014.

Foster, Hal. "Armour Fou." *October* 56 (Spring 1991): 64–97.

Foster, Hal. *Compulsive Beauty*. Cambridge, MA: MIT Press, 1993.

Foster, Hal. "Obscene, Abject, Traumatic." *October* 78 (Autumn 1996).

Foucault, Michel. *Madness and Civilization: A History of Insanity in the Age of Reason* (1960), trans. Richard Howard. New York: Random House, 1965.

Francis, Richard. *Epigenetics: How Environment Shapes Our Genes*. London and New York: Norton, 2011.

Fraser, Suzanne. *Cosmetic Surgery, Gender and Culture*. Hampshire and New York: Palgrave Macmillan, 2003.

French, Sean. *The Terminator*. London: British Film Institute, 1996.

Freud, Sigmund. "The Uncanny." *The Standard Edition of the Complete Psychological Works of Sigmund Freud*, ed. and trans. James Strachey et al. London: Hogarth, 1955a, 17:217–256.

Freud, Sigmund. *Civilization and its Discontents*, trans. James Strachey. In Peter Gay ed., *The Freud Reader*. New York: Norton, 1995b.

Furetière, Antoine. *Dictionnaire universel contenant généralement tous les mots François, tant vieux que modernes, & les termes de toutes les sciences et des arts*. The Hague and Rotterdam: Arnout & Reiner Leers, 1690. 3 vols., repr. Paris: Le Robert, 1978, 1984.

Fussell, Samuel. *Muscle: Confessions of an Unlikely Bodybuilder*. New York: Avon Books, 1991.

Gabriel, Markus, and Slavoj Zizek. *Mythology, Madness and Laughter: Subjectivity in German Idealism*. London and New York: Continuum, 2009.

Gallagher, Mark. *Action Figures: Men, Action Films, and Contemporary Adventure Narratives*. New York: Palgrave Macmillan, 2006.

Garber, Marjorie. "Out of Joint." In David Hillman and Carla Mazzio eds, *The Body in Parts: Fantasies of Corporeality in Early Modern Europe*. New York and London: Routledge, 1997: 22–51.

Garelick, Rhonda. "Fashioning Hybridity." *TDR* 53, no. 2 (Summer 2009): 150–157.

Garelick, Rhonda. *Coco Chanel and the Pulse of History*. New York: Random House, 2014.

Gasché, Rudolphe. *Georges Bataille: Phenomenology and Phantasmatology*, trans. Roland Végsö. Stanford: Stanford University Press, 2012.

Geczy, Adam. *Art: Histories, Theories and Exceptions*. Oxford and New York: Berg, 2008.

Geczy, Adam. "Straight Internet Porn and the Natrificial: Body and Dress." *Fashion Theory, The Journal of Dress, Body and Culture, Special Issue, Fashion and Porn*, Pamela Church Gibson and Vicki Karaminas eds., 2014, 18, no. 2, 169–188.

Geczy, Adam, and Vicki Karaminas. *Queer Style*. New York and London: Bloomsbury, 2013.

Geczy, Adam, and Vicki Karaminas. *Fashion's Double: Representations of Fashion in Painting, Photography and Film*. New York and London: Bloomsbury, 2015.

Geczy, Adam, and Jacqueline Millner. *Fashionable Art*. New York and London: Bloomsbury, 2015.

George, David. "Joan Brossa and the 'Commedia dell'arte'." *Anales de la literatura española contemporánea* 20, no. 3, Drama/Theater (1995): 331–349.

Gerfein, Herschel, Mel Gordon and Gennaro Tuci. "The Adriani Lazzi of the Commedia Dell'Arte." *The Drama Review. TDR* 22, no. 1, Italian Theatre Issue (March 1978): 3–12.

Ghelderode, Michel de. *Les entretiens d'Ostende*, ed. Roger Igleesias and Alain Trutat. Paris: L'Arche, 1956.

Ghelderode, Michel de. *Théâtre*. 5 vols. Paris: Gallimard, 1950–1957.

Gide, André. *Isabelle*. Paris: Gallimard, 1921.

Gilles, Annie. *Images de la marionette dans la littérature*. Charleville-Mézières and Nancy: Éditions Institut Internationale de la Marionnette and Presses Universitaires de Nancy, 1993.

Glotzbach, Maria. *"Strahlend und Herschend." Kleists Anspruche an die Grazie und Ihre Verkorperung im Mechanischen Wesen*. Nordstedt: Grin, 2004.

Goethe, Johann Wolfgang. *Faust*. Munich: Deutsche Taschenbuch Verlag, 2010.

Goodman, Gail, and Christine Aman. "Children's Use of Anatomically Detailed Dolls to Describe an Event." *Child Development* 61, no. 6 (December 1990): 1859–1871.

Gordon, Mel. *Lazzi: The Comic Routines of the Commedia Dell-Arte*. London: PAJ Publications, 2001.

Green, Eileen, and Alison Adam, eds. *Virtual Gender: Technology, Consumption and Identity*. London and New York: Routledge, 2001.

Gross, Kenneth. *The Dream of the Moving Statue*. Ithaca and London: Cornell U.P., 1992.

Gross, Kenneth. *Puppet: An Essay in Uncanny Life*. Chicago and London: Chicago U.P., 2011.

Gross, Kenneth, and Leslie Katz. "The Puppet's Calling." *Raritan: A Quarterly Review* 15, no. 1 (1995): 1–28.

Grosz, Elizabeth. *Volatile Bodies: Toward a Corporeal Feminism*. Bloomington: Indiana U.P., 1994.

Grovier, Kelly. "*Dead Dad* (1996–97): Ron Mueck." *100 Works of Art that Will Define Our Age*. London: Thames and Hudson, 2013.

Guidicelli, Carole, ed., *Surmarionettes et mannequins: Craig, Kantor et leurs heritages contemporains*. Lavérune and Charleville-Mézières: L'Entretemps Édtions and Institut International des Marionettes, 2013.

Halberstam, Judith, and Ira Livingston, eds. *Posthuman Bodies*. Bloomington: Indiana U.P., 1995.

Hallett, Judith. "Plautine Ingredients in the Performance of 'Pseudolis'." *The Classical World* 87, no. 1 (September–October 1993): 21–26.

Hansen, Günther. *Formern der Commedia dell'Arte in Deitschland*. Emsdetten: Verlag Lechte, 1984.

Harraway, Donna. *Simians, Cyborgs and Women: The Reinvention of Nature*. London and New York: Routledge, 1991

Harraway, Donna. *Modest_Witness@Second_Millennium.FemaleMan _Meets_OncoMouse(tm): Feminism and Technoscience*. New York: Routledge, 1997.

Harris, Daniel. "Some Reflections on the Facial Expressions of Fashion Models: 100 Years of Vogue." *Salmagundi* 98/99 (Spring–Summer 1993): 128–140.

Harris, Muriel. "The Doll." *The North American Review* 212, no. 781 (December 1920): 809–815.

Harris, Neil. *Humbug: The Art of P. T. Barnum*. Chicago and London: Chicago U.P., 1973.

Hauser, Arnold. *Mannerism*. Belknap Press of Harvard U.P., 1965.

Hayles, Katherine. *How We Became Posthuman: Virtual Bodies in Cybernetics, Literature and Infomatics*. Chicago and London: Chicago U.P., 1999.

Hazard, Paul. *La Crise de la conscience européenne 1680–1715*. Paris: Fayard, 1961.

Hellman, Helen. "'Hallucination and Cruelty in Artaud and Ghelderode." *The French Review* 41, no. 1 (October 1967): 1–10.

Henke, Robert. *Performance and Lietarture in the Commedia Dell'Arte*. Cambridge and New York: Cambridge U.P., 2002.

Herbrecheter, Stefan. *Posthumanism: A Critical Analysis*. London and New York: Bloomsbury, 2013.

Heudin, Jean-Claude. *Les Créateures artificielles: des automates aux mondes virtuels*. Paris: Odile Jacob, 2008.

Hillis Miller, J. *Versions of Pygmalion*. Cambridge, MA: Harvard U.P., 1990.

Hoffmann, E. T. A. *Der Sandman*. Stuttgart: Philipp Reclam, 1991.

Holland, Thomas. *Girls' Toys from the Fifties and Sixties: Memorable Catalog Pages from the Legendary Sears Christmas Wishbooks 1950–1969*. Sherman Oaks, CA: Windmill Press, 1997.

Hollier, Denis. *Against Architecture* (1974), trans. Betsy Wing. Cambridge, MA: MIT Press, 1989.

Hooker, Michael ed. *Descartes: Critical and Interpretative Essays*. Baltimore and London: Johns Hopkins U.P., 1978.

Ibsen, Henrik. *A Doll's House* (1879), (no trans.). Available at http://www.gutenberg.org/files/2542/2542-h/2542-h.htm#act3 (Last accessed February 15, 2015).

Ideal, Moshe. *Golem: Jewish Magical and Mystical Traditions of the Artificial Enthropoid*. Albany: State University of New York Press, 1989.

Ince, Kate. *Orlan: Millennial Female*. Oxford and New York: Berg, 2000.

Irigarary, Luce. *Parler n'est jamais neutre*. Paris: Minuit, 1985.

Irwin, Jones, and Helena Motoh. *Zizek and His Contemporaries: On the Emergence of the Slovenian Lacan*. London and New York: Bloomsbury, 2014.

Jackson, Kate. "Bizarre Confessions of real-life Barbie." *The Sun*. Available at http://www.thesun.co.uk/sol/homepage/features/4771200/real-life-barbie-valeria-lukyanova-on-her-obsession-to-be-like-iconic-toy.html (Last accessed February 15, 2015).

Jacobs, Laura. *Barbie™: What a Doll!* New York and London: Artabras of Abbeville, 1994.

Jean Paul, *Werke*, vol. 2, Munich: Carl Hanser Verlag, 1959–1963.

Jeffords, Susan. *Hard Bodies: Hollywood Masculinity in the Reagan Era*. New Brunswick, NJ: Rutgers U.P., 1994.

Johnston, John. *The Allure of Machanic Life: Cybernetics, Artificial Life, and the New AI*. Cambridge, MA: MIT Press, 2008.

Jones, Irwin, and Helena Motoh. *Zizek and His Contemporaries: On the Emergence of the Slovenian Lacan*. London and New York: Bloomsbury, 2014.

Jones, Meredith. *Skintight: An Anatomy of Cosmetic Surgery*. London and New York: Berg 2008.

Jordan, Peter. *The Venetian Origins of the Commedia Dell'Arte*. London: Routledge, 2014.

Joubert, Bernard. *La Commedia dell'arte et son influence en France du XVIe au XVIIIe siècle*. Paris: L'Harmattan, 1999.

Joyner, Michael. "Sam Fussell: An Interview with the Author of Muscle." *Human* Limits, June 10, 2014. Available at http://www.drmichaeljoyner.com/sam-fussell-an-interview-with-the-author-of-muscle/ (Last accessed February 15, 2015).

Kafai, Yasmin, Carrie Heeter, Jill Denner, and Jennifer Sun, eds. *Beyond Barbie and Mortal Kombat*. Cambridge, MA: MIT Press, 2008.

Kant, Immanuel. *Critique of Practical Reason*, trans. L. W. Beck. New York and London: Palgrave Macmillan, 1956.

Kermode, Frank. "The Dancer." *Romantic Image*. London: Routledge, 1957.

Kirkham, Pat, ed. *The Gendered Object*. Manchester: Manchester U.P., 1996.

Kirkova, Deni. "'I want people to treat me like a plastic sex doll': Woman has hypnotherapy to make her 'brainless like Barbie' after spending £25,000 on breast enhancements." Available at http://www.dailymail.co.uk/femail/article-2562870/I-want-people-treat-like-plastic-sex-doll-Woman-hypnotherapy-make-brainless-like-Barbie-spending-25-000-breast-enhancements.html (Last accessed February 15, 2015).

Kirschoff, Bodo. *Body-Building: Erzählung; Schauspiel; Essay*. Frankfurt am Main: Suhrkamp, 1980.

Kleist, Heinrich von (1810). "Über das Marionettentheater": *Sämtliche Werke*. Leipzig: Im Insel Verlag, n.d.

Kominz, Laurence, and Mark Levenson, eds. *The Language of the Puppet*, Vancouver and Washington: Pacific Puppetry Center Press, 1990.
Koss, Juliette. "'Bauhaus Theater of Human Dolls." *The Art Bulletin*, 85.4 (December 2003): 724.
Lactantius. *The Divine Institutes* 2, no. 4, trans. William Fletcher. In Alexander Roberts, James Donaldson, and A. Clevelend Coxe eds. *Ante-Nicene Fathers*. Buffalo, NY: Christian Literature Publishing Co., 1886. Revised and edited for New Advent by Kevin Knight. Available at http://www.newadvent.org/fathers/0701.htm (Last accessed February 15, 2015).
Lahusen, Susanne. "Oskar Schlemmer: Mechanical Ballets?" *Dance Research: The Journal of the Society for Dance Research* 4, no. 2 (Autumn 1986): 65–77.
Lea, Kathleen. *Italian Popular Comedy: A Study in the Commedia Dell'Arte 1560–1620*. New York: Russell and Russell, 1962.
Lecoq, Jacques. *Le Corps poétique: Un enseignment de la creation théâtrale*. Paris: Actes Sud, 1999.
Leopardi, Giacomo. "Dialogue Between Fashion and Death." *Dialogues*. Available at http://www.bartleby.com/380/prose/840.html (Last accessed February 15, 2015).
Levitt, Paul. "Ghelderode and Puppet Theatre." *The French Review* 48, no. 6 (May 1975): 973–980.
Lichtenstein, Therese. *Behind Closed Doors: The Art of Hans Bellmer*. Berkeley and London: California U.P., 2001.
Lord, M. G. *Forvere Barbie*. New York: William Morrow and Co., 1994.
Lovelace, Carey. "Orlan: Offensive Acts." *Performing Arts Journal* 17, no. 1 (January 1995): 13–25.
Lynch, Annette. *Porn Chic. Exploring the Contours of Raunch Eroticism*. London: Berg, 2012.
Lyotard, Jean-François. *L'Inhumain: causeries sur le temps*. Paris: Gallimard, 1988.
MacDill, Marjorie. "Ancient Dolls and Toys Tell Whole History of Race." *The Science News-Letter* 16, no. 454 (December 21, 1929): 380–381, 390.
Maeterlinck, Maurice. *Théâtre* I-III. Paris and Geneva: Slatkine, 1979.
Mann, Thomas. *Buddenbrooks* (1901). Frankfurt am Main: Fischer, 1993.
Manson, Michel. "Le mythe de Pygmalion est-il un mythe de la poupée?" *Colloque d'Ovide*, September 1980. Paris: Les Belles-Lettres, 101–137.
Manson, Michel. "Pour une Histoire de l'enfant dans l'antiquité." *Histoire d'éducation* 30 (May 1986): 3–12.
Manson, Michel. "Les Poupées Antiques." *Dossiers d'archaeologie* 168 (1992): 48–57.
Marzano, Michela. "Ceci mon corps: Orlan ou l'identité incertain" *Cités* 21, Refaire son corps: Corps sexué et identities, 2005, 89–101.
Masson, Céline. *La Fabrique de la pouppée chez Hans*. Bellmer, Paris: Harmatton, 2000.
Matthews David, Alison. *Cutting a Figure: Tailoring, Technology and Social Identity in Nineteenth-Century Paris*, Ph.D. dissertation. Department of Art and Art History, Stanford University, August 2002: 80–82.
Mazzio Carla, and David Hillman. *The Body in Parts: Fantasies of Corporeality in Early Modern Europe*. London and New York: , 1997.
McCorquodale, Duncan, ed. *Orlan: Ceci est mon corps . . . ceci est logiciel/This is my body . . . this is my software*, trans. Tanya Augsburg and Michel Moos. London: Black Dog, 1996.
McDowell, John. "Some Pictorial Aspects of Early 'Commedia dell'arte' Acting." *Studies in Philology* 39, no. 1 (January 1942): 47–64.
McGill, Kathleen. "Women and Performance: The Development of Improvisation by the Sixteenth-Century." *Theatre Journal* 43, no. 1 (March 1991): 59–69.
McNeil, Anne. *Music and Women of the Commedia dell'Arte in the late Sixteenth Century*. Oxford and New York: Oxford U.P., 2003.
Mears, Ashley. *Pricing Beauty: The Making of a Fashion Model*. Berkeley and London: California U.P., 2011.
Mendelsohn, Daniel. "The Robots Are Winning." *New York Review of Books* (June 4, 2015): 51–54.

Mic, Constant. *La Commedia dell'arte, ou le théatre des comediens italiens des XVIe, XVIIe et XVIIIe siècles*. Paris: Librairie Théatrale, 1980.

Michalzik, Peter. *Kleist: Dichter, Krieger, Seelensucher*. Berlin: Propyläen, 2011.

Mirzoeff, Nicholas, ed. *The Visual Culture Reader*, 2nd edn. London and New York: Routledge, 2002.

Molière. *Le Malade imaginaire: Œuvres complètes 4*. Paris: Flammarion, 1979: 379–460.

Monnet, Livia. "Anatomy of Permutational Desire: Perversion in Hans Bellmer and Oshii Mamoru." *Mechademia* 5, Fanthropologies (2010): 285–309.

Moody, C. "Vsevolod Meyerhold and the 'Commedia dell'arte'." *The Modern Language Review* 73, no. 4 (October 1978): 859–869.

Mosbergen, Dominique. "Real-Life Barbie Documentary: Valeria Lukyanova, 'Living Barbie': Featured by Vice (VIDEO)." *Huffington Post*, July 29, 2013. Available at http://www.huffingtonpost.com/2013/07/29/valeria-lukyanova-vice_n_3672260.html (Last accessed February 15, 2015).

Moser, Edward, and Richard White. "Seri Clay Figurines." *Kiva* 33, no. 3 (February 1968): 133–154.

Nancy, Jean-Luc. *Corpus*. Paris: Éditions Métailé, 2006.

Needham, Joseph. *Science and Civilization in China, vol. 2*. Cambridge and London: Cambridge U.P., 1986.

Nelson, Robert. "Sam Jincks: Distortions." *The Age*. August 31, 2005, repr. Available at http://www.samjinks.com/essay.html (Last accessed February 15, 2015).

Nelson, Victoria. *The Secret Life of Puppets*. Cambridge, MA: Harvard U.P., 2001.

Nicoll, Allerdyce. *Masks, Mimes and Miracles*. New York: Cooper Square, 1963.

O'Bryan, Jill. "Saint Orlan Faces Reincarnation." *Art Journal* 56, no. 4, Performance Art: (Some) theory and (Selected) Practice at the End of This Century (Winter 1997): 50–56.

Orlan. *De l'art charnel au baiser de l'artiste*. Paris: Jean-Michel Place & Fils., 1997.

Orwin, Clifford, and Nathan Tarcov, eds. *The Legacy of Rousseau*. Chicago and London: Chicago U.P., 1997.

Ovid. *Metamorphoses*, trans. Samuel Garth, John Dryden et al. Available at http://classics.mit.edu/Ovid/metam.10.tenth.html (Last accessed February 15, 2015).

Paasonen, Susanna, Kaarina Nikunen, and Laure Saarenmaa, eds. *Pornification: Sex and Sexuality in Media Culture*. Oxford and New York: Berg, 2007.

Palaver, Wolfgang. *René Girard's Mimetic Theory (Studies in Violence, Mimesis and Culture)*. East Lansing, MI: Michigan State U.P., 2013.

Park, Julie. "Unheimlich Maneuvers: Enlightenment Dolls and Repetitions in Freud." *The Eighteenth Century* 44, no. 1 (Spring 2003): 45–68.

Parker, Rhian. *Women, Doctors and Cosmetic Surgery: Negotiating the "Normal" Body*. Hampshire and New York: Palgrave Macmillan, 2010.

Parrot, Nicole. *Mannequins*. London: St. Martin's Press, 1983.

Paul, Jean. *Werke*, ed. Norbert Miller and Wilhelm Schmidt-Biggermann. Munich: Carl Hanser, 1976, pt. 2, vols. 1 and 2.

Peers, Juliette. *The Fashion Doll: From Bébé Jumeau to Barbie*. Oxford and New York: Berg 2004.

Perthuis, Karen de. *Dying to Be Born Again: Mortality, Immortality and the Fashion Model*, Ph.D. dissertation, The University of Sydney, 2003.

Phillips, Sandra. "Marionette Photographs by André Kertész." *Performing Arts Journal* 7, no. 3 (1983): 115–120.

Plassard, Didier, ed. *Les Mains de la lumière. Anthologie des écritssue l'art de la marionnett*. Charleville-Mézières: Institut International de la Marionnette, 1996.

Plato. *Laws* (360 B.C.E.), Book VII, trans. Benjamin Jowett, MIT Classics. Available at http://classics.mit.edu/Plato/laws.

Plessix Gray, Francine du. *At Home with the Marquis de Sade* (1998). London: Pimlico, 2000, 46.

Plutarch. *Makers of Rome*, trans. and ed. Ian Scott-Kilvert. Harmondsworth: Penguin, 1965.

Purschke, Hans. *Die Entwicklung des Puppenspiels in den klassischen Ursprungsländern Europas*. Frankfurt am Main: (Self Published), 1984.

Quinn, Michael. "Svek's Stage Figure: Illustration, Design, and the Representation of Character." *Comparative Drama* 31, no. 3 (September 1988): 317–338.

Quinn, Michael. "The Comedy of Reference: The Semiotics of Commedia Figures in Eighteenth-Century Venice." *Theatre Journal* 43, no. 5 (March 1991): 70–92.

Rand, Erica. *Barbie's Queer Accessories*. Durham, NC: Duke U.P., 1995.

Reinhardt, Leslie. "Daughters, Dress, and Female Virtue in the Eighteenth Century." *American Art* 20, no. 2 (Summer 2006): 32–55.

Reynolds, R. "Criticism of Individuals in Roman Popular Tragedy." *Classical Quarterly* 37, no. 1/2 (January–April 1943): 37–45.

Richman, Steven. *Mannequins*. London: Shiffer Publishing, 2005.

Rilke, Rainer Maria. *Sämtliche Werke* v. 5 and 6. Frankfurt am Main: Insel Verlag, 1965.

Rilke, Rainer Maria. *Die Gedichte*. Frankfurt am Main: Insel Verlag, 1986.

Riskin, Jessica. "The Defacating Duck, Or, The Ambiguous Origins of Artificial Life." *Critical Inquiry* 29, no. 4 (Summer 2003): 599–633.

Riskin, Jessica, ed. *Genesis Redux: Essays in the History and Philosophy of Artificial Life*. Chicago and London: Chicago U.P., 2007.

Rogers, Mary. *Barbie Culture*. London: Sage, 1999.

*Ron Mueck*, exn. cat. Paris: Fondation Cartier pour l'art contemporain, 2006.

*Ron Mueck*, exn. cat. Tokyo: Foil, 2008.

Rose, Barbara. "Is it Art? Orlan and the Transgressive Act." *Art in America* 81, no. 2 (February 1993): 82–87, 125.

Rosenberg, Marvin. "Elizabethan Actors: Men or Marionettes?" *PMLA* 69, no. 4 (September 1954): 915–927.

Rousseau, Jean-Jacques. *Collected Writings of Rousseau*, ed. Roger Masters and Christopher Kelly. Hanover, NH: New England U.P., 1991–2012.

Rousseau, Jean-Jacques. *Œuvres* completes, ed. Bernard Gagnebin and Marcel Raymond. 4 vols. Paris: Gallimard, 1964, v. 2.

Roussel, Raymond. *Locus Solus* (1914). Paris: Gallimard, 1979.

Ruprecht, Lucia. *Dances of the Self on Heinrich von Kleist, E.T.A. Hoffman and Heinrich Heine*. Hampshire: Ashgate, 2006.

Rushing, James. "The Limitations of the Fencing Bear: Kleist's 'Über das Marionettentheater' as Ironic Fiction." *The German Quarterly* 61, no. 4, (Autumn 1988): 528–539.

Sack, Adriano. "Was Will der spornosexualle Mann?: *Die Welt*, March 2, 2015. Available at http://www.welt.de/icon/article129588106/Was-will-der-spornosexuelle-Mann.html (Last accessed February 15, 2015).

Safran, Linda. *Heaven on Earth: Art and the Church in Byzantium*. Pittsburgh: Penn State Press, 1998.

Salecl, Renata, and Slavoj Zizek, eds. *Gaze and Voice as Love Objects*. Durham, NC, and London: Duke University Press, 1996.

Sandberg, Patrick. "Living Doll." Available at http://www.vmagazine.com/site/content/261/living-doll.

Sandy, Gerald. "Scaenica Petronia." *Transactions of the American Philological Association* 104 (1974): 329–346.

Schiebinger, Londa, ed. *Feminism and the Body*. Oxford and New York: Oxford U.P., 2000.

Schiller, J. C. F. von. *Über Anmut und Würde* (1793). Available at http://gutenberg.spiegel.de/buch/ueber-anmuth-und-wurde-3320/2.

Schlegel, Friedrich. *Lucinde*. Frankfurt am Main: Insel Verlag, 1985.

Schlemmer, Oskar, Laszlo Moholy-Nagy, and Farkas Molnár. *The Theatre of the Bauhaus*, ed. Walter Gropius, trans. Arthur Wensinger. Middletown, CT: Weslayan U.P., 1961.

Schröder, Heinrich Otto. "Marionetten: Ein Beitrag zur Polemik des Karneades." *Rheinisches Museum für Philologie* 126, no. 1 (1983): 1–24.

Secrest, Meryle. *Elsa Schiaparelli: A Biography*. New York: Knopf, 2014.
Segel, Harold. *Pinocchio's Progeny: Puppets, Marionettes, Automatons and Robots in Modernist and Avant-Garde Drama*. Baltimore and London: Johns Hopkins U.P., 1995.
Simmel, Georg. *Aufsätze und Abhandlungen 1894–1900*. Frankfurt am Main: Suhrkamp, 1992.
Smith, Marquard. *The Erotic Doll: A Modern Fetish*. New Haven and London: Yale U.P., 2013.
Smith, Winifred. "Italian and Elizabethan Comedy." *Modern Philology* 5, no. 4 (April 1908): 555–567.
Snaith, Guy. "Tom's Men: The Masculinization of Homosexuality and the Homosexualization of Masculinity at the end of the Twentieth Century." *Paragraph* 26 (2003): 73–82.
Sommer, Katharina. *Maskenspiel in Therapie und Pädagogik*. Bielefeld and Basel: Edition Sirius, 2009.
Speaight, George. *Punch and Judy: A History*. London: Studio Vista, 1970.
Speaight, George. *The History of the English Puppet Theatre*, 2nd edn. Carbondale: Southern Illinois U.P., 1990.
Sterling, Charles. "Early Paintings of the Commedia Dell'Arte un France." *The Metropolitan Museum of Art Bulletin*, New series, 2, no. 1 (Summer 1943): 11–32.
Swoboda, Helmut. *Der künstliche Mensch*. Munich: Heimeran, 1967.
Taviani, Ferdinando, and Mirella Schino. *The Secret de la commedia dell'arte*, trans. Fr. Yves Liebert. Florence: La Casa Usher, 1984.
Taylor, Sue. *Hans Bellmer: The Anatomy of Anxiety*. Cambridge, MA: MIT Press, 2002.
Thesander, Marianne. *The Feminine Ideal* (1994), trans. Nicholas Hills. London: Reaktion, 1997.
Toffoletti, Kim. *Cyborgs and Barbie Dolls: Feminism and the Posthuman Body*. London: I.B. Tauris, 2007.
Tonelli, Franco. "Molière's *Don Juan* and the Space of the Commedia dell'Arte." *Theatre Journal* 37(4): December, 1985, 440–464.
Torok, Maria. "The Illness of Mourning and the Fantasy of the Exquisite Corpse" (1968). In Nicholas Abraham and Maria Torok, *The Shell and the Kernel: Renewals of Psychoanalysis*, trans and ed. Nicholas Rand. Chicago and London: Chicago U.P., 1994: 107–124.
Trimpi, Helen. "Harlequin-Confidence-Man: The Satirical Tradition of Commedia Dell-Arte and Pantomime in Melville's *Confidence Man*." *Texas Studies in Literature and Language* 16, no. 1 (Spring 1974): 147–193.
Troy, Nancy. *Couture Culture: A Study in Modern Art and Fashion*. Cambridge, MA: MIT Press, 2003.
Tseëlon, Efrat. *Masquerade and Identities: Essays in Gender, Sexuality and Marginality*. London: Routledge, 2001.
Tylus, Jane. "Women at the Windows: 'Commedia dell'arte' and Theatrical Practice in Early Modern Italy." *Theatre Journal* 49, no. 3 (October 1997): 323–342.
Valéry, Paul. *Œuvres I*. Paris: Gallimard Pléiade, 1957.
Vaucanson, Jacques. *Le Mécanisme du fluteur automate*, trans. J. T. Desaguliers. The Netherlands: Buren, 1979.
Veneciano, Jorge, and Rhonda Garelick. *Fabulous Harlequin: Orlan and the Patchwork Self*. Lincoln and London: Nebraska U.P., 2010.
Verlaine, Paul. *Poèmes saturniens suivi par Fêtes galantes*. Paris: Livre de Poche, 1972.
Vernant, Jean-Pierre. *Mythe et pensée chez les Grecs II*. Paris: Maspero, 1965.
Vernant, Jean-Pierre. *Figures, idoles, masque*. Paris: Juillard, 1990.
Villiers de l'Ilse-Adam, Auguste. *L'Eve Future* (1886). Available at http://www.gutenberg.org/files/26681/26681-h/26681-h.htm (Last accessed February 15, 2015).
Wagner-Ott, Anna. "Analysis of Gender Identity Through Doll and Action Figure Politics in Art Education." *Studies in Art Education* 43, no. 3 (Spring 2002): 246–263.
Walton, Michael, ed. *Craig on Theatre*. London: Methuen, 1983.
Webb, Peter. *The Erotic Arts*, rev. ed. New York: Farrar, Strauss & Giroux, 1983.

Weiss, Pietro. "Venetian Commedia dell'Arte 'Operas: in the Age of Vivaldi'," *The Musical Quarterly* 70, no. 2 (Spring 1984): 195–217.
Weissman, Kristin. *Barbie: the Icon, the Image, the Ideal*. Universal Publishers, 1999.
Welsh, Talia. "Child's Play: Anatomically Correct Dolls and Embodiment." *Human Studies* 30, no. 3 (September 2007): 255–267.
Wetmore, "Sympathy Machines: Men of Feeling and the Automaton." *Eighteenth-Century Studies* 43, no. 1 (Fall 2009): 37–54. Available at http://search.proquest.com.ezproxy1.library.usyd.edu.au/docview/198664826?accountid=14757 (Last accessed February 15, 2015).
Wharton, Edith. *The House of Mirth*. London: Dent, 1993.
Windisch, Charles Gottlieb de. *Inanimate Reason, or A Circumstantial Account of that Astonishing Piece of mechanism, M. De Kempelin's Chess-Player*. London: S. Bladon, 1784.
Winge, Theresa. "Costuming the Imagination: Origins of Anime and Manga." *Mechademia*, 1, Emerging Worlds of Anime and Manga (2006): 65–76.
Winnicott, D. W. *Play and Reality*. London: Travistock Publications, 1971.
Wolff, Max. "Zur Commedia dell'arte," *Zeitschrift für Französische Sprache und Literature* 58, no. 7/8 (1934): 419–424.
Wollen, Peter. *Raiding the Icebox: Reflections on Twentieth-Century Culture*. London and New York: Verso, 1993.
Zamir, Tzachi. "Puppets." *Critical Inquiry* 36, no. 3 (2010): 386–409.
Zizek, Slavoj. *Tarrying With the Negative*. Durham, NC: Duke U.P., 1993, 12.
Zizek, Slavoj. *The Most Sublime Hysteric: Hegel with Lacan*, trans. Thomas Scott-Railton. London: Polity, 2014a.
Zizek, Slavoj. *Event: A Philosophical Journey Through a Concept*. Brooklyn and London: Melville House, 2014b.
Zupancic, Alenka. *The Odd One In: On Comedy*. Cambridge, MA: MIT Press, 2008.

# Internet sources not cited elsewhere

http://bodybuilding.about.com/od/bodybuildingcompetition/ss/The-Eight-Mandatory-Poses-In-Bodybuilding_8.htm#step-heading (Last accessed February 15, 2015)
http://www.i-am-bored.com/bored_link.cfm?link_id=98068 (Last accessed February 15, 2015)
http://www.justinjedlica.com/press.html#prettyPhoto[rv]/11/ (Last accessed February 15, 2015)
http://www.galleryhistoricalfigures.com/index.html (Last accessed February 15, 2015)
http://www.patriciapiccinini.net/104/61 (Last accessed February 15, 2015)
https://secure.realdoll.com/ (Last accessed February 15, 2015)
http://en.wikipedia.org/wiki/Zanni (Last accessed February 15, 2015)
https://www.youtube.com/watch?v=oLK0myrbSzQ (Last accessed February 15, 2015)
https://www.youtube.com/watch?v=MGVrLuMIbdc (Last accessed February 15, 2015)
https://www.youtube.com/watch?v=VO4M2VT4F-o (Last accessed February 15, 2015)
https://www.youtube.com/watch?v=vU4dGhF2cJE (Last accessed February 15, 2015)
https://www.youtube.com/watch?v=wow2utprEoM (Last accessed February 15, 2015)
https://www.youtube.com/watch?v=XQYF6HcnKdk (Last accessed February 15, 2015)

# Filmography

*A.I. Artificial Intelligence*, dir. Steven Spielberg, Amblin/Kubrick Productions, 2001.
*Annabelle*, dir. John Leonetti, New Line Cinema, 2014.
*Automata*, dir. Gabe Ibáñez, Millennium Entertainment, 2014.

*Avatar*, dir. James Cameron, Lightstorm/Dune/Ingenius Film, 2009.
*Blade Runner*, dir. Ridley Scott, Ladd Company, 1982.
*Conan the Barbarian*, dir. John Milius, Universal Pictures and Twentieth Century Fox, 1982.
*The Conjuring*, dir. James Wan, New Line Cinema, 2013.
*The Devil-Doll*, dir. Tod Browning, MGM, 1936.
*The Doll*, dir. Ernst Lubitsch, UFA, 1919.
*Dolly Dearest*, dir. Maria Lease, Patriot Pictures and Channeler Enterprises, 1991.
*Ex Machina*, dir. Alex Garland, DNA Films/Film 4/Scott Rudin Productions, 2015.
*First Blood*, dir. Ted Kotcheff, Anabasis Investments, 1982.
*Ghost in the Shell*, dir. Mamoru Oshii, Production I.G., 1995.
*Ghost in the Shell II*, dir. Mamoru Oshii, Production I.G./Studio Ghibli, 2004.
*Her*, dir. Spike Jonze, Annapurna Pictures, 2013.
*I, Robot*, dir. Alex Proyas, Davis and Overbrook Entertainment, 2004.
*Iron and Beyond*, dir. David McVeigh and Scott McVeigh, 2002, https://www.youtube.com/watch?v=wiXxifU5ilQ (Last accessed February 15, 2015).
*Machine*, dir. James Caradog, Red and Black Films, 2013.
*The Matrix*, dir. the Wachowski brothers, Village Roadshow, 1999.
*Metropolis*, dir. Fritz Lang, UFA, 1927.
*Pumping Iron*, dir. George Butler, White Mountain Films, 1977.
*Rambo: First Blood Part II*, dir. George Cosmatos, Anabasis Investments, 1985.
*Terminator*, dir. James Cameron, Hemdale and Pacific Western, 1984.
*Terminator 2: Judgment Day*, dir. James Cameron, Carolco Pictures et al. 1991.
*Thunderbirds*, TV series, dirs. Desmond Saunders, David Elliott, David Lane, Allan Pattillo, AP films, 1964–1966.
*Waxworks*, dir. Paul Leni, Neptune-Film A.G., 1924.

## Television series

*Almost Human*, Bad Robot Productions/Warner Bros. Television, 2013–2014.
*Humans*, AMC Britain, 2015.
*Orphan Black*, Temple St. Productions, BBC America, 2013–2016.

# INDEX